INVENTING AUSTRALIA

THE AUSTRALIAN EXPERIENCE: NO 3

THE AUSTRALIAN EXPERIENCE
Series Editor: Heather Radi

ALSO IN THE SERIES
Geoffrey Sherington   *Australia's Immigrants*
Geoffrey Bolton   *Spoils and Spoilers*
Richard Broome   *Aboriginal Australians*

RICHARD WHITE

INVENTING AUSTRALIA
Images and Identity 1688–1980

GEORGE ALLEN & UNWIN

SYDNEY LONDON BOSTON

155.8994

W 587i

First published in 1981 by
George Allen & Unwin Australia Pty Ltd
8 Napier Street
North Sydney NSW 2060

National Library of Australia
Cataloguing-in-Publication entry:

White, Richard
Inventing Australia

ISBN 0 86861 027 5
ISBN 0 86861 035 6 (pbk.)

1. National characteristics, Australian
I. Title. (Series: The Australian experience; no. 3).

155.8'9'94

Library of Congress Catalog Card Number: 81-66528

Set in 10 on 11.5 Times by Filmset Ltd, Hong Kong

Printed in Hong Kong by South China Printing Company

212954

Contents

To Linda

Acknowledgements

For their help in various ways, I am grateful to Mike Bosworth, Garry Disher, Alison French, Linda Frow, Jan Kociumbas, Susan McKernan, Judy Mackinolty, Anne O'Brien, John Rickard, Peter Spearritt, David Webster, Phil White and Janis Wilton; to the staff at Mitchell Library; to past students at Monash University; and in particular to Heather Radi, a patient and sympathetic editor.

For permission to use illustrations, I would like to thank The Mitchell Library, Sydney (pages 7, 12, 19, 60, 67, 99, 113, 120, 123); Fisher Library, University of Sydney (page 21); Birmingham Museums and Art Gallery (page 39); The National Library, Canberra (pages 74, 78, 80, 95, 110, 128, 142); The *Bulletin*, Sydney (pages 76, 122, 138); Mr R.A. Lorimer (page 99); National Gallery of Victoria, Melbourne (page 107); New South Wales Department of Education (page 145); Bondi Surf Bathers' Life Saving Club (page 156); Bruce Petty and the Australia Council (page 170).

Introduction

This is the history of a national obsession. Most new nations go through the formality of inventing a national identity, but Australia has long supported a whole industry of image-makers to tell us what we are. Throughout its white history, there have been countless attempts to get Australia down on paper and to catch its essence. Their aim is not merely to describe the continent, but to give it an individuality, a personality. This they call Australian, but it is more likely to reflect the hopes, fears or needs of its inventor. This book traces some of these efforts to explain what it means to be Australian, from William Dampier's description of 'the poor winking people of New Holland' to the corporate advertisements of the 1980s.

There are no prizes for getting it right. There was no moment when, for the first time, Australia was seen 'as it really was'. There is no 'real' Australia waiting to be uncovered. A national identity is an invention. There is no point asking whether one version of this essential Australia is truer than another because they are all intellectual constructs, neat, tidy, comprehensible—and necessarily false. They have all been artificially imposed upon a diverse landscape and population, and a variety of untidy social relationships, attitudes and emotions. When we look at ideas about national identity, we need to ask, not whether they are true or false, but what their function is, whose creation they are, and whose interests they serve.

Historians seeking to explain the origins of the Australian identity have often contributed to its mystification. We must remember that historians can be image-makers too. Many have sought to hunt out the 'real' Australia or the 'typical' Australian and, with their eyes fixed firmly on what is distinctive about the land and its people, have ended their search among the convicts, the bushrangers, the shearers, the gum trees and the wide open spaces. But these are merely some of the materials with which the images have been constructed. To understand why they have been put together in the way they have, we need to look at other forces, not particularly distinctive, contributing to the making of Australian identity. Three are especially important.

Firstly, national identities are invented within a framework of modern Western ideas about science, nature, race, society, nationality. Not only is the very idea of national identity a product of European history at a particular time, but each addition to the Australian identity has reflected changing intellectual needs and fashions in the West. In other words, not only is the idea of 'Australia' itself a European invention, but men like Charles Darwin and Rudyard Kipling have contributed as much to what it means to be Australian as Arthur Streeton or Henry Lawson. The national identity is not 'Born of the lean loins of the country itself', as one ardent nationalist put it, but is part of the 'cultural baggage' which Europeans have brought with them, and with which we continue to encumber ourselves.

The second influence moulding ideas about Australian identity is the intelligentsia, or that class of people—writers, artists, journalists, historians, critics—most responsible for its definition. As the composition and influence of that class changes, so does their image of Australia. The nineteenth-century man of letters, the *fin de siècle* professional artist, the mid-twentieth-century academic have all viewed Australia differently, and have all had an interest in claiming their image as the only valid one since it strengthens their position in society. To understand the images which they produce, it is necessary to keep in mind their perception of themselves as a group, and their economic relationship with the rest of society.

This brings us to the third influence on images of national identity: those groups in society who wield economic power. National identities emerge to serve a social function. While the intelligentsia create the images, they do not work in a vacuum. The most influential images are those which serve the interests of a broader ruling class, on whose patronage the intelligentsia rely. Every powerful economic interest likes to justify itself by claiming to represent the 'national interest' and identifying itself with a 'national identity'. In this view of the world there is no room for class conflicts, and sexual and racial exploitations are also obscured. The 'national interest' must appear to work for the good of all.

However the relationship between the 'ruling class' and the 'national identity' is much more complex than this suggests. For one thing, groups outside the ruling class can develop their own ideas of national identity, although they are unlikely to be dominant. For another, the ruling class is not united, but contains powerful economic interests often in competition with one another. The result is that the national identity is continually being fractured, questioned and redefined. The earliest debates about Australia's identity involved conflicting British interests. In Australia, from the late nineteenth century to the mid-twentieth, the competition was between the previously dominant pastoral interests and the increasingly powerful local manufacturing interests. Australia's flocks were being challenged by Australia's factories. It is no coincidence that this period saw the most effort being spent in the promotion of competing Australian identities.

So we will never arrive at the 'real' Australia. From the attempts of others to get there, we can learn much about the travellers and the journey itself, but nothing about the destination. There is none.

1   Terra Australis Incognita

I stood up ... and urged the unfairness of judging animals any
more than of men, only by those of our own country.

Fanny Burney, March 1774[1]

Centuries before Europeans first set foot on the continent we now
call Australia, the Greeks, the Arabs, the Chinese and the Indians
had elaborate ideas about a land somewhere to the south of Java.
These ideas were the product of imagination rather than experience.
Their stories of palaces of gold, of fabulous birds of prey, of a kingdom
of women or of dwarfs, were bound up in religious belief, or were
extensions of their science.

In the sixteenth and seventeenth centuries, more prosaic images
drew Western Europeans to seek this 'terra australis incognita': the
profits of the spice trade, the souls to be saved, and the scientific
curiosities awaiting discovery. Alvero de Mendana in 1567 and Pedro
Fernandez de Quiros in 1605 set out from Callao in Spanish Peru to
claim the unknown land for Spain and Catholicism but hesitated and
turned back without seeing it. The Portuguese may have sailed along
the east coast, to beat the Spanish to the continent's supposed riches,
but if so they did not find the riches they sought. From 1606 the Dutch
pieced together the coast-line of the continent in the north and west,
and called it New Holland. They found no gold or spices, only sand,
flies, naked savages and a few weird animals. In 1642, Abel Janszoon
Tasman saw better country with good water and timber in the south,
and named it Anthoony van Diemenslandt. Yet he thought so little
of it that, for the sake of brevity, he left no detailed description.
Although there was evidence that the land was inhabited, no contact
was made with the natives, and there seemed to be little possibility of
profitable trade.[2]

The Spaniards, the Portuguese and the Dutch saw little in the new
land to recommend it. They were to have no more to do with the
development of the idea of what it meant to be Australian. The picture
they drew stimulated no further interest, and the names that they

had given it—Terra Australis, Austrialia del Espiritu Santo, Zuidland, New Holland, Van Diemen's Land—fell into disuse. Instead it was the English image of the new continent which was to prove most powerful and most lasting, and which was to attract more interest, promote its exploitation, and bring settlers to it. This was not due to any greater perseverance by the English, nor even to the fact that they came to the more fertile eastern coast of Australia. It was due, rather, to a revolution taking place in European attitudes to, and curiosity about, man, nature and science.

Dampier Dismayed

That revolution can be seen clearly if we compare the images of the continent popularised by two Englishmen, by Dampier at the end of the seventeenth century, and by Cook towards the end of the eighteenth. William Dampier made two voyages to what was then called New Holland, in 1688 and 1699. On each occasion his descriptions of the land, its flora, fauna and inhabitants, were more detailed but just as unfavourable as those of the Dutch. Like them he was full of complaints. The land was barren and fly-pestered; the water was brackish if any could be found; the trees were stunted and bore no fruit; and the animals that might provide food were not plentiful.

He saved his most vivid language for the Aborigines, 'The poor winking People of *New Holland*', whose appearance and habits he set down in disgusted but picturesque detail:

> The Inhabitants of this country are the miserablest People in the world. The *Hodmadods* of *Monomatapa*, though a nasty People, yet for Wealth are Gentlemen to these; who have no Houses and Skin Garments, Sheep, Poultry, and Fruits of the Earth, Ostrich Eggs, & c. as the *Hodmadods* have: and setting aside their humane shape, they differ but little from Brutes. They are tall, strait bodied, and thin, with small long limbs. They have great Heads, round Foreheads, and great Brows. Their Eye-lids are always half closed, to keep the Flies out of their Eyes . . . They are long visaged, and of a very unpleasing aspect; having no one graceful feature in their faces. Their Hair is black, short and curl'd, like that of the Negroes: and not long and lank like the common *Indians*. The colour of their skins, both of their faces and the rest of their body, is coal black, like that of the Negroes of *Guinea*.
>
> They have no sort of Cloaths; but a piece of the rind of a Tree ty'd like a Girdle about their wastes, and a handful of long Grass, or 3 or 4 small green Boughs, full of Leaves, thrust under their Girdle, to cover their nakedness.

They have no Houses, but lye in the open Air, without any covering; the Earth being their Bed, and the Heaven their Canopy. Whether they cohabit one Man to one Woman, or promiscuously, I know not: but they do live in Companies, 20 or 30 Men, Women, and Children together. Their only food is a small sort of Fish, which they get by making Wares of stone, across little Coves, or branches of the Sea . . . Sometimes they get as many Fish as makes them a plentiful Banquet; and at other times they scarce get every one a taste: but be it little or much that they get, every one has his part, as well the young and tender, as the old and feeble, who are not able to go abroad, as the strong and lusty . . .

I did not perceive that they did worship any thing. These poor creatures have a sort of Weapon to defend their Ware, or fight with their Enemies, if they have any that will interfere with their poor Fishery . . . I saw no Iron nor any other sort of Metal; therefore it is probable they use Stone-Hatchets, as some *Indians* in *America* do.[3]

Clearly Dampier was not impressed. This passage, the first extended description of the Aborigines of Australia, was to set the pattern of European responses to the Aborigines for many years to come. His second voyage to New Holland confirmed his original opinion of the place, and again his description of the inhabitants was uncomplimentary: they had a 'natural Deformity' and 'the most unpleasant Looks and the worst Features of any People that ever I saw, tho' I have seen great variety of Savages.'[4]

However such criticism says as much about the writer as it does about the Aborigines. Dampier was disappointed at finding no gold or spices or anything else worth trading. That, after all, was his purpose in making contact with the inhabitants:

I intended especially to observe what Inhabitants I should meet with, and to try to win them over to somewhat of Traffick and useful Intercourse, as there might be Commodities among any of them that might be fit for Trade or Manufacture, or any found out in which they might be employed. Though as to the *New Hollanders* hereabouts, by the Experience I had had of their Neighbours formerly, I expected no great matters from them.[5]

There were no commodities fit for trade or manufacture, so it is not surprising that Dampier should stress the country's general barrenness, and the poverty and nakedness of its people. Even the possibility that the people might prove useful as labourers came to nothing. When Dampier performed lengthy charades to explain to the Aborigines that they should work for him, carrying barrels of water to the ship, they simply 'grinn'd like so many Monkeys'.[6] So the land and its people were dismissed: he was motivated by a desire for profit, and there was no profit to be had there.

Dampier's comments were also the product of a particular view of the relationship between civilised man and nature. He was a contemporary of Daniel Defoe, whose *Robinson Crusoe* was published in 1719, by which time Dampier's account of his first voyage was in its fifth edition. Both men's works reflected similar views of the world. The difference between European man and the savage was civilisation, or as Dampier put it, 'Wealth'. This was measured in material terms: clothes, weapons, permanent housing and creature comforts were the signs of civilised man, who was distinguished from barbaric souls by his industry, his respect for material possessions and his reading of the Bible. Proof of the barbarity of the Aborigines lay in the fact that 'these poor creatures seem not accustomed to carry burthens', that they failed 'to admire anything that we had',[7] and appeared to lack religion.

This outlook was to be challenged in the next hundred years. Even in Dampier's writing there were hints of a scientific interest that was much more marked in Cook's journals. When Tasman's hopes for trade were disappointed, he showed no further interest in his Van Diemen's Land, except for the wishful comment that in such an expanse there must be something of value somewhere. Dampier expressed his disappointment too, but the very length of his accounts of what he found reflected an interest that went beyond mere trade, and an awareness that there was a popular curiosity in new discovery.

Dampier's journal was a success among the small but growing public that was supporting the beginnings of a scientific revolution in England. Already the Royal Society of London, for the Improving of Natural Knowledge, was 40 years old, and was providing a focus for that revolution—Isaac Newton was about to become its president. The Society was largely made up of enthusiastic amateurs, but they were concerned to promote a professional approach to the collection of new knowledge:

> to study *Nature* rather than *Books*, and from the Observations, made of the *Phenomena* and Effects she presents, to compose such a History of Her, as may hereafter serve to build a Solid and Useful Philosophy upon.[8]

Thus they were interested in voyages of discovery for the sake of science, not for the sake of profit. They had formulated a set of 'Directions for Seamen, bound for far voyages' which were to be issued to men like Dampier so that science as well as commerce might profit from their discoveries.

So when Dampier published his account of the first voyage, it was not surprising that he dedicated it to Charles Mountague, President of the Royal Society, with the modest assessment of his discoveries:

As the scene of them is not only Remote, but for the most part little frequented also, so there may be some things in them New even to you; and some, possibly, not altogether unuseful to the publick.[9]

A Mine of Scientific Novelty

By the time of Cook's voyages round the world, this interest in science had become dominant. One naturalist, in introducing the public to the botany of New Holland, admitted that it so far offered little that was useful. Instead he put the case of Science for Science's sake:

It is the peculiar privilege of reasoning man, not only to extend his enquiries to a multiplicity of attainable benefits to himself and his species . . . but also to walk with God through the garden of crea-tion, and be initiated into the different plans of his providence in the construction and economy of all these various beings . . . In this point of view no natural production is beneath the notice of the philosopher, nor any enquiry trifling under the guidance of a scientific mind.[10]

There was much more to voyaging than mere trade. The whole purpose of Cook's first voyage was a scientific one—to visit Tahiti in order to observe the transit of Venus across the sun in the hope that, from measurements made there, the distance between the sun and the earth could be calculated. It was undertaken at the direct request of the Royal Society. For this the president of the Royal Society provided advice on how to collect specimens, record vo-cabularies and accurately observe the inhabitants, plants and animals. A second, more secret purpose was to try to settle the question of whether there was a continent in the south seas.

Cook set out with a large scientific party on board, in itself some-thing quite novel. There were two astronomers, two naturalists (Joseph Banks, later to be president of the Royal Society for a record term, and Dr Daniel Solander of the newly established British Museum), two professional artists and a scientific assistant. On their departure, John Ellis, an English naturalist, wrote excitedly to Linnaeus, the most renowned naturalist of the day:

No people ever went to sea better fitted out for the purpose of Natural History, nor more elegantly. They have got a fine library

of Natural History; they have all sorts of machines for catching
and preserving insects; all kinds of nets, trawls, drags, and hooks
... many cases of bottles with ground stoppers, of several sizes,
to preserve animals in spirits. They have several sorts of salts ...
in short, Solander assured me this expedition would cost Mr.
Banks ten thousand pounds. All this owing to you and your writings.[11]

They returned three years later, 'laden with spoils': 1000 new species
of plants, 500 fish, 500 skins of animals and birds, innumerable
insects, rocks and native artifacts and the vocabularies of unheard-of
languages.[12]

The scientific purpose of the voyage also meant that they returned
with a new image of Australia. Cook had not been able to find a
southern continent, but had sailed along the eastern coast of that
continent whose western side Dampier had so disparaged. As far as
commerce went, Cook agreed with Dampier; although the east was
not as barren and miserable as the west, and 'the hand of Industry'
could produce grain, fruits and cattle in the future, 'the Country it
self so far as we know doth not produce any one thing that can become
an Article in trade to invite Europeans to fix a settlement upon it'.[13]
So commercial interests continued to ignore Australia; for them it
was as barren as it always had been.

For scientists, however, there were vast riches. The specimens
which the naturalists took back from the new continent firmly established it in the minds of scientists as a land of oddities. To be native
to New Holland was to be, almost by definition, freakish and bizarre.
Cook had acknowledged the importance of the botanical discoveries
when he named their first landfall on the continent: 'The great quantity
of New Plants &ca. Mr Banks & Dr Solander collected in this place
occasioned my giveing it the name of *Botany Bay*.'[14] Linnaeus called
the plants that Banks and Solander took back 'a matchless and truly
astonishing collection, such as has never been seen before, nor may
ever be seen again'.[15] The most remarkable thing about them was
that they simply did not fit into the accepted botanical classifications
of the day, which were those devised by Linnaeus. As Sir James
Edward Smith, the first president of the Linnean Society, explained,
anyone working on the botany of New Holland found 'himself as it
were in a new world ... Whole tribes of plants ... prove ... total
strangers ... not only all the species that present themselves are new,
but most of the genera, and even natural orders'.[16]

Yet even more extraordinary were the animals, the marvellous
oddities of a topsy-turvy land. There was a fish which Banks found

'a very singular Phaenomenon', which not only jumped from rock to rock, but did not particularly seem to prefer water to land.[17] The activities of Australian ants were 'most curious' and 'most extrordinary[sic]' and 'probably in no countrey more admirable than in this'.[18] One of the seamen came across a flying fox, which he described to Banks as being 'about as large and much like a one gallon cagg, as black as the Devil and had 2 horns on its head, it went but Slowly but I dard not touch it'.[19] He would not have been the only member of the crew whose main concerns were drink and damnation.

But strangest of all was the kangaroo which they finally tracked down and killed. It was a complete novelty. As Banks wrote, 'To compare it to any European animal would be impossible as it has not the least resemblance of any one I have seen'.[20] Even the hard-to-

'The Kangooroo'

It was to be some time before the curious fauna of Australia was depicted accurately by European artists. From The Voyage of Governor Phillip to Botany Bay *(1789).*

please Dr Johnson was prepared to admit an interest in the kangaroo,[21] and soon 'this unparalleled Animal from the Southern Hemisphere, that almost surpasses Belief' was being exhibited in the Strand, admittance one shilling.[22]

The reason for the plants, animals and people of New Holland attracting so much scientific interest lay in the way they fitted into the eighteenth-century view of the universe. It was a common belief that every species of plant and animal had its own unique slot in a great chain of being that stretched from the highest form of life to the lowest, a chain which had been fixed at creation and would continue for all time. Naturalists believed that there were still gaps in the chain, and they looked to new botanical and zoological discoveries to fill them.[23] The Pacific seemed to be providing two crucial links in the chain, the link between the plant kingdom and the animal kingdom, and the link between the highest animal and man himself. The plant-animal link was thought to be the zoophytes, the minute creators of the fantastic corals taken back by Banks, Solander and others. The link between the monkey and man was thought by many to be the Australian Aborigine, for no better reason than that he seemed to be furthest from European civilisation, which in their arrogance they assumed to be the highest imaginable form of human life.

Thus when Banks described the Aborigines as being 'but one degree removd from Brutes'[24] he was mentally placing them on the chain just one step above the animal kingdom. Similarly George Shaw, the zoologist, thought them 'less elevated above the inferior animals than in any other part of the known world'.[25] Later visitors to New South Wales reinforced that view. Even in the 1840s it was still a common image of the Aborigine among the white invaders. They were 'the last link in the great chain of existence which unites man with the monkey'[26] to Augustus Earle, the artist, and Peter Cunningham asked if they should be placed 'at the very zero of civilization, constituting in a measure the connecting link between man and the monkey tribe?—for really some of the old women only seem to require a tail to complete the identity'.[27] It was an image that conveniently suited those who were gradually destroying Aboriginal society in the name of 'civilization' and the expansion of their sheep-runs.

At the same time though, Australia was supplying evidence which increasingly challenged the concept of the chain of being. Robert Brown, a naturalist with Matthew Flinders, had collected 3400 specimens in Australia, 2000 of which were new to science. When he published his findings in 1810, he abandoned the Linnean system of classification, arguing in nature the natural orders were linked 'more after the manner of a network than of a chain'.[28] François Péron, a French naturalist, also found that New Holland 'mocks our studies, and shakes to their foundations the most firmly established and most universally admitted of our scientific opinions'.[29] Here the order was confused. Here there were plants and animals that just did not fit into a place on the chain. Nature seemed to mix up the chain completely by, for example, attaching a duck's bill to a mole's body and calling it a platypus. For the logic of the chain to work, ducks should have nothing at all to do with moles, so when George Shaw saw his first platypus, he assumed it was a skilful hoax and tried to find the place where two different animals had been sewn together.[30]

Through such unnatural productions as the platypus, Australia, the land of oddities, contributed to the demise of the chain of being. Among scientists, it was to be replaced, later in the nineteenth century, by the theory of organic evolution, finally outlined in Charles Darwin's *The Origin of Species* in 1859. It is significant that the three scientists who contributed most to that theory—Darwin, J.D. Hooker and T.H. Huxley—had all visited Australia. The land of oddities had become an essential port of call for anyone working on the frontiers of science.

The idea that Australia was a land of oddities also had a more popular vogue. In 1817, the Reverend Sydney Smith thought it a joke:

> in this remote part of the earth, Nature (having made horses, oxen, ducks, geese, oaks, elms, and all regular productions for the rest of the world) seems determined to have a bit of play, and to amuse herself as she pleases.[31]

Much play was made of the idea that in Australia there was an inversion of natural laws, an old idea but one that was popularised by Australia's zoological oddities. So Australia was the land which was upside-down, topsy-turvy, where it was day when it should have been night, summer when it should have been winter, where, it was said, grass grew on trees and rivers flowed uphill.[32] It was an idea that continued to have a certain popular appeal for long afterwards.

Noble Savages

The image of the Aborigines also contributed to ideas of what it was to be Australian. Those who saw the country as barren tended to view the Aborigines with disgust. Those motivated by an interest in science saw the Aborigines as yet another oddity worthy of observation; indeed, among scientists, throughout the nineteenth century, the word 'Australian' referred to the Aboriginal rather than the white population. Both Banks and Cook viewed the Aborigines with a scientific curiosity and occasionally with the disgust of Dampier; but at other times there was something that almost bordered on envy. It was as if, since Dampier's day, people had grown bored with the civilised life of Europe. Intellectuals had begun to idealise man in what they regarded as his 'natural' state, in which he knew nothing of the burdensome demands of civilisation. Dampier had pitied the Aborigines because they did not know how to work—now men were asking might not a life without work, where all the necessities of life were provided by nature, be a very pleasant one? Dampier had been surprised that they had so few possessions, and pitied them when they did not admire European clothes and ornaments. Now Banks and Cook found they tore off and abandoned the clothes they had been given. To Banks this was proof that they could be quite happy without the clutter of European civilisation: 'Thus live these I had almost said happy people, content with little nay almost nothing'.[33] He wondered 'how small are the real wants of human nature, which we Europeans have increased to an excess'.[34]

As Cook left the Australian coast, turning back from the unknown to civilisation, he too began to idealise the life of the Aborigine:

> ... they may appear to some to be the most wretched people upon Earth, but in reality they are far more happier than we Europeans; being wholy unacquainted not only with the superfluous but the necessary Conveniencies so much sought after in Europe, they are happy in not knowing the use of them.[35]

These were a people who appeared totally uncivilised, without agriculture, without permanent homes, totally naked: according to Cook, 'even those parts which I allways before now thought nature would have taught a woman to conceal were uncover'd'.[36] Yet it seemed they had all they desired. This in itself made them interesting as scientific curiosities. However the information that Cook and his party brought back did not only interest scientists. In the official account of Cook's first voyage, written by John Hawkesworth and published two years after Cook's return, Hawkesworth apologises for the amount of detail that has been included for scientists, and comments:

> It is however hoped, that those who read merely for entertainment

will be compensated by the description of countries which no European had before visited, and manners which in many instances exhibit a new picture of human life.[37]

He knew that the new discoveries would interest not only those primarily concerned with science, but also a class of general reader who, as Hawkesworth suggested, would wonder about the nature of human life, just as Cook had.

Among such readers, Cook's voyages stimulated and reinforced a cult of the 'noble savage', a cult that was less scientific than philosophical. When Hawkesworth wrote his account, based on the journals of Cook and Banks, he blithely ditched scientific accuracy and used their comments about the Aborigines of New South Wales to describe the inhabitants of Tierra del Fuego.[38] He was not writing for scientists but for a readership attracted by novelty or interested in a philosophical debate about civilisation.

By the end of the eighteenth century there were several lines of thought concerning primitive man. First, there was an idealised picture of the noble savage and the simple life, which in Europe had been destroyed by civilisation. According to this view, natural man was far better off without the knowledge of civilisation. Supporters of this ideal were later able to point to the ravages inflicted on the original inhabitants of Australia and the Pacific by the introduction of European disease, weapons and technology.

Cook's voyages stimulated this tradition, although it was the reports of Tahiti which captured the European imagination rather than the harder lives of the Australian Aborigine or the Patagonian. Tahiti, where Cook's men cavorted with graceful 'dusky maidens', seemed like a Garden of Eden before the fall: shame and hardship were unknown; all the necessities of life were provided by a bounteous nature, with minimum exertion on the part of man. Hawkesworth's account of the first voyage, and the etchings that went with it, turned the people and places that Cook came across into noble savages and classical Arcadian landscapes for popular consumption. Then on his second voyage, Cook returned with a noble savage in the flesh, Omai, who did the rounds of London society, generally to the admiration of all who met him. A meeting with him at her father's house caused the young Fanny Burney to contemplate man and nature, and is typical of the way in which Cook's discoveries were received by the noble savage school. In her diary she compared Omai, who had 'no tutor but Nature', favourably with an acquaintance, who had received a rigorously systematic education from his father, and had had all the advantages civilisation could provide, yet had turned out remarkably awkward. She concluded: 'I think this shows how much more *nature* can do without *art*, than *art* with all her refinement unassisted by *nature*'.[39]

It was only to be expected that with the various populations of the Pacific confused in the popular mind, the Australians were sometimes seen in the same light. At other times they were seen as 'hard' primitives as opposed to the 'soft' primitives of Tahiti, but they remained just as noble, and to some—Cook, for example—preferable. So in the etchings produced for the publication of the journals of Phillip and Hunter, the Aborigines were given classical physiques, classical posture and classical poses, even if the original sketches were far less flattering. The image of the Australian was being forced into a classical mould for the men of taste who were expected to buy these expensive volumes.

This admiration filtered through to other perceptions. George Barrington, a convict whose aesthetic sense perhaps explains his propensity for picking pockets, left an admiring description of his

'Natives of Botany Bay'

This engraving caters for the men of taste who would read Phillip's Voyage. *It is based more on the conventional classical ideal of the noble savage than on the more realistic illustrations of Aborigines which were becoming available.*

Aboriginal companion in 1796:

> a form that might serve as a perfect model for the most scrupulous statuary; her face . . . of a perfect oval, or Grecian shape, with features regularly beautiful, and as fine a pair of eyes as can be imagined . . . she was likewise of a much lighter colour than any of her countrywomen.[40]

Similarly, Charles Pickering, who visited Australia with the United States Exploring Expedition between 1838 and 1842, thought that, while some individual Aborigines were 'of surpassing ugliness', others

> had the face decidedly fine; and several of the young women had a very pleasing expression of countenance . . . Strange as it may appear, I would refer to an Australian, as the finest model of the human proportions, I have ever met with; in muscular development, combining perfect symmetry, activity, and strength; while his head might have been compared with an antique bust of a philosopher.[41]

Pickering was aware when he wrote that his view of the Aborigine was no longer a generally accepted one. Even when Cook returned from his first voyage, the noble savage was being satirised in London. Dr Johnson was quite confident that civilisation was to be preferred philosophically, and in any case was rather more comfortable than the state of nature. He once dismissed the Aborigines as uninteresting on discovering they had no tails.[42] Other satirists continued to attack the idea. Banks became a butt of their verse, especially when it was known that he had found, as he put it, a 'snug lodging' with some of the Tahitian women, and had taken advantage of the 'opportunity of putting their politeness to every test'.[43] This satirical view of the noble savage led easily into a comic view of Aborigines, which was to be particularly popular in the colony itself. They were dressed in the comic cast-offs of Europeans, loaded with alcohol, taught a few words of English, and set up as grotesque figures of fun. The casual jokes about the land of oddities had a darker side which was cruel and vicious.[44]

A more powerful force than either the satirists or the admirers of the noble savage in shaping ideas about the Aborigines was the evangelical movement which was rapidly gaining influence at the end of the eighteenth century. The evangelicals condemned the idea of the noble savage because it implied that there were men who had escaped the fall. In their interpretation of the Bible, natural man was brutish and unregenerate, lacking shame and moral sense. They had evidence from Cook and other observers of nakedness, promiscuity, cannibalism and infanticide. When Captain Watkin Tench reflected on the

Australian Aborigine in 1793, for example, he wished that those philosophers who 'exalt a state of nature above a state of civilization' could learn that natural man was neither happy nor rational:

> a savage roaming for prey amidst his native deserts, is a creature deformed by all those passions, which afflict and degrade our nature, unsoftened by the influence of religion, philosophy and legal restriction.[45]

For such men, natural man was naturally evil. For some, that justified 'civilised' man's harsh treatment and dispossession of the Aborigines. It was a view which allowed British law to ignore the Aborigines' right to their own lands and was a popular belief when the Aborigines' lands became more valuable in the 1830s. For others, natural man needed to be civilised by Protestantism for the sake of his salvation. The accounts of the Pacific explorers jolted such men into action. The Missionary Society was founded in London in 1795, and soon missionaries were being sent to save the Tahitians from immorality and the Australians from ignorance. For the evangelicals, New Holland was a land sunk in depravity, a land awaiting salvation, and they set sail with a good supply of trousers.[46]

Even before European settlement in Australia, then, there were, among those who cared to think about it, well-established images of what it meant to be Australian. These images were the reflection not of a reality, but of the interests and assumptions of particular groups. For commercial interests, Cook had offered no advance on Dampier's damning picture of a continent which had nothing to trade. At most it could provide a base for whaling, and perhaps for the China trade, and the possibility that in the future something might turn up.

For scientists on the other hand, the continent held out great botanical and zoological riches, including key links in both the great chain of being and the theory of evolution which overthrew it. But it was also a strange land, full of natural oddities that did not fit into the accepted order of things, a topsy-turvy world where nature seemed at odds with herself. For some it was a land untouched by civilisation, a primitive land in a perfect state of nature. Its inhabitants could provoke fashionable envy for their supposed pristine happiness, cynical amusement at their comical antics, or pious disgust at their depravity and barbaric ignorance.

These various images ebbed and flowed through the minds of those few Europeans who ever thought about the continent before British settlement. Something of each of them was to remain part of the image of Australia in Europe, long after the British invasion and even into the twentieth century.

As these images jostled with each other the Aborigines lost out. The weird animals and plants became popular symbols of Australian identity. They were to appear on coats of arms and coins, and as company trade marks. They were elevated into the conventional, neutral symbols of Australia.

The Aborigines fared worse. In Europe they remained representative of Australia, placed beside the plants and animals as natural objects of curiosity. In Australia, as the idea of 'being Australian' developed among the European inhabitants, the Aborigines became less and less representative of 'Australia' until in the end they were quite dispossessed. For most of the settlers they were pests, sometimes comic, sometimes vicious, but always standing in the way of a civilised Australian community. Eventually they were to reach the indignity of being 'Our Aborigines', their image no longer representative of Australia except as garden ornaments in suburban backyards and ashtrays in souvenir shops.

2 Hell Upon Earth

Very strange tales
Are told of gentlemen of New South Wales.

Anon[1]

There was a terrible aptness about the decision that the new land of contrarieties should become, on the advice of Banks, a dumping ground for those who had gone against the established social order. The lowest element of British society was to be cast out among the lowest form of human life; unnatural vice was to be exiled as far from home as possible, where nature itself was inverted and nakedness knew no shame; thieves were to be condemned to a land where there was nothing at all of value. The macabre analogies meant that Australia remained, for a time, a mine of extravagant conceits for the cultured elite. Sydney Smith labelled it the 'land of convicts and kangaroos' and Charles Lamb, in a precious bit of clowning, explained how kangaroos were

> like a lesson framed by nature to the pick-pocket! Marry, for diving into Fobs they are rather lamely provided *a priori;* but if the hue and cry were once up, they would shew as fair a pair of hindshifters as the expertest loco-motor in the colony.[2]

The idea of antipodean inversion was extended to describe a land where 'vice is virtue, virtue vice'.[3] Minor poets such as William Bowles and Erasmus Darwin, Charles' grandfather, mused about how the new civilisation would turn out, with such inauspicious beginnings.[4]

The Botany Bay Bogey

Once convict transportation became reality, a new image of Australia was created, and it was an image which dwelt in the minds of people from an entirely different class to the scientists, the philosophers and the leisured class who read their works. For the semi-criminal lumpen proletariat, for the conventional middle class who feared them, and for the broad British working class, musings about the oddities of

nature and new empires in the Pacific were irrelevant to daily life.
For them, the image of Australia was summed up by Botany Bay,
and later by the even more horrific places of secondary punishment
such as Port Arthur, Moreton Bay and that 'dwelling place of devils
in the human shape, the refuse of Botany Bay, the doubly damned',[5]
Norfolk Island.

Such an image of exaggerated horror was an essential element in
the penal system of the day, which was based on the belief that the
severity of punishment, rather than the likelihood of being caught,
was the most effective deterrent to crime. Fear of the consequences
was the basis of the whole system of morality, and Botany Bay became one of the most fearful consequences. Along with Hell and the
gallows, Botany Bay was used to frighten children into being good
and displaying the great virtues of the day, industry, temperance and
humility.[6] And so, in the 'leaden little books' for children which
Dickens described, 'the good grown-up baby invariably got to the
Savings-bank, and the bad grown-up baby invariably got transported'.[7]
Hell and Botany Bay were supposed to have the same effect on the
working class, to keep them sober, industrious and humble: in *Hard
Times*, Bounderby's solution to trade unionism was to ship the leaders
off to penal settlements.[8] Even two genteel ladies, cut off from society
in North Wales, could wonder if their impecuniosity would find them
in Botany Bay.[9]

Given its place in the moral order, the authorities went out of their
way to make the threat of Botany Bay dreadful for anyone likely to
stray from the straight and narrow. They always stressed the severity
of punishment rather than the possibility of reform. Lord Stanley
boasted in 1833 that he would make transportation worse than death.
Colonial administrators had difficulty in convincing him that the
convicts were indeed as miserable as they could possibly be.[10] For
many Botany Bay did become an absolutely awful prospect, capable
of reducing hardened criminals sentenced to transportation to tears.

Once the settlement was well-established, accounts of the system
were publicised in Britain. Returned convicts acknowledged Lord
Stanley's success. In 1837, George Loveless, one of the Tolpuddle
Martyrs, wrote that it would have been doing men a kindness to have
hanged them in England rather than expose them to the cruelties
and miseries of Australia.[11] Joseph Holt, an Irish rebel leader, agreed
that the gibbet was a more merciful end than the penal settlements,
where men were

subject to the unmerciful treatment of human tigers, who tortured or killed those within their power, according to the caprice of the moment.[12]

There were two elements which made Botany Bay such a dreadful place in popular imagination. One was negative: the fact that Botany Bay was not England meant there was the fear of the unknown on the one hand and the misery of exile on the other. This element sustained many of the sentimental broadside ballads about transportation, such as the 'Farewell Address' of 'those unfortunate Men who received their several Sentences, of Transportation, at the Summer Assizes for the year 1842':

> Oh! 'tis a cruel sentence for a man to leave his wife,
> His children, and his dearest friends, all dearer than his life;
> To leave the land that gave him birth, to see it p'rhaps no more,
> And drag a wretched life in chains, upon a distant shore.[13]

The letters written by convicts also revealed a strong sense of exile. They were not necessarily representative of convict feelings since they were generally written by literate men, whose writing home, and having someone there to write to, would naturally have stimulated their thoughts of exile; yet a sentence to Botany Bay was likely to have affected others similarly. These letters appealed to the nineteenth-century taste for sentimental departures and many were published.

The other element in the dread of Botany Bay was the sheer brutality of the system. Its horror and depravity were well-publicised in England. Lurid descriptions of floggings and chain gangs were both a macabre entertainment and a warning to the working class:

> the hideous triangle is displayed with its gory associations and the scourger comes forth, he displays his brawny strength, grasps his scourge, draws his clotted fingers through the tangle of its many knots, the nine detested thongs descend, and after a fiftieth repetition, each more swift and cutting, he is taken down.[14]

Also popular in England were accounts of the general drunkenness and immorality in the settlements, of the vicious murders sometimes carried out in the hope of being hanged, and of cases of cannibalism among convicts. Pathetic attempts to escape by walking over the hills to China were widely reported, as was the amazing and terrible story of Mary Bryant and her companions who got as far as Timor in an open boat.

Whereas the voyages of exploration and the accounts of the botany and zoology of New Holland were published in expensively illustrated, richly bound volumes, the idea of Botany Bay as hell on earth was

Compare this rough woodcut, produced in a small chap-book for mass con-
sumption, with the delicate engravings of Phillip's Voyage. *The emphasis on the*
brutality of Botany Bay could be both an indictment of the system and a cautionary
lesson to the working class. Frontispiece from Edward Lilburn's Complete
Exposure of the Convict System, *published about 1841.*

spread for mass consumption in the very cheapest form, as sixpenny
chap-books or pamphlets, street ballads or simple illustrated penny
broadsides.[15] Their titles confirmed the popular picture of New
South Wales: *The Unhappy Transport, The Horrors of Transportation,
The Fell Tyrant, or the Suffering Convict* and *A Complete Exposure
of the Convict System, Its Horrors, hardships, and severities, including
an account of the Dreadful Sufferings of the Unhappy Captives.* Such
works borrowed freely from each other; some were genuine, others
not, but they shared similar assumptions, and generally reinforced
the same image of Botany Bay. Fairly typical was a broadside with
the rather overblown title:

> The Remarkable, Affecting, and Interesting LIFE, and Dreadful
> Sufferings of the poor unhappy Elizabeth Watson, The Daughter
> of a wealthy Merchant near Piccadilly, who was Seduced by a
> Gentleman, Under a promise of Marriage, at the early age of Six-
> teen, who afterwards abandoned her to all the horrors of infamy
> and poverty. Her Father refused her admittance to his house, and
> She was cast upon the Town, where, after enduring all the miseries
> of Prostitution, she was tempted through extreme distress to Rob

her Landlady, for which she was Convicted at the Old Bailey, and Transported to Botany Bay. Shewing the DREADFUL HARD-SHIPS which she underwent for Fourteen Years. Concluding with her return to England, a sincere Penitent, where she was kindly received by her Father.[16]

Such works were often clothed in conventional morality but, as with tabloid journalism today, the prime purpose was a commercial one. Their claims to moral respectability were often transparent. They purported to be dissuading the dissolute from their guilty practices, showing how easy it was to be led astray. They ended with penitent heroes hoping that their experiences would be a warning to others. The opportunity which this offered for titillating details of low life is apparent from the opening sentences of *The Life and Exploits of Ikey Solomons, Swindler, Forger, Fencer, and Brothel-Keeper*:

> This little work is held up as a warning beacon to keep the traveller from the sands of a poisonous desert, or from splitting on the rocks of infamy.
>   It is necessary in such a case to point out 'hells' and brothels, girls and bawds, and rogues, by name and situation, not as a direction for youth to steer towards them, but that he may take the contrary course—for no reasonable man would enter a whirlpool, when he could pass by it on the smooth surface of a summer sea.[17]

These books were pandering to a taste for tales of low life in London and of violence in Botany Bay, and were published in the hope of commercial success. Yet they reinforced the moral and economic function of Botany Bay as a weapon in the control of working-class crime in Britain.

Magwitch and the Middle Class

For the middle classes in England, Botany Bay posed a slightly different threat. The image remained one of depravity, but the great fear was, not that they themselves would end up there, but that they could unknowingly come into contact with a returned convict carrying the Botany Bay stigma. Peter Cunningham, a surgeon with the navy, explained the difficulty if you happened to mention to a fellow coach passenger, for example, that you had been to New South Wales:

> lo! the smile which played upon his face at once vanishes; he measures you over and over with a most suspicious eye; and with an anxiously inquisitive look grunts out, 'What! have *you* been out there, sir?'

Conversation suddenly flags, and while you attempt to change the subject, he 'takes advantage of your eye being off him to hitch himself gradually from you to the farthest corner of the coach; and, under pretence of fumbling after a pen-knife or tooth-pick, assures himself that all his pockets are safe'.[18]

The unexpected ex-convict haunted respectable England right through the nineteenth century. Charles Dickens played on that fear very cleverly in *Great Expectations*, published in 1861, when the fear was beginning to fade. While the young Pip is all alone on the dark, silent marshes, Dickens suddenly introduces Magwitch, 'A fearful man, all in coarse grey, with a great iron on his leg'. Although Magwitch emerges as the benefactor who turns Pip into a gentleman, Pip could not, even at the end, 'bring myself to bear the sight of him' imagining 'that he dragged one of his legs as if there were still a weight of iron on it, and that from head to foot there was Convict in the very grain of the man'.[19] In 1876 Thomas Hardy also played on this theme,

The middle-class horror of the convict stigma: Pip meets Magwitch in Great Expectations. *From a Chapman and Hall edition (circa 1870) illustrated by F.A. Fraser.*

when he satirised a conventional matron's dismay that she had dined unawares with her servant's daughter: 'to have honoured unawares the daughter of the vilest Antipodean miscreant and murderer would have been less discomfiting'.[20] It was beginning to fade by then, but the stereotype of the returned convict, who had known nameless horrors in Australia, and been guilty of nameless crimes, had almost been a convention of English fiction.

The Sins of the Fathers

The identification of the image of Botany Bay with the convict system caused it to be universally condemned. But what of the Australian society which was to emerge from the penal settlements? Eventually transportation would cease, to New South Wales in 1840, to the rest of eastern Australia in 1852, to Western Australia in 1868. Would these settlements remain for ever depraved? The common view was once a convict, always a convict: it was a stain that would never be removed. It was also commonly assumed that a bad character was inevitably passed from one generation to the next. Dr Thomas Arnold of Rugby thought it was 'a law of God's Providence . . . that the sins of the father are really visited upon the child in the corruption of his breed',[21] so the convict stain would last for generations. With such assumptions, most observers looked for the worst, and found it.

Depravity was not only inherited, but also contagious. John Turnbull, who visited Sydney twice between 1800 and 1804, found it had affected 'the general manners, or what may be called the national character' of the place. Free settlers caught the contagion, and lacked integrity and honour. Emancipists returned to lives of depravity, idleness, drunkenness and crime. Soldiers who chose to settle in the colony also 'abandoned themselves to drunkenness and other vices already too prevalent in the colony'.[22]

This was a relatively early assessment, but 40 years later, J.C. Byrne, who spent 12 years in the Australian colonies, came to the same bleak conclusion. The convicts failed to throw off their depravity, and not only were free settlers and the military infected, but even 'the higher classes of individuals'.[23] Indeed another writer feared— rather fancifully perhaps—that the prevalence of vice in the colonial upper class was 'quite beyond the reach of an unsophisticated English imagination'.[24] That the contagion reached even into the upper class, who were supposed to set the moral tone, seemed to confirm all the fears of the respectable observer about the depravity of New South Wales, fears which the notorious womanising of Governor Fitzroy and his sons in the 1840s did nothing to allay.

The whole society seemed affected. Vice was triumphant. The female convicts in particular were condemned, universally stereotyped as 'damned whores'.[25] The rot, it was said, had spread to the Aborigines, who were even more 'depraved' than the convicts,[26] and it was feared the contamination would spread through the Pacific.[27] Byrne saw no hope in the second generation:

> With convicts (emancipated) for their fathers, and convicts or prostitutes for mothers, little could be expected from the religion or morality of the rising generation, and but little has been realized; for on the face of the globe there does not exist such an accumulation of crime, of the most horrifying description, as in New South Wales. It is awful even to think of it; it pervades every class, revels in most abodes, from the solitary cell or the lonely bush hut, up to the homes of the magnates of the land.[28]

This was a predictable view from respectable nineteenth-century Englishmen, ready to measure morality by religious observance and sobriety. With the then recent great social changes in Britain, respectable people were especially sensitive to further upheaval. Byrne shared the horror of a Magwitch-like figure turning up unexpectedly:

> General society cannot be said to exist there, [in N.S.W.] particularly in the shape of public balls, *réunions*, and concerts, when you may expect to find the person on your right hand, a murderer; him on the left, a burglar.[29]

The critics were middle-class observers bringing their own values to a scrutiny of working-class life in Australia. They had not yet scrutinised English 'low life' in the same way, although they were shortly to be equally shocked by the revelations of Mayhew, Engels and parliamentary reports.[30] They thus established a pattern which was to be repeated: characteristics were seen as being distinctively Australian when in fact they were equally a part of the English social order. For such men, the result was that to be Australian, whether convict, native-born or free settler, was to be tainted with the brutality and depravity of the convict system.

These attitudes surrounded a campaign against transportation. By the 1830s, theories of both penology and colonisation were being vigorously debated, and the alleged depravity of the penal colonies was continually brought up by the reformers. A potentially wealthy colony was being turned into a 'vast heap of moral corruption'.[31]

The campaign culminated in the Molesworth Committee which condemned the 'curious and monstrous evil of calling into existence ... the germs of nations most thoroughly depraved'.[32] Richard Whately, Archbishop of Dublin and a leading colonial reformer, rejected the idea that future generations might improve: given 'the boasted fecundity of the worst description of females in New Holland', transportation bred more vice than if the criminals had been left at home. He shuddered at the thought that such a colony might one day grow to nationhood: 'think what stuff this people will have been made of; and who it is that posterity will then curse for bringing this mildew on the social intercourse of the world'.[33]

When the *Edinburgh Review* drew a similar picture, it was concerned instead to promote free colonisation: 'the rank deposit which we have left on these remote shores has blighted some of the fairest regions of the earth with its exhalations: the vices of the old and the new world have met there, in one fermenting mass'.[34] The only benefit to the colonies of the convict system—cheap labour—was not worth the cost. The reformers wanted to promote a different image of the colonies which would attract emigrants and turn these colonies into profitable markets. To do so, they needed to dwell on the horrors of the system at Botany Bay. In their own way, the arguments for reform, like the sentimental chap-books or the moral tracts, reinforced the idea that Botany Bay was a hell on earth, albeit a more bourgeois version of hell.

Nature or Nurture

There was at the same time a campaign both for and against transportation going on in Australia itself. Those who benefited from the cheap labour of convicts could not agree that depravity was contagious. As early as 1822, their views found their way into the Bigge Report. Bigge had concluded that the children of convicts were 'a remarkable exception to the moral and physical character of their parents'.[35] In 1838, in the New South Wales Legislative Council, the supporters of transportation resolved that it continue. They claimed the Molesworth Committee had misrepresented the moral condition of the colony, and that the rising generation, far from being corrupted by convict depravity, were impressing 'a character of respectability upon the Colony at large'.[36] Earlier these same men had been more disposed to argue the contagion of convict depravity as a reason to oppose free institutions in the colony: that, after all, would have detracted from their own influence.

However it was not only the colonial supporters of transportation who resisted the image of the colonies as corrupted for generations to come. There were local capitalists who saw more benefit in skilled free immigrants than in convict labour, and they knew that 'sober and industrious' workers would not be attracted to a moral dunghill.[37] But more than simple economic interest was involved. Those who identified themselves with Australia were naturally disposed to look more favourably on the character of native-born—'currency' Australians of convict stock—who held the key to the future. Alexander Harris had found spiritual comfort in religion, and social comfort in mateship, in the unlikely sanctuary of New South Wales. Identifying with the colony as an immigrant, not as a mere visitor, he commented on the local image of the 'currency':

> I have never heard or seen the fact noticed out of the colony, but it was one well-known within it ... that from convict blood, on either or both sides, has sprung much more than the average of the strength and beauty of the colony.[38]

Such a view directly challenged the dominant view in Britain, as expressed by men such as Turnbull, Byrne and Whately. It also questioned the assumption that character was inherited, that the sins of the parents must pass on to the children.

Within the colony, there was a predisposition to accept the enlightenment belief in the influence of environment on character. A small group of intellectuals were conscious of themselves as future leaders. They were setting out to produce the 'first fruits' of literature, writing the first 'historical' accounts of Australia, proclaiming themselves the honest interpreters of the new society. None went so far as the moral philosopher who declared transportation was 'a great experiment in ... renovation in the human character',[39] but they did view the second generation favourably. They naturally preferred to see themselves as midwives to a culture that would lead rather than deprave the world.

As early as 1823, when W.C. Wentworth wrote his 'Australasia' for the Chancellor's Prize at Cambridge, he proudly signed himself 'An Australasian' and modestly noted that his poem was 'the first fruits of Australasian poesy'. He betrayed at the same time a sense of inferiority, an awareness that his inflated hopes for his 'new Arcadia' did not accord with the conventional wisdom about a society based on convict stock. He simply claimed that Australia's glorious future would not only outshine, but actually grow out of, its ignoble beginnings:

> Land of my hope! soon may this early blot,
> Amid thy growing honours, be forgot . . .
> Nor more the outcast convicts' clanking chains
> Deform thy wilds, and stigmatize thy plains . . .

If imperial Rome was 'Hatch'd in an aery fouler far than thine', Australia had nothing to fear from its convict parentage:

> So, Australasia, may thy exil'd band
> Spread their young myriads o'er thy lonely land.[40]

Clearly Wentworth did not share Whately's fears about convict fecundity, and trusted that the characteristics of the convicts would not be passed on to succeeding generations.

He had some support for this view from Peter Cunningham who had taken up land in the colony. He identified with it to the extent of calling it '*Australia* as we colonials say' and even found himself looking on gum trees with pleasure! He found the currency children 'a fine interesting race'; they were 'little tainted with the vices so prominent among their parents! Drunkenness is almost unknown with them, and honesty proverbial'. He failed to convince Archbishop Whately, particularly when he let slip that the currency lasses 'do not commonly appear to class chastity as the *very first* of virtues' and the young men were fond of boxing.[41] Whately leapt on this as evidence that the sins of the parents had been passed on to the children.[42]

Whately in his turn was rounded on by John Dunmore Lang, that ardent proto-nationalist with the attachment of a proselyte to his adopted country. He condemned Whately's attack on convict colonies such as New South Wales. Such 'wrong-headed people' were forming

> in their fertile imagination, a sort of inclined plane, descending from the actual level of society to the bottomless pit, down which a colony so formed would be sure to descend, with the perpetually increasing velocity of a falling body.

Lang shared Cunningham's more charitable view of the second generation and quoted the English radical Cobbett to support his case that crime was due to poverty not inherited characteristics.[43] Just as Byrne[44] and others looked for the worst, Wentworth, Cunningham and Lang looked for the industry, sobriety and respectability which were the great virtues of the age, and found them in the new generation. Lang claimed that he knew of many instances where the children of convicts became 'reputable, industrious, and virtuous members of society'. And naturally, like Wentworth, he was supremely confident of the future:

> I should have no fears whatever for the morals even of a convict colony, in the second, and still less in the third and fourth genera-tion ... The colonies of New South Wales and Van Diemen's Land ... are destined ... to take a high place, both in morals and in everything else, in the great family of nations.[45]

Now the interesting thing about this is that both arguments accepted the same low opinion of the convicts. Essentially they shared the popular English image of a depraved and vicious convict society. It was only towards the end of the nineteenth century that a new argu-ment became popular in Australia. Writers such as Marcus Clarke and Price Warung condemned the brutality of the system, rather than the depravity of the convicts, and for them this reflected on the morality, not of Australia, but of England. It was then a short step to the view put by G.A. Wood, the historian, that 'the atrocious criminals remained in England, while their victims, innocent and manly, founded the Australian democracy'.[46] This had always been a popular view among the convicts themselves, and was expressed in many convict ballads, and popular eighteenth-century rhymes such as

The law locks up the man or woman
Who steals the goose from off the common,
But leaves the greater villain loose
Who steals the common from the goose.[47]

Those intellectuals setting out to create an image of Australia in the early nineteenth century were still a long way from regarding the convicts themselves as respectable and manly. They shared the English view of convict depravity, but where they differed was in their estima-tion of the second generation, the 'fine and numerous families' of the convicts. They strove to distinguish between being convict (and British) and being Australian. In so doing they revealed a propensity within Australia to regard environment as a greater moulder of character than inheritance. Their attempt to redefine the image of the second generation was less successful outside Australia. What was to have more effect on the accepted view of Australia was the opportunity it presented, particularly to men in England of some capital, for investment and social mobility. Despite its disreputable occupants, the land was modestly plentiful. Or as Sydney Smith noted in 1819, 'this land of convicts and kangaroos is beginning to rise into a very fine and flourishing settlement'.[48]

So perhaps Frank the Poet summed up one image of Australia

when he left Van Diemen's Land with a conditional pardon in his pocket. Before leaving, he climbed the paddle-box of the boat and proclaimed to his friends:

> Land of Lags and Kangaroo,
> Of 'possums and the scarce Emu
> The Farmer's pride but the Prisoner's Hell,
> Land of Bums—Fare-thee-well![19]

It was significant that his destination was New South Wales which, at least for Frank the Poet, had outgrown the reputation under which Van Diemen's Land still laboured. It could now be seen as a land of opportunity for the ex-convict, as well as for England's 'surplus population' and for the sturdy and ambitious men who felt their prospects in England were limited.

3 A Workingman's Paradise?

To hear him talk you'd think it was a heaven upon earth,
But listen and I'll tell you now the plain, unvarnished truth.
'Immigration', anonymous ballad[1]

Between 1830 and 1850, Hell was turned into Paradise. A gradual shift in the needs of both the British and local economies resulted in a new, more complimentary image of Australia competing with, and eventually overwhelming, the old convict image. The establishment of the wool industry turned the gaol into a vast sheep-run which by 1850 was providing half of Britain's wool. Along with other local industries, it continued to demand labour from Britain at the same time that British manufacturing interests were seeking profitable overseas markets. Emigration suited them both, offering labourers as well as markets. From 1832 various schemes of assisted migration were set up and by 1850, had attracted about 100,000 migrants to New South Wales and Van Diemen's Land, while another 50,000 had paid their own way. They were lured by a new image of Australia as a land of opportunity for all comers, and above all for the working man. This image continued to attract—and deceive—migrants for the rest of the century. No longer a land of convicts and kangaroos, Australia was now depicted as the land of the emigrant. And the emigrants came: by 1851 convicts represented only 1.5 per cent of the population of New South Wales, emancipists 14 per cent and free immigrants 41 per cent.[2]

Arcadia in Hell

Even while the convict image of Australia had been dominant, there had always been an undercurrent of admiration for the new country. It was commonly expressed in relation to the landscape, the favourite comparison being to an English gentleman's park. Underlying this admiration we can detect the aspiration of men of capital to establish themselves in Australia as landed gentlemen. Sydney Parkinson, artist on the *Endeavour*, had made the comparison in his journal, published in 1773.[3] Arthur Bowes, surgeon in the first fleet, reported that the country around Port Jackson excelled in beauty 'any nobleman's grounds in England'[4] and Elizabeth Macarthur that 'the greater part of the country is like an English park'.[5] In 1802 Port Phillip was thought to fall 'nothing short, in beauty and appearance, of Greenwich Park',[6] while in 1828, country further east was seen as resembling 'the park of a country seat in England, the trees standing in picturesque groups to ornament the landscape'.[7] Thomas Mitchell, exploring 'Australia Felix' in 1836, thought the country 'had so much the appearance of a well kept park' that he was loath to drive his carts across it.[8] Such comments reflected fashionable taste for the neo-classical and the picturesque in judging landscape. The irony was that the Aborigines, whose systematic burning-off was largely responsible for giving the country its park-like appearance, were to be seen as pests, obstacles in the way of men realising their dream of becoming landed gentlemen.

The attractions of the settlement were also spread by convicts returning home. Some told tales of horror, but some suggested that a poor man might make good in the Antipodes. As one ballad put it, there was 'a lot of jolly living over there'.[9] There was enough truth in the rumours of the rags-to-riches convict to give some consolation to those about to be transported, and considerable heart-burning to the penal system's administrators. Given the increasingly desperate plight of the British working class from 1815 to the 'Hungry Forties', it was easy for the ruling class to believe that transportation was a 'boon' rather than a deterrent, and to worry endlessly that convicts in New South Wales were better off than free labourers in Britain. They even told themselves that people were committing crime in the hope of being transported. Although the idea had wide currency among those who thought the system too lenient, it seems that this might have been yet another myth associated with the Australian colonies.[10]

Attempts were made to tighten up the system but the real problem was that an image which was supposed to strike terror into the heart simply could not be reconciled with one which was to attract sober and industrious workers. William Molesworth had explained the problem in 1840, after his committee had recommended an end to transportation to New South Wales:

It not unfrequently happens that whilst a judge is expatiating on the miseries of exile, at the same time, and perhaps in the same place, some active agent of emigration may be found magnifying the advantages of the new country ... telling of the high wages to be obtained, the enormous fortunes that have been made, and offering to eager and willing listeners, as a boon and especial favour, the means of conveyance to that very place to which the convict in the dock has been sentenced by the judge for his crimes.[11]

Others also had difficulty reconciling the two images. George Loveless attempted to distinguish between the people and the place: in one breath he condemned the prevalence of corruption, drunkenness, robbery and rape among the inhabitants, and in the next praised the country's beauty, climate, 'rich and luxuriant' soil and evergreen trees.[12] David Mackenzie faced the same problem. He had been recruited by J.D. Lang to teach at Lang's Australian College, but preferred making money out of sheep to making gentlemen out of his students. In his 1845 guide for emigrants, he asked his readers to

Picture to yourselves ... a vast forest diversified with mountains and valleys; innumerable plains without a tree ... large tracts of open forest-land, resembling a gentleman's domain in England ... extensive lagoons, darkened with legions of wild duck and teal, the property of any man who may choose to shoot them; innumerable birds of the most beautiful plumage, chirping on every branch around you; flowers of every hue and shade of colour strewing your path, wherever you go; above you an Italian sky, without a cloud or speck, and the air you inhale pure and balmy; a fearful silence pervading the forest around you, and vividly impressing upon your mind the idea of solitude and desolation—*that is Australia.*

He realised that such a pleasant picture, full of all the fashionable exemplars of beauty, was open to ridicule. A 'mischievous wag' could just as easily paint a picture of a land of convicts and bushrangers, swindling and drunkenness, selfishness and irreligion, mosquitoes and drought, a land of '*never*-green' rather than evergreen. In the end Mackenzie reverted to the image of Australia as a land of contrarieties.[13]

The need for a new, more complimentary image was accompanied by a search for more appropriate names. Originally the names Botany Bay, New Holland and New South Wales were popularly but inaccurately used to refer to the whole continent. All were associated with the convict system and none could be expected to attract many migrants. As Archbishop Whately pointed out, 'The name of *Botany Bay*, &c. could not, for generations, become connected in men's minds with honesty, sober industry, the higher qualities of the British character'.[14] In 1814 Matthew Flinders, whose circumnavigation had proved New Holland and New South Wales to be part of the same land mass, had suggested the name Australia, 'being more agreeable to the ear, and an assimilation to the names of the other great portions of the earth'.[15] It stuck. Vague classical allusions were felt to be more acceptable than the prosaic names provided by Cook, names which had so quickly lost their meaning in their disreputable associations. Men like Wentworth and Lang began to make an ostentatious habit of signing themselves 'an Australian' without the fear of being taken for a pick-pocket or a savage. For the same reasons, the name Van Diemen's Land was replaced by Tasmania, from the 1820s in popular usage, formally in 1854. When the Moreton Bay District became a colony in 1859, it was hoped that the convict stigma would be buried by renaming it Queensland.[16] The changes were not always successful: as late as 1882, a Tasmanian was complaining that 'not one in a hundred . . . knows this island by the name of Tasmania; but it is well known as Van Diemen's Land; the land of white slavery'.[17]

Salvation for All-Comers

Several groups contributed to and stood to benefit from the portrayal of Australia as a land of opportunity for the emigrant. Men of capital in England could see profit to be had. There were many of them in the 1830s and 1840s with accumulated profits burning holes in their pockets.[18] Manufacturers could see in colonisation 'an enterprise which would convert . . . paupers into customers'.[19] Colonial reformers saw emigration as a means of easing poverty and distress in England, which otherwise threatened to erupt in revolution. Caroline Chisholm's proud boast was that she had convinced a Chartist that the solution to social problems in England was to emigrate.[20] Shipping agents benefited more directly, particularly from the assisted passage schemes of the 1830s. Their posters exaggerated the virtues of New South Wales to such an extent that in 1840 the Colonial Office stepped in to regulate their activities.[21] The Colonial Office itself saw emigration as an economy: it was a cheaper solution to working-class distress than police and gaols, since it was paid for by land sales.[22] Finally colonial capitalists themselves, seeking to attract workers and respectable families, were not averse to a little exaggeration in their attempts to advertise Australia as a land where all could make good. It should be added that working-class organisations, in both Britain and Australia, often opposed the encouragement of emigration to Australia: as one English working-class paper put it, 'we will not quit our fatherland to companion with demi-savages and kangaroos', but such efforts to undermine Australia's new image did not generally succeed.[23]

The supporters of emigration to Australia painted a picture of an idealised Arcadian society, a rural Utopia, an Eden before the fall. Very different imaginations could produce surprisingly similar visions of Australia's future. W.C. Wentworth, full of Oxford scholarship and classical allusions, hoped the 'new Arcadia' would soon 'teem with simple swains'.[24] He had already written *A Statistical, Historical, and Political Description of the Colony of New South Wales* in 1819, in which he tried to show the advantages for migrants of New South Wales over America. 'What a cheering prospect' he thought

> for the philanthropist to behold what is now one vast and mournful wilderness, becoming the smiling seat of industry and the social arts ... What a proud sight for the Briton to view his country pouring forth her teeming millions to people new hives.[25]

J.D. Lang, the staunch Presbyterian, published his *Historical and Statistical Account of New South Wales* in 1834. With his more biblical style, he described his vision of currency lads, 'each of whom, on attaining man's estate, goes forth with his axe into the vast forest to extend the limits of civilization, and to fill the wilderness and the solitary place with the habitations of men'.[26] It was a vision reminiscent of the America he admired and believed Australia should imitate, and it was more appropriate to the American mid-west than the Australian outback, particularly when he spoke of 'peopling her vast solitudes with a numerous, industrious and virtuous agricultural population' and causing 'her moral wilderness to blossom as the rose'.[27]

A third vision was that of Caroline Chisholm, a convert to Catholicism, who saw Australia as a refuge for the poor, particularly the Irish poor. Almost one million Irish starved to death in the Great Famine of 1846–47. Lang believed she was simply trying to populate the place with Papists, but her own vision of her work was of a 'God-like undertaking', establishing 'a well-fed peasantry',[28] bringing 'Comfort to the Poor' and the benefits of rural family life to an uncivilised wilderness. Her appeal was to sentiment—she was, after all, an associate of Charles Dickens. So after the famine she asked:

> Is it not sad,—is it not awful,—is it not harrowingly painful, to think, to know, that since that period,—within the twelvemonth,

—that a vast, a magnificent tract of country, rich in pasture, inter-
sected by fine rivers, untrodden by European foot before, has been
discovered by that indefatigable and successful explorer, Sir Thomas
Mitchell, in the heart of New Holland, able to maintain millions
of families, and yet that thousands upon thousands of poor have
died around us of starvation?[29]

The remarkable thing about these varied visions of simple swains,
pioneering families and well-fed peasantry was that they had nothing
at all to do with the Australian reality. In fact, Australia's economy,
and British interest in the colonies, was to be based on big sheep-
runs, mining and large cities. Nor was Australia to be an extension
of rural England: Australia's connection was with industrial England,
providing wool for its factories and markets for its goods. These
hard realities were ignored. Rather the romantic visions were an
imaginative response to industrialisation in England. Behind all the
admiration for Australia's fresh air, its greenness, its sense of space,
its Arcadian innocence and its imagined social harmony, there lurked
an unstated comparison with a cold, crowded, polluted, industrialised
and socially-divided England. The industrial revolution was still, for
many, a traumatic shock. The visions of rural innocence in Australia
appealed to a deep-seated emotional resentment against industrialisation.

The result was that the supporters of emigration saw Australia
becoming the sort of society they imagined England to have been in
the past, before it disappeared under the grime of the industrial
revolution. The *Edinburgh Review* made it quite clear: 'by colonization nations are able to retrieve the past'.[30] For E.G. Wakefield, the
most influential of the systematic colonisers, Australia was to be the
means of recreating a rural squirearchy; for Samuel Sidney, another
propagandist for emigration, it would allow the labouring classes to
reclaim their patrimony, recreating a more equal society, for men at
least, with 'every striving man who rears a race of industrious children
... living on his own land, looking down to the valleys to his herds—
towards the hills to his flocks, amid the humming of bees'.[31] The
romantic image of an ideal rural society would continue to influence
Australia, and helps account for the continuing opposition both to
vast sheep-runs and to large cities. Dispersal and urbanisation were
equally crimes against the Arcadian dream. In 1883 someone who
had never been to England was still dreaming of Australia 'casting
off her un-British fashion of lonely sheep-walks' and becoming 'with
green fields and neighbourly, contented country life, like the England
of Shakespeare and Milton'.[32] Through the Selection Acts of the

1860s, through closer settlement schemes and talk about decentralisation, the image lingered on, and continued to attract its share of immigrants.

Although often carried away with their own powers of description, most writers with first-hand knowledge of Australian conditions sounded a note of warning. Only particular classes of emigrants could be expected to succeed, although there was some confusion over exactly which classes these would be. In 1827 Peter Cunningham thought only families with at least £1200 should migrate to Australia —otherwise, America offered better prospects.[33] In the 1830s, when the colonies were trying to attract free labourers and female emigrants, respectable single middle-class women were warned that they could not be assured of finding wealth and happiness—in the form of a husband—in New South Wales.[34] Unskilled labourers were told that Van Diemen's Land was not 'the garden of Eden for emigrants the deluded people of England imagine'.[35] In 1834 'respectable young men' hoping to be clerks, were warned off by J.D. Lang who thought New South Wales 'the preferable country for a gentleman-farmer' or for 'respectable families of moderate capital',[36] while in 1839 it was said there were good prospects for 'labourers of all classes'.[37] By 1848 one visitor was accusing wealthy landowners of deceiving the poor with 'distorted and exaggerated accounts ... of the flattering prospects afforded to all classes ... and the almost certain wealth which awaited them', although 'Any good tradesman, of whatever denomination, can do very well'.[38] Another Emigrant's Friend advised that Australia was 'flooded with clerks' but 'mere labourers and shepherds', small farmers and large capitalists were all likely to succeed.[39]

Time would alter the reality behind some of these judgments. The depression of the early 1840s in Australia meant that no group could expect much. The abolition of transportation eventually improved the chances of labourers since they no longer had to compete with cheaper convict labour. The gold rushes at first offered the slim chance of a fortune to men on the diggings and later, in a more complex society, openings were created for a wider range of groups. But even in 1873, Anthony Trollope made a point of warning off 'The would-be government clerk, the would-be governess, the would-be school-master, lawyer, storekeeper or the like'.[40]

The warnings usually went unheeded. While visitors were at pains to stress that Australia could only offer salvation to a few, too often it was seen as offering salvation to all. From the 1830s until the 1890s, the image of Australia as a land of opportunity for all-comers remained the popular one, and it was one which was encouraged by colonial employers seeking labour. Over that period the image changed little although for a time it acquired a distinct golden tinge. The discovery of gold had enormous social and economic effects on Australia, but it did not greatly alter the prevailing view of Australia: Samuel Sidney simply extended it to 'an El Dorado and an Arcadia combined'.[41] Gold popularised the image immensely, increased the numbers attracted by it, and hastened the demise of the convict image. But still, Australia was portrayed as the land of opportunity, a paradise for those to whom Britain offered nothing, and the hope remained, as the Selection Acts made clear, that the idealised vision of small farms and pioneering families would be given substance in Australia.

The pervasiveness of the idea that Australia offered salvation, indiscriminately, to all-comers, can perhaps best be seen in the English novel: emigration, to Australia, the United States and elsewhere, became a rather hackneyed literary convention for getting rid of embarrassing characters, particularly sympathetic characters such as fallen women or worthy workers who, through no fault of their own, found themselves unable to arrive at a conventional happy ending in English society as it was. Since few writers advocated overturning the system, they were left with three alternatives. Such characters could be killed off, with an appropriate effusion of Victorian sentimentality; they could come across an unexpected, but rarely convincing, inheritance; or they could be sent off as emigrants. Emigration was not an issue in the novel, simply a convention, a solution to an artistic problem which in fact reflected deep-seated problems within English society.[42] Australia was portrayed as a haven from industrial capitalism, the easy solution, not just for those who might succeed in Australian conditions, but indiscriminately, for all and sundry.

The result was that many authors packed off a great cavalcade of minor characters to Australia. The most remarkable mass exodus is found in Charles Dickens's *David Copperfield*, published in 1850. At the time he was giving active support to Caroline Chisholm's emigration schemes. All his characters who could not expect a happy ending in England were packed off to Australia: Martha, the kind-hearted prostitute, the fallen Emily and the Peggottys ('No one can't reproach my darling in Australia'),[43] old Mrs Gummidge, who even got a husband, and most successful of all, Mr Micawber and family, who thrived in Melbourne although they could never make ends meet in England. Other writers sent out declining landed gentry, the too-well-educated, black sheep 'to be whitewashed',[44] socially embarrassing relations, suspected thieves, middle-class bankrupts, the hopelessly incompetent, and steady labourers who could not find advancement.[45] Often they were the very groups warned not to emigrate, but most writers knew or cared little about the colonies. Some sort of salvation had to be found for the 'failures' inevitably produced in the struggle to survive while Britain industrialised. Once the character was on the ship, success was assumed.

The Emigrant as a Failure

The result of this was to give a further dimension to the image of the emigrant, and so to that of Australia. There were two main attitudes to the emigrant in Victorian Britain, both of which reflected bourgeois attitudes to the working class. The more conventional view was that the emigrant was a failure whose economic difficulties in Britain were caused by personal instability rather than an unjust system. It was an attractive view for the complacent middle class, one that can be clearly seen in the novels of Henry Kingsley who migrated to Australia, without much success, in 1853. Five years earlier his brother Charles, the more successful novelist, packed his most famous working-class character off to America.[46] Henry displayed great fawning sympathy for the landed gentry forced to Australia to bolster their declining incomes, but he despised the ordinary class of emigrant: 'their mere presence in this colony proves them to be unable to manage their own affairs with any success';[47] they were 'a lazy independent class . . . with exaggerated notions of their own importance', and were addicted to 'independence, godlessness, and rum'.[48] In 1843, James Backhouse, the Quaker missionary, had taken a similar view. His harsh puritanism gave cold comfort to the poor of the 'Hungry Forties'. In his view, migrants were fired with 'a restless spirit', an immoral refusal to submit themselves to the places ordained for them by God; dissatisfied with their lot, they were 'unwilling to believe that the fault is in themselves'. While he admitted that some 'sober, industrious and prudent persons' could legitimately improve their lot in Australia, he held out little hope for the majority, whose 'inefficiency and instability' would soon lead to 'hopeless degradation'.[49] In 1852, Earl Grey, the Secretary of State for Colonies told Charles Dickens that emigrants were 'necessarily far below the average of the working population in respect to steadiness and strictly moral conduct . . . in every rank of life it is not the steady and well conducted that are the most disposed to emigration'. He conceded that emigrants might have more 'energy and intelligence', but these were not qualities the middle class sought in workers.[50] The logical extension of this view of the emigrant was the portrayal of Australia as simply the 'dustbin of the unwanted and unsuccessful'.[51]

Many colonists shared this uncharitable view of the working-class immigrant, since they shared the social attitudes of the British middle class. Concerned to attract labour, they complained that the assisted migrants arriving after 1831 were not the 'sober and industrious' workers they desired; they accused Britain of 'shovelling out paupers', of dumping in the colonies 'the very refuse of the counties', and they demanded the introduction of a more 'moral and industrious population'.[52] In Van Diemen's Land in 1835, convicts and immigrants were considered equally depraved, a 'mingled mass of vice and villainy'.[53] The attitude to female immigrants was even more harsh, since it embodied Victorian attitudes to sex as well as class. J.D. Lang's view that female immigrants were turning New South Wales into 'a sink of prostitution'[54] was a common one among the colonial bourgeoisie.

The more charitable view of emigrants was that, failures though they were, it was rather the British social system which was at fault. This was the view that appealed to Victorian sentiment, depicting migrants as more sinned against than sinning, forsaken by their homeland which offered them only poverty or exile. It produced the sort of sentimental verse which comforted the young Henry Parkes when he boarded an emigrant ship, the sort of verse which began:

Oh! Emigration! Thou'rt the curse
Of our once happy nation's race!
Cannot our fatherland still nurse
Its offspring ... [55]

It produced the sentimental painting, *The Last of England*, painted by Ford Madox Brown after farewelling a friend to the Australian gold-fields. As Brown himself suggested, the sentimental view was an appropriate one when the emigrant was middle class: he had, 'in order to present the parting scene in its fullest tragic development, singled out a couple from the middle classes, high enough through education and refinement to appreciate all they are now giving up'.[56] But the image of the departing emigrant, of whatever class, was not just an excuse for sentimentality. Many writers, particularly in the 1840s, condemned the system which forced people into exile to find openings, and the result was an image of Australia and other emigrant societies as the saviours of what was callously called Britain's 'redundant population'.

Ford Madox Brown's painting, The Last of England *(Birmingham Art Gallery), was painted after farewelling his friend, Thomas Woolner, a sculptor who emigrated to the Australian goldfields in 1852. The sentimentality is reserved for the middle-class couple in the foreground, the implication being that the working-class migrants behind them felt nothing of the refined emotions of respectable people.*

However the two attitudes to migrants were not always so clear-cut. Dickens's Micawber, for example, was sympathetic, good-hearted and deserving of something better; but he was also pompous, hopelessly impecunious, financially incompetent, and really a joke. The system did not allow him to succeed in England, but nor did Dickens see him as deserving of the success he had in the colonies. The joke rubs off on Australia: it might be a haven for the poor but, as a society where someone like Micawber could make a splash, it cannot be taken seriously.

It is an intriguing, but ultimately fruitless, question to ask whether either of these images of the migrant was accurate—fruitless because in the final analysis such images reflect social prejudices rather than reality. Did Australia attract only the deserving and undeserving failures, the Micawbers and the good-for-nothings? Was there in fact something fundamentally second-rate about Australia? Certainly many migrants achieved far more in colonial life than they ever could have in Britain, particularly the group of gold rush immigrants who transformed themselves into a bourgeois establishment. Certainly there is something Micawberish and rather whimsical about the fortune of men such as Henry Parkes, who left England after business failures, graduated to business failures in Sydney, but ended up the grand old man of Australian politics, regarding himself as another Gladstone; or Redmond Barry, squeezed out of an over-crowded Irish bar, who could become a Supreme Court judge, founder of the Public Library, University Chancellor and, most respectable of all, the sentencer of Ned Kelly, yet still not marry the mother of his four children. On the other hand, what of men such as Robert Lowe, radical New South Wales Legislative Councillor, or Hugh Childers, first Victorian Auditor-General, men who could return to Britain and still be at the centre of things, both coincidentally becoming Chancellors of the Exchequer and Home Secretaries in later life? Clearly their prominence in Australian public life cannot be considered unmerited, yet the image of Australia as a haven for the second-rate was always strong in Britain, and was often shared by intellectuals in Australia. It helped justify their disdain for those they considered their social or cultural inferiors.

Myth and Reality

The success of men such as Parkes and Barry raises another issue: was Australia, in fact, the land of opportunity it was so often painted? While Australia never did conform to the popular dream of small farms and pioneer families, did it nevertheless offer to all-comers, and especially the working class, a better way of life? The image of Australia as a 'workingman's paradise' had long been fostered, particularly in the colonies. Even in 1844, in the midst of depression, Archibald Michie, later a prominent Victorian liberal politician, could proudly compare the working man's lot in Australia with that of

London, where he would 'linger out a short and shivering existence, and pine and starve and die, in courts, and alleys, and mouldy garrets of cheap lodging houses'.[57] During the gold rushes when immigration was at its height, it had been suggested that 'a voyage to Australia is the working man's only road to the future'.[58] By the 1880s, when the phrase 'a workingman's paradise' was most often heard and immigration was again high, self-congratulation was in the air. In 1881, H. Mortimer Franklyn, editor of the *Victorian Review*, judged that, for domestic servants, 'Australia is, indeed, the paradise of Bridget and Sarah Jane' and 'No working man, who is prudent, temperate and industrious, need occupy a house that is not his own . . . To the operative classes, Australia is a veritable land of promise'.[59] During the Centennial Celebrations of 1888, the *Sydney Morning Herald* observed that 'poverty is a comparatively rare thing among us . . . If elsewhere there is a possible danger of people getting too little, we are not entirely free sometimes from the danger of having too much'.[60] By 1893, during another depression, the New South Wales statistician was compiling aggregate figures that showed impressively that the general standard of living was higher in Australia than in Britain, Europe and even America.[61]

However, although this picture of a 'workingman's paradise' was a widely accepted one, there was always a thread of resistance to it, particularly among some working-class spokesmen. In 1843 a large group of workers, possibly 700, emigrated from Australia to Chile, 'under the firm conviction that in no other part of the world can their present condition be worse, or their future prospects less cheering'; they 'astonished' W.C. Wentworth, and pastoralists denied that conditions were really so bad, but the workers went all the same.[62] In the late 1850s, the Queensland government's attempts to attract labour by portraying the colony as a 'land of promise' met with the response from a popular ballad that:

> . . . men who come a living here to try
> Will vegetate a little while, and then lie down to die.[63]

In the 1880s Australian trade unions attempted to dissuade would-be emigrants from leaving England,[64] while in 1888, in response to all the self-congratulation, Henry Lawson was writing in the *Bulletin*:

> They lie, the men who tell us, for reasons of their own
> That want is here a stranger, and that misery's unknown.[65]

During the depression of the 1890s the resistance was still stronger. William Lane, the trade union activist, wrote a novel attempting to expose 'the much-prated-of "workingman's paradise"' by describing in detail the slums of Sydney.[66] Another writer commented that 'if Australia at present presents the Working Man's Paradise, I should hardly care for a glimpse even of the Workingman's Hades'.[67]

Clearly both sides were prepared to exaggerate. The idea that Australia was a 'workingman's paradise' gives a clear illustration of the way in which images can be constructed to serve the interests of particular groups. Colonial governments and employer groups sought to attract labour by painting a picture of a land of promise; equally it was in the interests of trade unions to maintain their members' conditions by discouraging immigration and constructing a bleaker image. But it is more complex than this. Historians disagree on the question of working-class affluence,[68] but it is true that, despite the general assumption that the Australian standard of living was high, there were very large areas of both rural and urban poverty throughout the nineteenth century. Comparisons with Britain are hazardous, but Australian slums were just as bad—in 1859 Sydney's health officer thought them even worse.[69] Factories could be just as confined, exploitative and unsanitary, and conditions deteriorated as much in an Australian summer as in an English winter. Public health could be further behind when, for example, the state of the water supply was bad enough for a judge to dismiss a charge of intoxication on the grounds that beer was all there was to drink.[70] Yet, despite the evidence of inquiries into social conditions, factories and public health, there are several reasons why, when compared to England, Australia continued to be seen as a 'workingman's paradise', apart from the direct economic interests of employers.

In the first place, all migrants compare their adopted country with the country they left, but often the comparison is a false one because it is based on a dated idea of the old country, and ignores changes that have taken place since they left. So when migrants talked about a 'workingman's paradise' in Australia in the 1880s, the England they pictured in their minds as a working man's hell was not contemporary England, but the England that they had known 20 or 30 years earlier. For non-migrants the comparison was even less valid, being based on hearsay, their parents' memories or the vagaries of a national myth. This time element is crucial in making any comparisons with Victorian Britain because, from the 'Hungry Forties' until about 1900, real wages had shown a steady and marked improvement. Industrialisation in Britain had reached the stage where it was turning workers into consumers, of transport, clothing, food and household goods. The use of a basic commodity such as sugar, for example, rose from

17lb per head per year in the early 1840s, to 90lb 50 years later.[71] There was a gradual, although painfully slow, improvement in hours and conditions of work and in the political influence of the working class.

The image of the typical worker changed too. In the 1840s the worker was seen as dirty, wretched, exhausted, demoralised—and dangerous. By the end of the century, a new image had developed: vulgar, independent, self-confident, flashily-dressed, newly-literate, sports-mad, technologically-competent. They were less likely to be called mere 'hands': given the Victorian middle class's passion for the machine, its operator was held in higher regard and called an 'operative' or a 'mechanic'. James Smith reflected such attitudes when he observed in 1866 that 'The operative is rapidly being transformed into the guide, controller and director of infinitely ingenious and inestimably efficient mechanical agencies'.[72] Those two common images overstated the change: the first reflected the fears of the middle class, the second their complacency and condescension. Working-class life remained hard, the improvements often only applied to particular groups of workers, and at the end of the century government investigations and social reformers could still 'discover' great areas of appalling poverty in both Britain and Australia. Nevertheless, the change was there, gradual but noticeable enough over any period of a decade or more in the later nineteenth century. G.C. Mundy, the conservative New South Wales Adjutant-General, had asked as early as 1852:

> [if] the feodality of feeling existing between master and man has departed altogether out of the land?—departing out of *all* lands? I have been inclined to think so ever since the last groom and valet I had at home—a modernising fellow, who attended his club twice a week—taught me to look upon myself, not as his master but as his *employer*.[73]

Other observers noticed the change in Australia, but assumed it was distinctively Australian, and proof that they were in a 'workingman's paradise'. In fact, as Mundy suggests, it was a more general change taking place in Britain, North America and parts of Europe as well. Believers in the 'workingman's paradise' often confused changes over a period of time with differences between England and Australia.

The second reason for the persistence of the image of Australia as a 'workingman's paradise' is the way in which it legitimised the role of the colonial bourgeoisie. Emigration often did result in individual social mobility. Those migrants who had risen into the colonial bourgeoisie from more humble origins in Britain, who found themselves in positions of influence they would not have reached at home, were the one group most likely to foster the idea that Australia was a 'workingman's paradise'. They viewed their own experience as proof of it. They were now in a position to suggest that they too had suffered the oppression which was identified with England, and had risen in the freer air of Australia. This meant that some would improve the conditions of their own workers: master stone-masons who had themselves started as workers could help initiate the movement for the Eight-Hour Day in their industry.[74] However it also meant that others could turn a blind eye to oppression alleging that in a working man's paradise it was the working man's fault if he failed to prosper. Thus in 1883, W.H.S. Blake, a tailor and a leader of the Early Closing Association, favourably compared Australian conditions with the England he remembered, where he had been forced to work 100 hours a week.[75] In that year, mill engine-drivers in Australia still worked up to 100 hours a week.[76] But more significant is Blake's exploitation of his own workers as a master tailor: in 1902 he was working female apprentices without pay (for theoretically a 60 hour week), paying the best of them five shillings a week after 18 months and dismissing the others.[77] The 'workingman's paradise' clearly suited Mr Blake.

The conviction that Australia was a 'workingman's paradise' helped preserve the social order.[78] It helped reconcile the working class to an unequal distribution of wealth. When poverty could not be ignored, it helped at least to explain it away. H.M. Franklyn argued that poverty in Australia was caused by an 'immense amount of that unthrift and self-indulgence' which accompanies 'abundance'.[79] Poverty in the land of promise was explained by personal failings. The local bourgeoisie could not justify their position by pretending they were born to it; rather, in a land of promise where all white men were equal, success and failure were the result of individual character. And so they could believe, as one of them said, that 'whenever men fell from health and happiness into disease and misery, in nine cases out of ten it was through their own fault and misconduct'.[80] In a land of promise there was no reason to resent the social order; indeed, employers muttered to themselves, a 'workingman's paradise' suggested that if anything workers were too well off.

Finally the image of a 'workingman's paradise' was supported at the time by evidence that some sections of the working class simply *were* better off in Australia. It was common to point to better food, working-class home ownership, pianos in working-class parlours. Such evidence needs to be treated cautiously. The fact that, with the help of building societies and land speculators, a minority of workers did own their own homes does not mean they were necessarily better off since rents in Australia were generally higher.[81] Caroline Chisholm's much-trumpeted promise of 'meat three times a day'[82] could be a mixed blessing, as one Rockhampton labourer pointed out to Trollope: 'If you knew what it was,' he said, 'to have to eat mutton three times a day, day after day, week after week, month after month, you would not come here and tell us that we ought to be contented with our condition'.[83] It was not, in any case, a very healthy diet.

More important is the fact that most of the benefits of a 'workingman's paradise' were only available to a minority of the working class, to sections of the skilled, white, male workforce. The benefits did not extend to men out of work, when employment could be very insecure. In 1859, two-thirds of Sydney's building trades workers, some of whom had achieved the Eight-Hour Day, were out of work.[84] The benefits did not extend to women and children who worked; the hours and conditions of work for women could be appalling, while in the 1870s in Melbourne, despite a factory act and compulsory education, there were still children working 60 hours a week for $1\frac{1}{2}$d an hour.[85] Nor did the benefits usually extend to unskilled labourers whose hours were longer, wages lower and employment more precarious than skilled men. Often, they did not extend to lower white-collar workers, the 'shabby genteel', the clerks and shopmen whom Nat Gould thought 'far worse off than the labourers'.[86] Even worse off were the kanakas in the sugar industry, the Chinese in laundries, market gardening and furniture manufacture and, worst of all, the Aborigines who were working extensively in the pastoral industry often for less than subsistence rations. England did not contain equivalent racial groups exploited for their labour. Finally there were many selectors and their families, scratching hopelessly at poor, inadequate land, who had struggled closest to the dream of small agricultural holdings. For many it was a shattering, miserable existence. Among them was Ned Kelly.

The benefits of the 'workingman's paradise' only went to a minority. The workers' cottages described by Twopeny, with all their 'manifest virtues',[87] were owned by skilled workers: building societies described their clientele as 'thriving artisans and prosperous tradesmen with neither too much nor too little of worldly goods'.[88] The Eight-Hour Day, another central feature of the 'workingman's paradise', only applied to the skilled building trades when it was first negotiated in Victoria in 1855, and only to stone-masons in New South Wales. Its gradual and haphazard extension only applied to the aristocracy of labour. The popular image obscured the very different conditions of workers; it implied the 'workingman's paradise' was open to all, at all times. That veneer of prosperity was ominously thin, and could easily be shattered by unemployment, recession, illness or old age.

The idea of Australia as some sort of paradise could mean many things. For sections of British society it could be an imaginative reaction against industrialisation, or a convenient salvation for the failures of industrial society, or merely a scrapheap, a dustbin for the sweepings of the poor-house. For migrants it held out hopes that would often have been illusory. In Australia it could be used deceptively, to attract labour and ignore poverty, or complacently, to prop up the system, and imply that the worker had all he or she could possibly hope for. Needless to say, it also reinforced discrimination against women, children, non-whites, the unemployed and other sections of the working class, since only the successful, adult, white male fitted the image of the 'workingman'. It was rarely an accurate description of the Australia that the working class knew.

But for that one group, white, skilled males in secure jobs, it had more meaning, especially when some of them became employers themselves. In Australia's different social structure, they had more prominence and more status than in England, and this was perhaps why they were always noticed by visitors, and taken as evidence of egalitarian prosperity. In 1883, Twopeny had seen the plumber as typical of 'the Australian working-man', struck by the fact that he had to try four before he could get one to take on a job, who then did not turn up.[89] In the twentieth century the plumber continued to be seen as typical, particularly when regarded by the middle class as a perfect example of workers earning too much. A long string of observers also saw the plumber as a symbol of equality, because when the plumber called he frequently drank tea with the housewife.[90] Perhaps he does, but if it proves anything, it is not that Australia is an egalitarian paradise, but that the upper working class attract more than usual respect in Australia. It remains true that no-one ever asks the garbage man to tea.

4   Another America

The people of this colony resemble the Americans in their presumption, arrogance, ignorance, and conceit.

G.T.W.B. Boyes[1]

The question of Australian identity has usually been seen as a tug-of-war between Australianness and Britishness, between the impulse to be distinctively Australian and the lingering sense of a British heritage. However this attitude to the development of an Australian identity only became common towards the end of the nineteenth century, when self-conscious nationalists began to exaggerate what was distinctive about Australia. The result has been that those aspects of the Australian identity which were not distinctive have been underestimated ever since. In fact, during most of the nineteenth century, it was generally accepted that Australia had a clear political and cultural 'image' which was considered neither particularly British nor Australian. Australians saw themselves, and were seen by others, as part of a group of new, transplanted, predominantly Anglo-Saxon emigrant societies. The basis of this shared image varied. Sometimes the emphasis was on being new; at other times, on being colonial; later a more explicitly racial element was added, so the emphasis was on being Anglo-Saxon or, as these societies grew more confident, on being the most vigorous branch of Anglo-Saxondom. The Irish had a slightly different view of them as societies freed from British repression. But certainly, the question of a distinctively Australian identity was not the burning issue it was to become for later historians.

Australia as a New Society

It was accepted, both in Europe and in the new societies themselves, that they all—the United States, Canada, Australia, New Zealand, southern Africa, occasionally Argentina, Uruguay and other parts of

South America—had much in common. Words such as brash, young, egalitarian, materialistic, provincial, braggart, were applied to all of them. They were commonly thought of as the children of Britain or Europe, as strapping sons, dutiful daughters or juvenile delinquents. Politically they were considered 'in advance' of Europe; culturally they were more often thought to be inferior. Their inhabitants developed a counter-image of Europe or the 'Old World': oppressive and decadent, but also sophisticated and intellectually intimidating, the old world could be sentimentalised or identified with poverty and privilege.

The new societies had a similar ancestry. The Australian colonies were by no means the only lands of opportunity offered to the British working class, nor the only solution to a Victorian novelist's problems. Indeed in 1850 the Australian colonies were only attracting 6 per cent of British emigrants, and even in the gold rushes, they only attracted a third of the number going to the United States.[2] Emigrant societies were to be distinguished from dependencies existing purely for economic exploitation. Thus in Trollope's definition of colonies, as 'countries outside our own, which by our energies we have made fit for the occupation of our multiplying race'[3], he included the United States but excluded India. These new settlements were continually supplemented by new arrivals throughout the nineteenth century, so that they retained their character as emigrant communities: before 1871 over half the white population of Australia was born elsewhere, and the adult population was not predominantly Australian-born until some time later.

For most of those emigrants, the difficult decision was the one to leave Britain, to emigrate: the question of where to go was probably a relatively minor one, determined by such accidental factors as climate, cost or proximity, and the vagaries of imperfect knowledge, advice and rumour or the likelihood of help from friends or relatives who had already emigrated. Few would have arrived with any strong attachment to their new home—any of the others would have done as well—but they would have shared a sense of exile and the feeling that their old home had failed them. An additional link between the new societies was the fact that migrants to any one of them often had friends and relatives in others.

Another shared characteristic was the newness of these societies. They *were* new, physically. They had no town walls, castles, ancient churches, Gothic or Roman ruins, or stately old homes, the material evidence of ancient Western civilisation. Their cities were marked by rapid growth, often built from the ground up within the memory of

living men and women. The wonder of visitors at Melbourne's spect-
acular growth was echoed in praise of Chicago and Toronto. These
sparkling symbols of Anglo-Saxon progress were stamped on what
was, to European minds, uncivilised wilderness. They were also new
in a more important sense: their institutions were established afresh.
Rather than being the accretion of centuries, as in Europe, they were,
at least in the minds of the colonists, free of the hidebound traditions
of older societies. In the liberal's view of progress, they were generally
'in advance' of Europe, being more democratic and more radical, and
they attracted a lot of interest for that reason. They shared a different
class structure from Europe, lacking an aristocracy, a peasantry and
a large, English-style industrial proletariat, but with the addition of
an exploited native population. Finally they had a similar economic
relationship with Britain, exporting raw materials and providing
markets for British industry and openings for British investment. By
the end of the century, however, the United States had industrialised
and was overtaking Britain as an industrial power.

It was the United States which stood out among these new societies.
Because of its position as the oldest, biggest, and most advanced of
the new societies, it was commonly considered to be, as the *Australian*
put it in 1831, 'a model for all new countries and New South Wales
(hereafter) in particular'.[4] It was a model, not only in the sense of
being worthy of imitation, but also in the other nineteenth-century
sense of being the archetypal example of a new society, and therefore
the one to which the others would assimilate simply because they were
all thought to be going through the same experience. Thus separation
and an Australian republic were often seen as being as inevitable as
democracy and federation—America had provided the model. So
when observers made a comparison between Australia and the United
States, they were in fact indicating Australia's status as a new society.

In political and social terms, the United States was often seen as
the model for much of Europe as well: America had advanced furthest
along the road to equality and Europe would inevitably follow. This
was by no means a development that was universally welcomed:
'Americanisation' was to become a dirty word in British politics.
Europe and the United States were placed on opposite ends of a
spectrum, and the usual assumption was that the other emigrant
societies were somewhere in the middle. The result was that almost
anyone whose impressions of Australia were published in the nineteenth century—and even well into the twentieth—at some stage
implicitly located the Australian colonies on this spectrum. One
important implication of this was to deny Australia an independent

identity: the less it was like Britain, the more it was like the United
States, and vice versa. It was there between the two, and had to
approach one or the other.

Both ideas of America, as the archetypal new society, and as one
end of the spectrum, were bound up with and often confused in the
continual comparison of Australia with America. Throughout the
nineteenth century, Australia was being depicted as 'another America',
a 'new America', 'the America of the South', 'the Future America',
'a humble imitation of the United States', 'that great America on the
other side of the sphere', 'the United States of Australia', 'a newer
America' and 'The Yankee-land beneath the Southern Cross'.[5]
American visitors tended to stress the similarities,[6] while those from
England were generally comforted that the similarities were not as
great as they might have been. Sir Charles Dilke disagreed with the
oft-stated comment that 'In Australia . . . we have a second America
in its infancy',[7] while in 1886, J.A. Froude decided that, in thought,
manners and speech, Australians were 'pure English and nothing
else'.[8] E.C. Booth thought Australia 'Another England',[9] while
another observer was pleasantly surprised 'that the Australian has
not more resemblance to the American'.[10] Most forthright was Sidney
Webb, the socialist, who was convinced in 1898 that 'Australia is
utterly and completely unlike America in every respect'.[11]

There were variants of these ideas. At first, before the flood of
mid-century emigrants revealed their preference for America, Australians hoped they would one day far exceed America in wealth and
power.[12] By 1861, the *Sydney Morning Herald* was content for Australia merely to equal American greatness, in which there was something 'rather flattering' to Australian eyes, 'something premonitory
of Southern Glories yet to dawn'.[13] By the end of the century the
dream that Australia would emulate America in prosperity was fading.
It was replaced by the idea that Australia had overtaken America
along the road to equality: it was the world's social laboratory.
American academics could now see Australia as 'the representative
of the new order of things, toward which the modern world is advanc-
ing'.[14] On the other hand, there were those who wondered whether
Australia was not in fact more English than England: Trollope
pointed to the 'English-mad' Tasmanians who were sure of their own
Englishness, but suspected that Britain itself had been 'Americanised'.
Trollope's own view was a typical English one, that Australia was so
slightly 'in advance' of England that it was 'rather a repetition of
England than an imitation of America'.[15] Another variant was the
distinction between Melbourne, considered on the whole to be more

American, and Sydney, seen as closer to the British end of the spectrum.[16] In the twentieth century, these positions were usually reversed, an interesting illustration of the way in which America remained the standard of modernity.

It seems that almost every aspect of Australian life was, in hope or despair, at some stage compared to its American equivalent. American examples could be introduced by all sides into almost any political argument. American experience was taken into account in a wide range of colonial legislation, in such areas as land policy, immigration, tariffs, education, railway construction, state aid to religion, irrigation, technical colleges, female suffrage, temperance and dog licences.[17] The debate over the tariff question, probably the most divisive issue in colonial politics, was often reduced to a contest between British free trade and American protectionism.[18] The American example was raised on everything from the most portentous issue—Deakin estimated that at least four-fifths of the Australian Constitution was based on American example[19]—to the most trivial —Twopeny saw Australians following their 'American cousins' in their preference for champagne, remarking that 'it requires some education to acquire a taste for claret'.[20]

Even responses to the Australian flora and fauna could have American models. In 1818 William Cobbett had described American 'birds without song, and flowers without smell'.[21] Twenty years later George Loveless used the same words to describe the Australian bush,[22] and it became an Australian cliché, with Mackenzie talking about 'our birds without music, many of our flowers without any smell',[23] Adam Lindsay Gordon writing poetry about the land 'where bright blossoms are scentless, And songless bright birds',[24] and Marcus Clarke trying to find beauty in 'our flowers without perfume, our birds who cannot fly'.[25]

America was also a model for the landscape, and for the type of civilisation—the small farms, the pioneer families—to be imposed upon it. In 1802 it was suggested that New South Wales 'might . . . in the course of a few centuries present as it were another America, a country of rising knowledge and civilisation, in the midst of a benighted and savage region of the world'.[26] Despite the geographical differences that became more apparent as the century passed, both countries were conceived as pre-industrial Arcadias for an industrialising Britain. In many ways America was a more suitable country for that sort of rural idyll, although it was difficult enough to realise it there. Nevertheless the pattern was followed in Australia: words such as 'squatter', 'homestead' and even 'the bush' were borrowed from

America, while the American slogan 'Homesteads for the People' was used in Victoria to encapsulate the ideal behind the Selection Acts.[27].

Democracy and the Mob

The view of America as a model for new societies was particularly relevant to the political relationship between Britain and the Australian colonies. It was never forgotten, by colonial politicians and British administrators, by radicals and conservatives alike, that disputes between Britain and the American colonies had led to war, separation and republicanism. Many thought the Australian colonies would inevitably take the same road. For some, that was an inspiration, for others it was an unfortunate mistake which Britain should not make again.

It was in this context that what is often regarded as an incipient Australian nationalism developed. From the 1820s, a number of issues—freedom of the press, trial by jury, control of Crown Lands, the extension of self-government, opposition to transportation—were framed in terms of conflict between the British government and colonial opinion. In fact those issues surfaced in a power struggle taking place between factions within the colonies themselves. In that power struggle, it was in the interests of colonial liberals to portray themselves as the 'Australian' party. In 1835 the Australian Patriotic Association was formed to embrace a range of liberal policies, and the term 'Australian' began to be used to refer to liberal sentiment.[28] However there was nothing particularly Australian about their politics. In 1827 they petitioned for the 'Rights of Englishmen, Trial by Jury and Taxation by Representation'; they talked of the British government's 'tyranny', 'the rights and liberties of Englishmen' and the 'birthright of a British Subject'.[29] What the 'Australian' case was founded on was not national sentiment nor a sense of being distinctively Australian; rather it was based on the notion of a growing colony, at some stage along the road taken by all British colonies. That road was best exemplified by the United States.

On both sides there was conscious and constant reference to the sentiments and catch-phrases of the American rebellion. In 1820 a Tory such as Barron Field, Supreme Court Judge and author of *First Fruits of Australian Poetry* (distinctly not a nationalist *cri de coeur*), feared one thing leading to another along the familiar road to republicanism:

> I see the shadow of the spirit of American revolt at taxation rising in the shape of the petition for trial by jury; it will next demand legislative assembly; and ... end in declaring itself a nation of freebooters and pirates.[30]

On the radical side, Wentworth could imagine an Australian War of Independence being fought out in the Blue Mountains when he put the case for representative government.[31] The American spectre appeared again in the campaign against transportation: Robert Lowe climbed on top of a tramcar at Circular Quay and warned 'The injustice forced upon the Americans is not half so great as that forced upon this colony'.[32] Finally there was J.D. Lang, converted to outright republicanism after visiting America, fulminating on British tyranny and calling for a republic and an Australian Declaration of Independence. For Lang there was no other course: 'The fact is, there is no other form of government either practicable or possible, in a British colony attaining its freedom and independence, than that of a republic'.[33]

Independence was not the same as democracy. Increasingly from the 1840s, the burning issue became the extent to which colonial institutions should be democratic. Once again the United States, where manhood suffrage had operated since the 1830s, became the example which everyone quoted. Once again Australia's identity became a matter of how much it resembled Amercia. From 1835, all sides could turn to the single most influential account of how democracy worked, Alexis de Tocqueville's *Democracy in America*.[34] De Tocqueville was an aristocratic French liberal who, like many others, accepted the view that history was a movement towards equality, and that Europe itself, for better or for worse, would follow America towards democracy. He had visited the United States to see the future, but also to discover for himself how the 'less desirable consequences' of democracy could be avoided. He both admired and distrusted democracy, and his cool, sophisticated account of what he found established a pattern of response, not only to America but to other new societies and to democracy itself. He expressed and refined what a broad section of the middle class was thinking. The concepts he popularised, 'the tyranny of the majority' and 'the middling standard' in the arts, were part of a formidable liberal ideology.

His book reflected the two common fears of democracy among the middle class. One was political, the fear of the mob; the other cultural, a fear of a decline in civilisation. De Tocqueville, and many others like him, argued that a tyranny of the majority could rule in these new democratic societies, that popular opinion was easily manipulated, that political corruption was likely, that the liberty of the individual was at risk, that mob rule was incompatible with good government, that the working class, if given power, would rule in its own interests, and that other interests (property, religion, education) and the interests of the nation as a whole would be overwhelmed unless somehow protected.

What applied to America also applied to Australia. American democracy, as interpreted by de Tocqueville, remained the standard by which the local variety was judged, for better or worse, for the rest of the century. De Tocqueville's influence was felt in the Colonial Office and in the British Parliament when self-government was gradually being extended to the Australian colonies in 1842 and 1850.[35] It was also felt in the colonies themselves when they set about drafting their own constitutions. These were democratic but contained provision for upper houses and plural voting, the sort of in-built constitutional protection for the middle class that de Tocqueville approved. Once again the United States was, as Wentworth put it, 'in every man's mouth in reference to the constitution fitted for this colony'. In his speech on the New South Wales Constitution Bill, he quoted great slabs of de Tocqueville. But on the question of democracy, Wentworth was no longer the radical that he had once been:

> I sincerely hope that the Constitution the Council is about to frame will be a constitution that will be a lasting one—a conservative one—a British and not a Yankee constitution.[36]

From the British point of view, American and Australian democracy were often seen as identical. This was most clearly borne out in the debates on the extension of the British franchise in 1867. Supporters of reform such as John Bright pointed to Australia to prove that democracy did not threaten 'a regard for law and property', and made similar comments about Canada and the United States. There were vestiges of an older image of Australia in his suggestion that an extended franchise would improve the attitude of the British Parliament to the bulk of the nation: 'the Botany Bay view of their countrymen would be got rid of'.[37] At the same time the most effective opponent of reform was none other than Robert Lowe, whom we last saw on top of a tramcar at Circular Quay. No longer the colonial radical, he now stood for respectability and the absolute rights of property. He also turned to the new democracies to prove his case that democracy threatened property and lowered the character of parliament: 'I do not want to say anything disagreeable, but if you want to see the result of democratic constituencies, you will find them in all the assemblies of Australia, and in all the assemblies of North America'. Later he tried to prove, by citing Australia, that democracy led to protectionism and instability: 'Victoria and N.S.W. are both governed by universal suffrage, and it is as much as we can do to prevent their going to war with each other'.[38]

Such was the attitude in Britain: the Australian colonies merged into the generalised attitude to the new societies, the dubious democracies. Liberal opinion within Australia also accepted the equation between the colonies and America. Although there was greater sympathy for democracy among the colonial middle class, they still shared de Tocqueville's qualms about mob rule and popular government. However, they increasingly took comfort in one aspect of Australian democracy which de Tocqueville, being a mere Frenchman, did not appreciate. This was the fact that America was tainted by being 'foreign', whereas the Australian colonies were indubitably, impeccably British. The very worst could be believed of American democracy, while the Australian (and Canadian and New Zealand) variety could still be regarded as safe. As Earl Grey put it, the good sense and reverence for parliamentary institutions 'which distinguish the English race' would enable Australians to correct 'any evils that may arise from the political institutions they have adopted'.[39]

This distinction between American and Australian (or British) democracy began to be made in the 1850s, when the gold-fields of Australia, discovered so soon after those of California, again invited the inevitable comparisons with America. The slightest hint of mob rule—and there was more than a hint—was condemned by conservatives and liberals alike. Here was all they feared of democracy, and fact and fancy surrounding Californian lynch law coloured the response to the situation in Australia. The overturning of the social order, and the lack of respect for authority which culminated in Eureka were equated with, and used to discredit, democracy. Yet often a distinction was made: 'the highly commendable morality and good conduct of the miners generally, strikingly contrasted with the savage violence, the lynch law, and the brute force said to be dominant at California'.[40] Lynchings could be stopped by appeals to miners' better feelings as Englishmen,[41] and even Eureka could be excused as the work of 'foreigners'. John Fawkner, radical and patriotic, blamed the uprising on the Americans who were 'accustomed . . . to resist the laws by armed mobs', while the Royal Commission which investigated Eureka concluded that 'foreigners formed a larger proportion among the disaffected than among the miners generally' and that they had drawn the diggers into 'courses that, among the British people, are happily as rare as they are disgraceful'.[42]

The idea that Australian democracy was safe because it was British became more important as the century wore on. The colonial bourgeoisie were proud of their political achievements, which they commonly saw as the product of British democracy. Eureka itself was seen as the assertion of the rights of British subjects against tyranny: it was only towards the end of the century that it acquired a distinctly Australian flavour. The inflated estimate of the British political character, puffed up by late nineteenth-century imperial expansion and racial attitudes, reached ever more ridiculous proportions. By the end of the century many Australians would have shared the view held by Rudyard Kipling, the laureate of imperialism, about the border between British Canada and the 'foreign' United States: 'Always the marvel . . . was that on one side of an imaginary line should be Safety, Law, Honour, and Obedience, and on the other frank, brutal decivilisation'.[43]

Culture and Mediocrity

Ultimately, the political implications of *Democracy in America* were to be less damaging than its cultural implications. Britain itself tardily embraced deomocracy, with only the die-hard conservatives regarding the result as disastrous. Even *The Times* came round in 1914.[44] Culture was a rather more delicate thing. The new societies, thought of and thinking of themselves as the outposts of a great European culture, were inevitably regarded as culturally inferior. There were two reasons: they were democratic and they were new.

Although de Tocqueville was not entirely pessimistic about culture in America, his work encouraged many English intellectuals to despise American culture and to regard democracy and high culture as totally incompatible. He argued that democratic societies lacked the aristocratic elite which made great art and literature possible. Democratic societies were materialistic, habitually preferring 'the useful to the beautiful'. Despite their constant bustle and their prosperity, their cultures would stagnate, swinging 'backwards and forwards forever without begetting fresh ideas'. Their 'doctrine of the equality of the intellect' would lead to a persecution of minority tastes. The tyranny of the majority would impose a culturally debilitating middling standard which, while enlightening the ignorant, would replace excellence with mediocrity.[45]

De Tocqueville's comments were tempered by his good-will towards America and his fairness, but they nevertheless amounted to a damning critique of democratic culture, a critique which was to be widely accepted by liberal intellectuals in the democratic societies them-selves.[46] If the political spectrum went from undemocratic Britain to democratic America, then the cultural spectrum led from the refined and educated British gentleman (or aristocratic Frenchman) to the loud-mouthed, ill-bred American philistine. The Australian colonies were once again considered as lying somewhere in the middle, pro-tected from complete cultural mediocrity by the fact they were 'British', although Matthew Arnold once suggested that Australia rather than America represented the nadir of cultural debasement.[47] This alleged decivilising influence of democracy was often based on simple snobbery; nevertheless the snobbery was so ingrained that it became one of the most effective arguments paraded against political reform, and one that democrats at first found difficult to dispute.

There was another argument which even democrats could use against the culture of America and Australia—its very newness. The simpler form of this argument was heard most often in the early nineteenth century, when the historical novels of Sir Walter Scott and the picturesque paintings of Claude Lorraine set the standard: true inspiration could only be found in the contemplation of ancient castles and picturesque ruins, which were amenities that new societies clearly did not possess. So John Ruskin could not contemplate even visiting the United States, 'a country so miserable as to possess no castles'.[48] A more sophisticated form of the same argument appeared later in the century. Henry James, the expatriate American novelist, argued in 1879 that:

> the flower of art blooms only where the soil is deep, that it takes a great deal of history to produce a little literature, that it needs a complex social machinery to set a writer in motion.[49]

Or, as an American art critic put it in Australia in 1890, 'A nation must be somewhat ripe in years before it develops appreciation of the refinements of life'.[50] Both ideas would continue to crop up in the twentieth century.[51]

It was a romantic view of culture which was being challenged by a more earth-bound view from the 1840s, not only in Britain but also in the colonies. In 1856, in one of the first extended analyses of the possibilities of an Australian literature, Frederick Sinnett, a young English-born journalist, facetiously parodied the conventional ro-mantic argument:

No storied windows, richly dight, cast a dim, religious light over
any Australian premises . . . No Australian author can hope to
extricate his hero or heroine, however pressing the emergency may
be, by means of a spring panel and a subterranean passage, or such
like relics of feudal barons . . . There may be plenty of dilapidated
buildings, but not one, the dilapidation of which is sufficiently
venerable by age . . .

He put in a plea for the 'realism' of Dickens against the romanticism
of Scott, and argued that the passions, character types and human
life which were the true subject of fiction were quite as in evidence in
Australia as anywhere else.[52]

Australian intellectuals could then challenge the view that new
societies, simply because they were new, could not produce great
literature. They had a natural refuge in realism, and in the new societies
there was a continuing commitment to ordinary life as the true subject
of art and literature. In 1871, Marcus Clarke was suggesting that 'in
a new country . . . there are opportunities for fresh and vigorous
delineation of human character',[53] and he continued to affirm the
virtues of realism. In 1896 Australian writers were again being urged
to take note of the American brand of realism, where 'nobody murders
or debauches anybody else',[54] while Australian painters were also
exhorted to discard the 'grand style' and stick to a more realistic
depiction of 'the intimate facts of our own life and environment'.[55]

It was more difficult for Australian intellectuals to come to terms
with the charges of materialism, anti-intellectualism and mediocrity
levelled at the new democracies. Sinnett's qualm was that a new
society might prefer ledgers to books;[56] another observer worried
that a migrant society was inevitably motivated by the 'engrossing
desire for wealth';[57] many were persuaded that democracy and
mediocrity were inseparable. On the whole, local intellectuals accepted
the charges as true, and joined British visitors in an incessant complaint
about Australian philistinism, a complaint which is still aired. Indeed
so many joined in that criticism that it is tempting to ask: can Australia
really be considered an anti-intellectual society when it contains so
many intellectuals ready to condemn it? The constancy of the complaint simply demonstrates the size of the intellectual class, not the
nature of Australian society.

It was all, of course, part of the European intellectual's stance;
attacks on materialism, philistinism, industrialism or on modern
society itself increasingly became part of the intellectual's stock-in-
trade in the nineteenth century. Whether romantics, utilitarians,
social critics, bohemians or aesthetes, creative artists and thinkers

could distinguish themselves by this stance from a rising middle class; it could also include a conservative, disdainful response to the material improvement of sections of the working class. Understandably, intellectuals in the new societies adopted a similar position: their cultural heritage, their social role, their financial worries, their sense of neglected genius were all pretty much the same. However they did not share England's bleak industrial towns, and these were central to the English intellectual's condemnation of nineteenth-century society. The new societies were unable to see themselves as part of the Industrial Revolution, despite the appearance of mills and factories in their cities and the importance of their primary produce for British industry. There was no tradition of village life being destroyed by industry's 'satanic mills'. They had to find something else to blame for the materialism they saw around them, and they chose to blame the very newness and democratic nature of places like Australia. For this, they had a ready-made critique in the work of de Tocqueville, and they put it to good use.

There is little point repeating much of the criticism of Australian materialism: it remained remarkably similar from around the 1830s on. What is important is to notice how similar their criticism was to criticism of industrial society in Britain. Charles Harpur, conscious of his role as the first Australian-born poet, could complain of having 'to mingle daily amongst men . . . who have faith for nothing in God's glorious universe that is not, in their own vile phrase, "money's worth"'[58]—much as Keats or Wordsworth might have done. The difference was that they identified materialism with industrial society, whereas Harpur saw it as peculiarly Australian, but the romantic image of the intellectual was the same. Similarly, in a later generation, Francis Adams attacked the 'philistinism' of Australian society. When his mentor, Matthew Arnold, had first used the term, his target had been modern Britain. Again the sense of heroic intellectual isolation from the materialistic majority was shared. The result was that local writers set up a false contrast between materialist Australia and cultured Britain.[59] And so a familiar pattern has appeared: materialism was seen as being integral to the Australian identity, when in fact it was being discovered in Britain as well.

Taming the Philistines

Splendid isolation was one response to materialism. The other response, common among the leaders of the colonial bourgeoisie, was to become the evangelists of 'Culture'. Defining 'Culture' as 'the machinery of intellectual and moral improvement',[60] they set about constructing the machinery that would improve the democratic populace. In 1849, they explained, 'This new country of ours must ... be moulded to our minds; not our minds to the country',[61] and they proceeded to set up mechanics' institutes, public libraries, art galleries and museums, schools, universities and systems of self-improvement. Even the Eight-Hour Day was justified on the grounds that it would 'secure time for intellectual improvement and moral culture'.[62] The machinery of moral improvement was as necessary to the old societies as to the new; the diffusion of culture would lead to a refinement in the manners and morals of society, and so, in the industrial cities of Manchester and Birmingham, as in the democratic cities of Sydney and Melbourne, art galleries and libraries sprang up to tame the philistines.

In a utilitarian age, 'Culture' was given a purpose. It existed, not for its own sake, but for the sake of morality. The prophet of this new 'moral aesthetic' was John Ruskin, whose ideas on cultural

'The New Reading Room at the Sydney Mechanics' School of Arts'. One of the many monuments to culture built by the colonial bourgeoisie. Note that a range of social groups (all male) are depicted improving themselves. From the Australian Town and Country Journal, *14 June, 1879, p. 1128.*

matters were to dominate Britain for half a century from the 1840s. With a substantial private income he could afford to scorn materialism. He had found moral purpose in art: the greatest art was that which conveyed 'the greatest number of the greatest ideas'.[63] The moral purpose of culture was also widely accepted in the Australian colonies, and it was with that justification that they vied with each other to erect cultural monuments. The first wave of universities, the major art galleries, the museums, the large public libraries and the government education systems all appeared between the 1840s and the end of the century. All were intended, as W.C. Wentworth said of the University of Sydney, opened in 1852, 'to enlighten the mind, to refine the understanding, to elevate the soul of our fellow men'.[64]

Established to defeat materialism, these cultural symbols themselves embodied the view that culture was measured in material terms. One reason for this was that national greatness and nationality were commonly measured by the extent to which a nation had erected the machinery for the moral improvement of its population. In the 1830s the colonies were urged to cultivate science and literature in order to gain 'a high standard of National character';[65] superior education was necessary lest 'our national (Colonial) character . . . eventually be one of rustic boorishness'.[66] The important thing was for a nation to have the visible trappings of culture; the idea that a national culture ought to be original and express a distinctive national sentiment only gained acceptance towards the end of the century. Thus there was often a strange mixture of moral idealism and crass patriotic pride, of keeping up with the Joneses, involved in the building of cultural monuments. The mixture is apparent in the reasons given for the establishment of the University of Melbourne in 1853: its supporters, men like Hugh Childers and Redmond Barry, expected it to

> go far to redeem their adopted country from the social and moral evils with which she is threatened: to improve the character of her people: to raise her in the respect and admiration of civilised nations.[67]

Similarly the *Age* saw the foundation of the Melbourne Public Library as marking 'an epoch in our social advancement . . . another stride forward in civilization . . . Victoria should not be content to be a single step behind America'.[68]

Such visible symbols of 'Culture' encouraged the immense pride of the colonial bourgeoisie in their own progress. It bolstered their position: they were the leaders of a cultured, not a debased, community, and they saw themselves as responsible for its moral improvement. The temples to culture they had built were central to the broad strand of cultural patriotism which reached its peak in the 'Marvellous Melbourne' of the 1880s, and which never ceased to be astonished at its own achievement. While the materialist tone of this pride must be admitted, it should not be allowed to obscure the intense moral seriousness with which men such as Redmond Barry established public libraries and galleries, and encouraged all classes to use them.

It meant that, in their own terms, accepting the cultural values of the period, the colonies did have claims to cultural respectability, so much so that in 1885 one visiting journalist advised Victorians to worry less about cultural societies and more about building better hotels.[69] Despite British contempt for 'colonials' and intellectuals' contempt for philistinism, the renowned boasting of the colonial bourgeoisie was not entirely baseless. We can sneer at their imposing edifices filled with valueless copies of sculpture, but this was their means of getting 'the greatest number of the greatest ideas' at a price they could afford. In their own terms they had resisted materialism and built reasonably cultured societies. Libraries flourished and were widely used—according to Mackenzie, 'Every body reads',[70] although he was disturbed that they read Dickens rather than more serious works. Australia absorbed about one-third of Britain's entire output of books,[71] and the number and quality of newspapers and journals published in the colonies were remarkably high—Trollope thought Australia had 'the best daily papers I have seen out of England'.[72] What was not high was the quality of original work produced, although there was plenty of it. However, originality for its own sake was not valued as much as moral content. The point is that the accusation that nineteenth-century Australian culture was philistine was essentially a criticism of nineteenth-century cultural values in general. To continue to condemn it on those grounds is merely to condemn it because its values are not our own.

It is clear that in the nineteenth century the Australian colonies had a political and cultural identity that, it was thought, could be distinguished from Britain's. For the most part though, this identity was not considered to be peculiar to Australia. It was an identity that Australia gained by virtue of the fact that it was a new society, politically democratic, culturally materialistic. In this, it was not creating anything distinctive, but simply following in the footsteps of the archetypal new society, the United States, footsteps which the older societies were also following in the nineteenth century.

5 The National Type

The Australasian will be a square-headed, masterful man, with full temples, plenty of beard, a keen eye, a stern and yet sensual mouth. His teeth will be bad, and his lungs good. He will suffer from liver disease, and become prematurely bald ... His religion will be a form of Presbyterianism; his national policy a democracy tempered by the rate of exchange.

Marcus Clarke, 1877.[1]

Know, O friendly generalizer, that there be tall Australians and short Australians ... faint or fierce, feeble-clinging or deathless strong ... speculative, rash Australians; also cautious, *very wary* Australians ... There is *no* generic native Australian.

Rolf Bolderwood, 1901[2]

It was difficult in the nineteenth century to pin down what was distinctive about Australia, apart from its unique flora and fauna. On the one hand, the Australian colonists were busy identifying themselves with wider loyalties, considering themselves primarily as British, or as being one of the new societies, another America. On the other hand there were narrower loyalties competing with the sense of being distinctively Australian. Politically Australia had no formal existence until Federation: the colonies were separate political entities owing their allegiance directly to Britain. Colonial rivalries were often surprisingly strong and until the 1880s, the general trend was towards a widening of the gap between the six colonies, at least politically. The first decades of self-government were marked by customs barriers, competition for investment and the short-sighted and expensive decision to build colonial railways on different gauges. At the same time, independent colonial identities were developing. Victoria was proud that it out-shone the others in political and economic progress; South Australians felt superior because they were without the convict taint; Queensland was the new frontier; Tasmania was the most English; Western Australia the most isolated and suspicious of the rest. New South Wales was less certain of a separate identity, being the background against which the other colonies defined themselves, and often simply regarding itself as Australia.[3] Even in the 1970s, New South Wales took longest to join the fad of finding an identity suitable for its cars' number-plates.

An Australian Type?

Nevertheless, some sense of Australian identity did develop in the nineteenth century, especially towards its end. Its basis was a belief in the existence of an Australian 'type'. The idea that it was possible to isolate national 'types' was the most important intellectual pillar supporting the complex structure of ideas about national character which developed in the nineteenth century. The national type was given not only physical and racial characteristics, but also a moral, social and psychological identity. Nationality was seen in concrete terms: the swarthy moustachioed Italian 'type' was given a reputation for shiftiness and passion, the tall blond German 'type' came to be seen as arrogant and assertive, and the educated English gentleman of noble forehead, fine nose and stiff upper lip gave himself the characteristics of justice, culture and refinement. Today we are more likely to see such images as hackneyed and very dubious 'stereotypes', but the idea of national 'types' remained strong well into the twentieth century, and was still influential in the writing of Australian history in the 1950s.

The fact that nineteenth-century Australians could see themselves in terms of a developing national type does not mean that this is necessarily an accurate and objective explanation of what was happening. The concept of national types fitted snugly into the nineteenth-century intellectual landscape, a central feature of liberal, national and racial ideology. It was a product of an obsession for categorisation which dominated the science of the day. The scientific classification of plants and animals into 'types' had begun with Linnaeus in the late eighteenth century. Only in the early nineteenth century did the word 'type' itself begin to be used in the sense of 'the general form or character', after which it gained technical meanings in natural history, chemistry and mathematics.[4] The enthusiasm for categorising types spread to geology and the study of climate. Scientists attempted to divide man into racial, psychological and physiognomical types. John Ruskin even attempted to reduce art criticism to a catalogue of the moral 'types' found in art.[5]

The idea of 'national types' was an extension of this enthusiasm, but it also embraced two other central features of nineteenth-century thought. In the first place, it is clearly related to the rise of nationalism in Europe, announced by the French Revolution in 1789, spreading with the revolutions of 1848, and finally adopted as the fundamental organising principle for Europe by the Treaty of Versailles in 1919. The very words 'nationalism' and 'nationhood' were nineteenth-century inventions, as were the states of Germany and Italy. Gradually the idea that a state embodied a nation replaced the old monarchical alliances and dynastic empires. However the problem of how to define a nation remained, and assumptions about national character and national types helped to provide an answer. Secondly, the idea of a national type reinforced ideas about the importance of 'character' in the lives of men and women. In the same way that poverty was blamed on individual failings rather than social upheaval or environmental factors, national prosperity, morality, and so on were thought to result from the national character. The belief in the moral superiority of particular national types helped justify imperial expansion and the exploitation of other peoples.

The idea of a national type was very much the product of a particular view of the world at a particular time. When attempts were made to discern a national type in Australia the first candidates were the Aborigines. Their physical appearance was linked to moral character. Some saw them as 'remnants of the ancient heathen nations', or 'as the men of Sodom, sinners exceedingly'.[6] Others, particularly from the 1830s to the 1850s, were influenced by the popular pseudo-science of phrenology which attempted to relate intellectual and moral character to the shape of the head. It had obvious application to national types, and became a simplistic justification for racism. George Combe, the popular phrenologist invited by Queen Victoria to read the heads of her children, would point during his lectures to the skulls of an Australian Aboriginal and an 'ancient Greek' to demonstrate what were supposed to be the lowest and highest examples of human intelligence and thus 'prove' the validity of phrenology.[7] Other followers of phrenology could see similarities between the skulls of Aborigines and ancient philosophers,[8] but the Combe view suited the interests of white settlers best, and proved more popular.[9] In 1844 it was said of the Aborigines that their 'characteristic vice and failing is indolence ... phrenologically speaking, their temperament partakes largely of the lymphatic quality'.[10] Another phrenologist measured their skulls and concluded they were 'rather deceitful, suspicious, slippery, time servers or dissemblers'.[11]

The convict 'type' was also studied phrenologically. J.C. Byrne

found among convicts an unmistakable 'peculiarity of visage, different
from all other men',[12] and such comments encouraged the idea that
criminal types should be transported before they had the opportunity
to commit serious crime. It also reinforced the idea that Australia
would be permanently tainted, an idea which many in Australia
strenuously rejected. They found the 'currency' quite unlike their
parents, with 'a certain characteristic trait of countenance' of their
own. They were quick, volatile, loquacious and fair, with 'scarcely a
single exception to this national, as we may call it, distinction'.[13] In
1827 Peter Cunningham enthused about the 'fine interesting race'
appearing in New South Wales, praising their 'open manly simplicity
of character' and commenting on their similarity to the Americans, in
stature, complexion and the fact that the girls lost their teeth early.[14]

Quite early in the century then, observers felt they could distinguish
a new character type in Australia. Some considered it distinctive to
Australia. Some, like Cunningham, saw it as sharing the characteristics
of other new societies. The important question was how the new type
compared to the British type, a question which was always asked in
the context of British imperial expansion. In that expansion, the
supposed superiority of the British racial type was the supreme justification: as the *Edinburgh Review* put it in 1850, 'It is through the
noblest nations that nature extends the race'.[15]

By the middle of the century in Britain, race had become the crucial
feature in the national type: in 1855 it could be said 'Race is everything: literature, science, art—in a word, civilization depends on it'.[16]
The educated English gentleman was quite certain that mankind had
reached his highest peak in the educated English gentleman. Lord
Macaulay's *History of England* was presenting him with history as
the story of progress, in which civilisation had progressed to its
highest point in England as he knew it, due to the genius of the English
character. The arrival of the railway age had confirmed his belief that
England and Progress were inseparable. In London, the Great Exhibition of 1851 set the stage for an orgy of self-congratulation. A year
later, the Engraver in Ordinary to the Queen announced, in praise
of British women, 'in this highly-favoured isle lies the very home and
centre of Beauty, and from this point, take what direction we please,
the further we travel the further we are off'.[17]

The Progress of the Species

Such attitudes raised intriguing questions about the development of

"THE COMING MAN."

An early version of the ennobled, independent worker. From Melbourne Punch, *13 May, 1858, p. 133.*

new types from British stock. When transplanted to other parts of the world, did the Anglo-Saxon racial type continue to progress, or did it degenerate? What would these developments reveal about the progress of the species as a whole? These were important questions for the British, who were beginning to assume that their superiority involved a duty and a destiny to populate the rest of the world. They were even more important questions for the transplanted communities themselves.

The fact that questions about the progress of the species could be posed at all shows the extent to which the old Linnean idea of a chain of being had been abandoned. It had assumed that the species were fixed and unchangeable. Now, however, the progress of the species was all the rage among English gentlemen convinced of their own superiority. They had the evidence from agricultural experiments that improvements could be made in nature, and they adapted that terminology to themselves, talking of 'the old stock', 'new strains', 'transplantation'. Thus in 1859 Henry Kingsley has one of his heroes contemplate Melbourne, a symbol of Anglo-Saxon enterprise, and calculate 'by his mathematics that the progress of the species is forty-seven, decimal eight, more rapid than it was thirty-five years ago'.[18] Kingsley did have doubts about the coming Australian type: the daughters were 'dowdy hussies', the sons 'lanky, lean, pasty-faced, blaspheming blackguards, drinking rum before breakfast, and living by cheating one another out of horses'.[19]

That year 1859 saw the publication of a rather more important book than Kingsley's, Charles Darwin's *The Origin of Species*. It had a devastating impact on the old certainties about mankind, God and nature. Darwin had fully worked out, and offered substantial proof for, a theory of evolution which scientists and philosophers had been uncertainly hinting at for 50 years. The species, including man, were not permanently fixed, as Linnaeus had assumed; they were all undergoing change by natural selection; if a species did not adapt successfully, it was liable to become extinct; only the favoured survived and prospered in the struggle for life. The book's impact went far beyond scientific circles. Jokes soon abounded about our grandparents being apes. Lord Tennyson, the poet laureate, struggling with its religious implications suggested Nature was at strife with God:

So careful of the type she seems,
So careless of the single life.[20]

Although revolutionary in many respects, *The Origin of Species* was very much a book of its time. It fitted easily with the general faith in progress. Macaulay's history could almost have shared Darwin's conclusion:

as natural selection works solely for the good of each being, all corporate and mental environment will tend to progress towards perfection.[21]

Darwin's theories also suited the social order. Even before 1859, the idea of 'The Survival of the Fittest', a phrase coined by Herbert Spencer, was being used to justify ruthless competition, between individuals, classes, nations and races. Although *The Origin of Species* did not relate natural selection to man, it seemed to give a scientific— and therefore moral—sanction to despotic social relationships. For the rest of the century, Social Darwinism, as this misapplication of Darwin's ideas came to be called, was used to justify the oppression of one group by another: by businessmen to condemn government interference in 'natural' competition; by conservatives to explain away poverty; by militarists to justify war as maintaining the vigour of superior races; by eugenicists to promote the sterilisation of the 'unfit' in the interests of racial progress.[22]

Above all, Darwin's ideas seemed to justify precisely what happened when the British expanded their empire, populated new lands and dispossessed native races. After all, the sub-title of *The Origin of Species* was *The Preservation of Favoured Races in the Struggle for Life,* and Darwin did write that:

> it inevitably follows, that as new species in the course of time are formed through natural selection, others will become rarer and rarer, and finally extinct. The forms which stand in closest competition with those undergoing modification and improvement will naturally suffer most.[23]

It seemed clear to the educated English gentleman that the spread of his race at the expense of other races, like the dominance of his class over other classes, although it might be abhorrent to sentimental morality, was in fulfilment of a natural and higher law.

Australia, like America, proved an attractive spawning ground for Social Darwinist ideas since it was an area of new Anglo-Saxon settlement where racial conflict needed to be explained away. Although Darwin only gained real acceptance in Australian scientific circles towards the end of the century,[24] at a more popular level his ideas enjoyed a very wide currency. In the first place, they provided a comforting, seemingly scientific explanation for the actual destruction of Aboriginal society. Previously Europeans had been convinced of the inferiority of the Aborigines, but that did not justify their extinction. Social Darwinism did. Racial conflict was reduced to a question of the Struggle for Life and the Survival of the Fittest. Darwin himself, visiting Australia in 1836 while groping towards his theory of evolution, had seen the havoc inflicted on Aborigines by white technology, white customs and white disease. For him, it was evidence of 'some more mysterious agency at work ... The varieties of man seem

to act on each other in the same way as different species of animals—
the stronger always extirpating the weaker'.[25] Before Darwin had
published *The Origin of Species*, the extinction of Aborigines was
being explained away as 'the design of Providence'.[26] Darwin's
theories gave such sentiments an aura of scientific legitimacy.

The dramatic decline of the Aboriginal population in the nineteenth
century still troubled some, but Darwin's ideas meant that moral
scruples could be overcome by a mixture of science and self-interest.
Thomas Major, for example, a 'squatter of the old school', found his
conscience troubled: 'Peace be with them—they have less to answer
for than we!' Yet he could also describe, with obvious relish, his
participation in an attempt to teach the Aborigines a lesson for stealing
cattle. Although completely outmanoeuvred by the Aborigines, his
party did manage to shoot one Aborigine in the back, and they de-
corated a hut with his skull and cross-bones. To Major, the episode
proved, once again, the superiority of the civilised white to the savage
black:

> Our treatment of the natives may be deemed unjustifiable by some.
> Naturally they may say that it was their country, and ask what
> business we had there? Quite so; but the same argument may be
> used in all new countries. It will not hold water, however, nor can
> we change the unalterable law of Nature. For untold centuries the
> aborigines have had the use of the country, but in the march of
> time they, like the extinct fossil, must make way. They now encumber
> the ground, and will not suit themselves to altered circumstances.
> The sooner they are taught that a superior race has come among
> them, and are made to feel its power, the better for them . . . The
> survival of the fittest is Nature's law and must be obeyed.[27]

Social Darwinism was also popular in the new societies because it
had implications for the continuing debate about the progress of the
Anglo-Saxon. Did the new types springing up in Australia and other
new environments preserve all the noble features of that old British
type from which they had sprung? Some argued that it was the cold
northern climate that kept up the vigour of the British race. In the
debilitating climate of the sunny south, the race would degenerate.
'Proof' was found in the fact that colonial men of mark were generally
socially-mobile immigrants, not Australian-born: the wonders they
accomplished in the colonies were due to the energy and the natural
superiority of men born in Britain.[28] Redmond Barry set up an
inquiry to discover whether 'the race in its transplantation to Australian
soil retains undiminished the vigour and fire and stamina of the
strong old stock of which it is an offshoot'.[29] In 1879 at least one

observer was 'prepared for the inevitable degeneration of the Anglo-Saxon stock',[30] and even at the turn of the century, Dr Alexander Buttner was noting that 'in cases where both the parents are Australian born, the weakening effect of the climate shows itself more and more strikingly with each succeeding generation'. The 'original vigour of physique and mental stamina' of the race would only be maintained with the constant addition of European migrants to the Australian population. He himself, with 'great paternal and material sacrifices', had sent all of his six children to Europe in their teens, 'for the purpose of there fortifying their constitution during the period of their principal development'.[31]

The whole question was treated very seriously indeed, but most Australians were more optimistic about the future Australian type. They were confident that Australia had maintained the purity of the old stock by active discrimination against Aborigines and Chinese immigrants: indeed it was the fact that Australia was '98 per cent British' that many saw as the most 'distinctive' thing about the place. Other areas of British settlement included larger populations of natives and non-British emigrants. As long as racial purity was maintained, as long as only the noblest racial strain was permitted to flourish in Australian soil, then the future of the Australian branch of the British race was secure. Even the *Bulletin*, never a paper to indulge in Empire toadyism, admired 'British blood, grit and force' when it suited: the Australian was 'as much a full-blown, white British subject as the Britisher himself', perhaps more so because, according to the *Bulletin*, Londoners were often Poles or Jews.[32] Far more certain in their loyalty to Empire and to the Anglo-Saxon race was a broad middle section of Australian opinion, neither fawningly Anglophile nor aggressively Anglophobe, but proud of both Australian and imperial achievement. It was their confidence in the superiority of the Anglo-Saxon race and 'the crimson thread of kinship' that gave them their confidence in the future of the Australian type.

Australians shared the racism and the Social Darwinist ideas which provided the intellectual underpinning for British imperial expansion in Africa and Asia in the late nineteenth century. They shared the creed of Joseph Chamberlain, Secretary of State for Colonies and archetypal imperialist:

I believe in this race, the greatest governing race the world has ever seen; in this Anglo-Saxon race, so proud, so tenacious, self-confident and determined, this race which neither climate nor change can degenerate, which will infallibly be the predominant force of future history and universal civilization.[33]

They shared the conviction of a 1901 school text, which explained it was not mere commercial greed that led to the growth of the British Empire, but rather 'the all-impelling power for good that drives the common aspiration of the Anglo-Saxon race'. The British Empire demonstrated 'a great scientific truth, in the survival of the race whose natural aptitude best fits it to carry on and maintain the best form of human government'.[34]

Testing the Type

Most Australians saw themselves as evidence of that scientific truth. Nevertheless they greeted with obvious relief any indication that the race was not degenerating under the Australian sun. They were positively eager to demonstrate how they measured up to anything which might be seen as a test of the race. In particular, Australian successes at 'test' cricket were used to prove the pessimists wrong. From 1874 on, victories over English teams proved to many minds that Australians retained 'the manhood and muscle of their English sires', that 'the manly qualities of the parent stock flourish as vigorously in these distant colonies as in the mother country', and that there was no longer evidence to support fears about 'the possible physical degeneration of the English race in the bright Australian climate'.[35] Sportsmen such as Spofforth, the 'demon bowler', and rowing and athletic champions became colonial heroes, the vindicators of the national type.

It did not convince everyone: indeed an inordinate love of sport could be considered one of the worst features of the new type.[36] So the performance of Australian students at Oxford and Cambridge was followed with interest as a measure of the intellectual develop-ment of the type. In the 1890s, Nellie Melba's operatic career was seen as demonstrating the race's cultural potential. However, at a time when military superiority was accepted as the ultimate measure of national fitness, by far the greatest, most glorious test was war. The greatest heroes, in the colonies as in Britain, were soldiers of Empire. When General Gordon was killed in the Sudan in 1885, the colonies went into mourning, Melbourne school-children wrote essays on 'General Gordon as a Hero' and statues were erected to com-memorate his sacrifice for Empire.[37] Ruskin glorified war as 'the foundation of all the high virtues and faculties of men'.[38] Sport might be a useful training ground for the race, but Australian children were told in their school books:

> there's a sterner task
> Than playing a well-pitched ball;
> That the land we love may someday ask
> For a team when the trumpets call.
> A team that is ready to take the field
> To bowling with balls of lead,
> In a test match grim, where if one appealed,
> The umpire might answer 'dead'![39]

Most Australians wholeheartedly supported British imperial expansion in the late nineteenth century, believing the Empire was their only defence. Contentedly bathing in the reflected glory of empire, they saw themselves as proof of the fitness of the British race to govern the world. But Britain's imperial wars were also the opportunity for the new Australian type to face the accepted test of nationhood. Various colonial contingents—700 New South Welshmen sent to avenge Gordon in the Sudan in 1885, 500 to China to help crush the Boxers in 1900, 16,000 to the Boer War—were farewelled with cheers and welcomed back with relief. James Service, Premier of Victoria, put aside inter-colonial rivalry and said that Sudan had 'precipitated Australia, in one short week, from a geographical expression to a nation'.[40] By the time the Boer War contingents had returned in 1902, the type had proved itself: 'although we have changed our skies we have not changed our strength. We are not degenerating, but are of that old British bull-dog breed . . . worthy descendants of that noble stock'.[41]

By this time, many Australians were not content simply to be proved worthy of the old stock: some were so bold as to suggest that the new type was in fact a decided improvement on the old. From the 1870s on, a self-conscious local patriotism developed, often linked with the emergence of local manufacturing, which had an obvious interest in endorsing the local product. In 1871 the Australian Natives' Association was formed, partly in opposition to the idea that all colonial men of mark were immigrants. Led by young businessmen, it became more influential in the 1880s, when it supported Australia's own imperialist adventures in New Guinea and the Pacific, and introduced the slogan 'Australia for the Australians'.[42] Its growth coincided with an increasing cultural fetishism for the distinctively Australian: architects were adapting native animals to building decoration; colonial composers imitated bell-birds in their music and competed with each other to produce Australian anthems; Aboriginal place-

ADAPTATION OF THE LYRE-BIRD TO SCULPTURAL PURPOSES.

(From a Panel modelled by Mr. Lucien Henry)

The fetish for decorative national motifs reached a peak in the 1880s. This example combines two popular Australian symbols, the lyre-bird and the sun. From the Centennial Magazine, *October, 1889, p. 161.*

names were preferred to English borrowings; waratah motifs appeared in cast-iron balconies and local poets sang hymns to the wattle. W.J. Sowden, a leader of the Australian Natives' Association, suggested Australians should give 'three cooees' rather than the traditional 'three cheers' whenever the opportunity arose.[43]

One result of this patriotic nativism was a reassessment, not only of the new type, but also of his antecedents. The emigrants were no longer portrayed as the failures, the Micawbers of Britain, but as the enterprising vanguard of the race. Local poets presented them, not as sentimental victims, but as

> bold adventurous bands,
> Bearing courageous hearts and vigorous hands.[44]

Later W.M. Hughes talked of the Australian type being 'bred from the hardy, the enterprising and the resolute'—the 'weaklings' stayed in Britain.[45]

They had the word, not only of local patriots, but of visitors as well. In 1873, Trollope was convinced 'that the born colonist is superior to the emigrant colonist . . . the emigrant is superior to his weaker brother whom he leaves behind him. The best of our workmen go from us, and produce a race superior to themselves'.[46] The old Tory in him idealised the Australian worker, although he was rather harder on young colonial gentlemen. Twenty-five years later, Michael Davitt, a radical Irish M.P., went 'so far as to say that the Australian, born of British or Irish parent, is the best physically developed man of either of these races'.[47] The revision even extended to the convicts, whom the *Lone Hand* described in 1907 as 'lusty and vigorous', the 'rough-hewn foundational stones of the best kind'.[48] Eventually the virtues of the convicts, their enterprise and self-reliance, were said to have been passed on to the Australian type, while their faults had been bred out.[49]

The new type was thought to have the advantage of a favourable environment as well as a superior stock. The sunnier climate and the outdoor life, which some thought debilitating, could also be used to help 'explain the vigorous frame, manliness of bearing, and stamp of independence of the average Australian'.[50] In 1880 the influence of the climate on the coming type was compared to progress made in Australian products such as wheat, wine, wool, beef and sugar: the hope was that 'the Anglo-Australian race will develop in like ratio'.[51] For the optimists, the new Australian type would combine the best of both worlds.

'*A drought-resisting stock*'

It was hoped that evolution would lead to improvements in the Australian type as he adapted to his environment. From the Bulletin, *10 December, 1903, p. 13.*

The Coming Australian

In the on-going debate about the new type, there was much disagreement: some thought he was taller, others that he was short,[52] some thought he had arrived, others were still waiting, some were hopeful, others pessimistic. Yet there was also substantial agreement on a particular group of characteristics: independence, manliness, a fondness for sport, egalitarianism, a dislike of mental effort, self-confidence, a certain disrespect for authority. These qualities were considered to be distinctively Australian, and many historians have since accepted them as accurate. However, there are other reasons why these particular characteristics came to be identified as Australian. The debate about the type overlapped with two other debates: the younger generation and the coming man.

In 1880 James F. Hogan decided that the three main characteristics of 'The Coming Australian' were

1. An inordinate love of field-sports.
2. A very decided disinclination to recognise the authority of parents and supervisors.
3. A grievous dislike to mental effort.

It does not take much effort to deduce that he was a school-teacher who did not much like his pupils. Nor is it surprising that he went on to suggest corporal punishment in the schools to remedy 'a dangerous feeling of independence'.[53] What is surprising is how often these characteristics were seen as being peculiarly Australian when they can more properly be ascribed to the age-old dismay with which one generation greets the ascendency of the next. In nineteenth-century Australia, where the younger generation always contained a noticeably larger proportion of Australian-born than their parents' generation did, it was perhaps understandable that criticism of the young should be transferred to the Australian character. In fact, when Dr Perry 'trembled' for the rising generation[54] he was simply exercising one of the prerogatives of an Anglican bishop; when others condemned larrikinism they did so in the same terms in which their counterparts in Britain and America condemned the appearance of relatively affluent working-class youth.

Similarly when visitors commented on the Australian girl, they praised her freshness, beauty, good sense and lack of affectation. The colonial miss was the salvation of English visitors trapped into endless colonial balls and tea parties. What delighted most observers was what they called her independence. (They deplored independence when they met it in domestic servants.) Although Twopeny argued that there was 'a distinctive Australian girl', the same qualities were associated with the 'new woman' who was beginning to make her mark in Britain in the late nineteenth century. The difference was that whereas in Britain these qualities were attributed to youth in Australia, where the question of national type was so prominent, they were more likely to be attributed to Australianness.

The second debate, on 'The Coming Man', raised issues concerned

A COMPARISON

The Melbourne Girl   The Sydney Girl

It was generally agreed that the Australian girl was a good sort, but were the Melbourne and Sydney girls the same species? From the Lone Hand, *2 December, 1912, p. 90.*

with class, sex, race and empire. The dominant middle-class English attitude to colonials was one of disdain, often mere social snobbery. This was to be challenged towards the end of the nineteenth century, not only by the colonials themselves, but by a new group of staunch imperialists, and above all by Rudyard Kipling, himself an Anglo-Indian and the most popular writer of the day. He was the laureate of the new imperialism, setting out to 'compose the greatest song of all—The Saga of the Anglo-Saxon all round the earth', coining the phrase 'the white man's burden' and embroidering the romance and adventure that accompanied it. He criticised the complacent Englishman who knew nothing of the empire: 'what should they know of England who only England know?'[55] It was the empire which made Britain great, but its greatness, Kipling argued, rested not on the natural superiority of the educated English gentleman but on the man of action, the intelligent 'Common Man', the adventurer ready to take up the burden of empire, the ordinary soldier at the outposts of empire, the settler civilising its fringes.

The contrast between the effete Englishman and the manly colonial was a popular one in colonial literature, but it went deeper than that. Colonial themes were very popular in English boys' stories in the 1880s and 1890s. The English writer, E.W. Hornung, drew a contrast between the English, an 'abominable, insular nation of humbugs' and 'the typical Australian . . . one of the highest if not *the* highest development of our species'.[56] In 1901 at the Commonwealth Inaugural Celebrations, Sydney's *Daily Telegraph* made the same contrast, but was less rude about it: 'The Englishmen, with their brilliant uniforms and perfect marching were a counterpoise to our own men, not so efficiently trained but more hardy, with greater self-reliance, quicker judgements, larger resource. Together they formed the sort of force that the Empire needs'.[57]

The Coming Man Saves the Day

It was during the Boer War that 'The Coming Man' came into his own. The war raised serious doubts about Britain's conventional military might, the Boers proving to be much more formidable opponents than had been expected. Many became convinced of the superiority of the British colonial troops over those from Britain. They were fitter, easier to train, and showed more initiative. As one Australian correspondent put it, 'they fought so pluckily, and yet so unconventionally, that . . . colonial stock went up fifty per cent in the military market'.[58] Kipling shared that view. He visited South Africa, mixed with the colonial contingents and made use of colonial writers such as A.B. Paterson on the paper which he edited for the troops. With Kipling's help, 'The Coming Man' emerged from the war as a new type of hero, in stark contrast to the complacent and sterile English:

> And ye vaunted your fathomless power, and ye flaunted your iron
> pride,
> Ere—ye fawned on the Younger Nations for the men who could
> shoot and ride!
> Then ye returned to your trinkets; then ye contented your souls
> With the flannelled fools at the wicket or the muddied oafs at the
> goals.[59]

Naturally this perspective on the empire was popular in all of Britain's colonies, and to some extent in the United States as well. Indeed, from the Australian point of view, their Boer contingents represented, not simply a contribution to Britain's war, nor simply

'Two types: the Imperial and Colonial intelligence officer'

The conventional contrast between the effete Englishman and the sturdy colonial was particularly popular during the Boer War. From Frank Wilkinson, Australia at the Front, *1901, p. 242.*

the opportunity to test the vigour of the national type, but also support for another progressive, colonial branch of Anglo-Saxondom. They could identify with the English uitlanders, who saw themselves as bringing progressive rule to South Africa, pitted against the anachronistic ways of the Dutch Boers who represented old reactionary Europe. Australians could readily share the view of the uitlanders that they were deprived of their democratic rights as 'The Coming Man' by the decaying Boer regime. Similarly Australians could identify with the American cause in the Spanish-American war of 1898–99. Again 'The Coming Man' was replacing the old order; a progressive young nation was taking up the 'white man's burden' in the Philippines and Latin America, sweeping away the anachronistic tyrannies of the Old World. Australia interpreted its own imperialistic interests in New Guinea and the New Hebrides in the same way. King O'Malley, the flamboyant Labor politician, proclaimed that 'the controlling destiny of the islands of the southern seas is sacredly vested in the Australian people'.[60] A shared identity as one of the new societies had been converted into support for other representatives of 'The Coming Man'.

The *Bulletin* distinguished Australians from both the Old World and 'lower' races, but did not limit its definition to the Australian-born:

> All white men who come to these shores—with a clean record—and who leave behind them the memory of the class-distinctions and the religious differences of the old world . . . are Australian. In this regard all men who leave the tyrant-ridden lands of Europe for freedom of speech and right of personal liberty are Australians before they set foot on the ship which brings them hither . . . No nigger, no Chinaman, no lascar, no kanaka, no purveyor of cheap coloured labour is an Australian.[61]

In 1887 there was nothing distinctive about the *Bulletin*'s Australian: it simply gave that name to its version of 'The Coming Man'.

The basis of this interest in 'The Coming Man' was a deep-seated racism. Nagging doubts about the fitness of the race and the challenge posed by other more vigorous races were sharpened by mounting evidence that the white race was not as virile as supposed.[62] The birth-rate in Australia, Europe and America was declining markedly by the turn of the century. In the Russo-Japanese War of 1905, a white nation was defeated by a coloured nation for the first time. And in Sydney in 1908, the famous Burns-Johnson title fight, the first ever between a white and a black boxer, resulted in an easy victory for the Negro. It was all very perturbing, and after the fight one Methodist minister prayed: 'God grant that the defeat on Saturday may not be a sullen and solemn prophecy that Australia is to be outclassed and finally vanquished by these dark skinned people'.[63]

Many pinned their hopes for continued domination of the world by white men on the more progressive branches of Anglo-Saxondom. Here, racial progress was evolving 'The Coming Man'. This broader Social Darwinist concern about the future of the race as a whole was used to justify the racism of the 'White Australia' policy. According to the *Bulletin* in 1902, the policy was fundamental to Australia's existence. It was based on

> the instinct against race-mixture which Nature has implanted to promote her work of evolution . . . Once a type has got a step up it must be jealous and 'selfish' in its scorn of lower types, or climb down again. This may not be good ethics. But it is Nature . . . the Caucasian race, as a race, has taken up the white man's burden of struggling on towards 'the upward path', of striving at a higher

stage of evolution . . . If he were to stop to dally with races which
would enervate him, or infect him with servile submissiveness, the
scheme of human evolution would be frustrated.[64]

In this light, the characteristics of the Australian type were not
peculiar to Australia, but were shared by other groups in the vanguard
of racial progress. Exactly who else shared those characteristics was
not always clear. Some, including Melbourne's Professor W.E. Hearn,
expressed a growing admiration for Germany and Aryan blood,
'confessedly the foremost in the world'.[65] Others limited the characteristics to the Anglo-Saxon or British races, although E.W.
O'Sullivan, Australian-born but of Irish background, insisted on
referring to the 'Anglo-Celtic'.[66] Others distinguished between the
old races and the new, and were able to overlook the United States'
'cosmopolitanism'. Some simply extended the privilege to all white
men. 'White man' became a term to apply to any worthy character,
although some distinguished 'real' white men from 'the lower Latin
type' who was only technically white.[67]

A set of values had been identified with 'The Coming Man' and
these were commonly attributed to the Australian 'type'. They were
the values of the new popular literature of the day, the literature of
mass literacy and democracy, of Kipling, Robert Louis Stevenson,
Conan Doyle and Rider Haggard, of the Harmsworth press and Boys'
Own Annuals. The heroes were men of action such as Cecil Rhodes
or Scott of the Antarctic, men concerned less with good manners
than with getting things done, and sharply distinguished from moralis-
ing liberal intellectuals. This same philosophy produced the Boy
Scouts movement, which grew out of the Boer War and spread rapidly
throughout the empire and America. It also produced the youth
hostels movement which developed in Germany around the same
time. In Britain and Australia, it gave added impetus to the formation
of school cadet corps and rifle clubs. It was the philosophy behind
Cecil Rhodes's scholarships, which aimed to educate a leadership for
'The Coming Man', significantly drawing its candidates from young
men (only) in the British Dominions, the United States and, until the
Great War, Germany. Behind them all was the movement at the turn
of the century to improve National Efficiency; what President Theo-
dore Roosevelt called 'The Strenuous Life' when he exhorted America
to face up to 'the hard contests where men must win at hazard of
their lives . . . [or] the bolder and stronger peoples will pass us by, and
will win for themselves the domination of the world'.[68]

This cluster of values surrounding the idea of 'The Coming Man'
could be shared by political philosophies ranging from Kipling's—

conservative, Anglophile, imperialist—to the *Bulletin's*—radical, republican and nationalist. It helps explain why the *Bulletin* could so easily become an extremely conservative paper in the twentieth century. Their values were generally democratic, although not necessarily radical, emphasising the worth of the 'Common Man', often at the expense of his political and military leaders. Common sense and decency were seen as virtues belonging to the 'man in the street', who became a popular authority in the new journalism of the day.[69] Increasingly it was 'the Soldiers of the Queen', not the officer class, who were the heroes. For Kipling, in the shadow of imperial war, it would be 'the common people in the 3rd class carriages—that'll save us'.[70]

Men embodied these values. The emphasis was on masculinity, and on masculine friendships and team-work, or 'mateship' in Australia. All the clichés—man of action, white man, manliness, the common man, war as a test of manhood—were not sexist for nothing. Women were excluded from the image of 'The Coming Man', and so were generally excluded from the image of the Australian 'type' as well. They could acquire a kind of second-rate masculinity by being clever with horses or being a 'tomboy', a phenomenon which began to appear in the late nineteenth century. More often, women were portrayed as a negation of the type, at best as one who passively pined and waited, at worst as one who would drag a man down.

Initiative was preferred to blind obedience, the practical to the theoretical, independence to subservience. There was an identification with new technology, a love of machines, a sort of schoolboy's interest in ships and cars and planes: according to Henry Lawson, Australian boys were 'Dreaming of great inventions—always of something new; With brains untrammelled by training'.[71] There was also a strong anti-urban, anti-metropolitan feeling. Both the cities and England were seen as unhealthy, debilitating, over-crowded, the antithesis of the outback, the veld, the prairie. These and other fringes of empire offered heroic struggle, adventure and the wide open spaces, the exhilaration of camp life and the thrill of war, in short all the tests of manhood.

It was little wonder that a new nation such as Australia, searching at the time for an identity of its own, should appropriate these popular virtues to itself. 'The Coming Man' became 'the typical Australian'. Almost as a parody of that process, a schoolboys' annual called *Young Australia* began to be published in London in 1893. The same book, chock-full of gripping tales of virile men fighting the wilds in Australia, Canada, New Zealand, India and Africa, was sold throughout the empire, but was packaged with a different title for each country.[72] Similarly, 'The Coming Man' was packaged for Australian consumption as 'the Australian type'. In his monumental *Australia Unlimited*, E.J. Brady, a self-consciously nationalist radical of the *Bulletin* school, could sum up what it meant to be Australian in terms of Romance and Boys' Own Adventure:

> Under clear cold stars their camp fire had been lighted. On the edge of odorous eucalyptus forests, their broad axes had flashed in the sunlight. Mountain fastnesses had echoed the report of their rifles. Over great plains their horses had galloped—north, south, east and west they had been staking out a continent for the White Race.[73]

Only the eucalypts were distinctively Australian; otherwise he could have been referring to the frontier of white settlement anywhere in the world.

6   Bohemians and the Bush

The brave Bohemians, heart in hand,
March on their way with spirits free;
They count not moments, sand by sand,
But spill the hour-glass royally.
With wine and jest and laughter long,
Their lives appear to pass, may be;
But still beneath the river's song,
There sounds the sobbing of the sea.

Victor Daley[1]

From the 1880s, just as 'The Coming Man' was coming into his own, a conscious attempt was being made in Australia to create a distinctively national culture. At the same time, it should be remembered, literary, artistic and musical nationalists in Europe and North America were also ransacking history, nature and folklore to construct national cultures. It was an outcome of the rise of European nationalism and, as in Australia, it was often associated with the growth of local manufacturing industry and an urban bourgeoisie. In Australia this would result in a new image which was to prove more powerful than any other. It was essentially the city-dweller's image of the bush, a sunlit landscape of faded blue hills, cloudless skies and noble gum trees, peopled by idealised shearers and drovers. Australians were urged to respond to this image emotionally, as a test of their patriotism. For the first time, a basic distinction was made between the image of Australia created by Europeans, and that created by Australians themselves. Now European images were condemned as necessarily alien, biased, blurred; only the new Australian image could be clear, pure, true. The irony was that this new image inevitably remained trapped, as we shall see, within a European intellectual milieu.

A Cultural Generation Gap

The new image was painted in against a background of dramatic changes in Australian life. A series of liberal measures—payment of M.P.s, graduated income tax, old age pensions, wages boards—saw an expansion in the role of government, and made the colonies the world's social laboratory, a title they occasionally shared with Germany. The long boom, which had led to a steady improvement in the overall standard of living from the time of the gold rushes, came to a sudden end in 1891. In the depression which followed, amid the great strikes, the bank crashes, drought and unemployment, the old faith in constant progress collapsed. Labour parties were formed to carry the voice of the unions into the colonial parliaments, where they established themselves surprisingly quickly, and gave a new direction and tone to political life. At the same time, a middle-class federation movement held its first convention in 1891, and by the end of the decade, without much fuss or enthusiasm, the six Australian colonies had voted to become a nation.

These changes in political direction were accompanied by a new vitality in the development of art and literature from the mid-1880s. A new generation of writers and painters was giving creative expression to a fresh approach to Australia. It was claimed that the Heidelberg School of painters, which emerged after 1885, saw Australia for the first time with Australian eyes. The same was to be said of the coterie of writers and artists attached to the *Bulletin*: the Australia they described was supposed to be more 'real', more in tune with the democratic Australian temper. Too often this vitality is explained by saying Australian culture had reached its adolescence, marked by youthful exuberance, cockiness, pimples and all. But the analogy is a dubious one because it implies that a national culture 'grows' of its own accord, quite apart from the rest of society. The reason that cultural life changed direction at this time, and produced a new image of Australia, is much more complex than that.

In the first place, a new generation had arrived. Most of the writers and artists coming into prominence in the late 1880s and 1890s were born in the 1860s, as Australian society settled down after the upheavals of the gold rushes. In 1890, J.F. Archibald, the *Bulletin*'s editor, was 34, A.B. Paterson was 26, A.G. Stephens and Edward Dyson were both 25, and Henry Lawson, Bernard O'Dowd, Steele Rudd, Randolph Bedford and E.J. Brady were all in their early twenties; among the artists, Tom Roberts was 34, Fred McCubbin 35, Arthur Streeton 23 and Charles Conder 22. Of the previous generation of artists, writers, teachers and critics, whose cultural values were being challenged, Marcus Clarke, Henry Kendall, Adam Lindsay Gordon and Louis Buvelot were already dead. Rolf Boldrewood was

64, Brunton Stephens 55, Ada Cambridge 46, Tasma 42 and Rosa Praed 39. Among those who taught the members of the Heidelberg School, Eugen von Guérard was 79 and G.F. Folingsby 60. Among other artists of that generation, William Strutt and Nicholas Chevalier had returned to Europe and W.C. Piguenit was 54, while James Smith, the most influential critic of the day, was 70, and the young Charles Conder was looking forward to the day when 'the irrepressible Mr. J.S. [would] be gathered to his fathers'.[2] It was little wonder then that the younger generation saw themselves as rebelling against an outdated and stale set of cultural standards. They could believe they were presenting a vision that was new and fresh, and could make much of the virtue of youth.

The difference between the generations was accentuated by the fact that the older generation was centred in Melbourne while the younger generation generally looked towards Sydney. Indeed the sheer dominance of the cultural values of an older generation in Melbourne helped to drive many—Archibald, Julian Ashton, Roberts, Streeton, Victor Daley, and later Hugh McCrae and the Lindsays—to make the move to Sydney. There they found a more ready acceptance than in the Melbourne cultural establishment, centred on respectable journals or the National Gallery of Victoria. There was more work available for both writers and artists on the *Picturesque Atlas of Australia*—a large-scale project of the 1880s—and the *Bulletin*; and the New South Wales Art Gallery, with Ashton's encouragement, began to buy the work of the Heidelberg School. However, the differences between the generations and between Melbourne and Sydney, while emphasising the break made by the writers and artists of the 1890s, does not explain the direction they took.

What helps explain their direction towards what has been seen as a distinctively national culture, is the fact that the younger generation was more likely to be Australian-born. The Melbourne cultural establishment was largely made up of men who had arrived in Victoria around the time of the gold rushes, and who saw in culture a means of civilising and educating a materialistic democracy. The 1890s generation, predominantly native-born, felt more at home in the Australian environment and felt more need to promote an indigenous culture.

But this is a far from adequate explanation for the new direction, although some later writers have made do with it. Harpur, Kendall, Boldrewood, Praed, Tasma and Piguenit were all born in Australia or migrated as children, yet they still shared the cultural values of their immigrant contemporaries. On the other hand, important names among the new generation—although not the most important—were immigrants: Conder, Daley, Will Ogilvie, D.H. Souter and Price Warung all left Britain as adults. Both groups still looked to Europe for cultural attitudes and philosophies: Australia remained, undeniably, part of a broad Western culture. Both groups, in varying degrees, looked to Australia for imagery and inspiration, and although that perhaps came more naturally to the 1890s generation, it could still be artificial and painfully self-conscious, a matter of hunting around for 'local colour'. It is significant that the younger generation itself liked to attribute its image of Australia to the entrance of the Australian-born on to the cultural stage. However it is not enough to argue simply that a native culture had replaced an immigrant one.

The Professionals' Revolt

The real break between the two generations can be found in the changes taking place in the late nineteenth century—in Europe and Australia—in the role of the artist and his audience, in the way in which 'culture' was produced, its *raison d'être*, the meaning of the word itself. The intelligentsia in Western society was being professionalised. Science, art and literature were increasingly the province of full-time professionals rather than educated amateurs or men of letters with a private income. Although the process was a gradual one, the sheer growth of the professional intelligentsia is striking. In Britain for example, the number of 'authors, editors and journalists' listed in the census rose from 2148 to 14,000 in the 40 years after 1871.[3]

That increase owed much to the new readership created by virtue of the 1870 Education Act, and to technological changes which lowered the cost of paper and type-setting. The market for British writers, like the market for British manufacturers, was expanding internally. The new literature of Kipling, Conan Doyle, Rider Haggard and Robert Louis Stevenson catered for a new class of consumer, as did the new journalism with its illustrations, advertising, sensationalism and immediacy. The standard mid-Victorian novel—what Kipling called the 'three-decker' because it normally filled three volumes[4]—was giving way to shorter novels, short stories and popular ballads in cheap illustrated editions. Their aim was not to moralise to the middle class, but to attract and entertain a mass market. At the other extreme, the aesthetic movement around Oscar Wilde and J.A.M. Whistler reacted to the same changes by promoting 'Art for Art's Sake' and flaunting their intellectual exclusiveness and studied decadence. Even so, Wilde's *The Picture of Dorian Gray* could still appear in *Lippincott's Monthly Magazine* in the same year (1890) as novels by Doyle and Kipling.[5] A mass audience paid too well to be ignored.

The same changes were taking place in Australia and throughout the Western world. In Victoria between 1881 and 1891, the number of 'authors and literary persons', including journalists and reporters, rose from 461 to 1292, while 'artists' rose from 734 to 1502. After 1891 the census categories were altered, so they are no longer comparable with the earlier ones, but the figures given in the table below give a rough indication of what happened to the local 'intelligentsia' after 1891.

		1891	*1901*	*1911*
Authors, editors, journalists:	N.S.W.	530	595	955
	Vic.	534	606	702
Artists, painters, art students:	N.S.W.	341	427	684
	Vic.	471	545	609

It is clear that the 1890s depression slowed down the growth of the intelligentsia in both colonies, but after that, the greater cultural vitality of New South Wales is marked. It is also noticeable that Australia was supporting a much larger 'intelligentsia' for its size than was Britain: in 1911, authors, artists and journalists accounted for about one in 3200 of Britain's population, while in Australia the figure was about one in 2100.[6]

Most striking is the fact that a large new community of professional writers and artists had emerged in Australia in the 1880s. Writing was no longer done for the love of it. It was even possible for a few, in their peak years, to live off their earnings from creative work as opposed to journalism, while others could use creative writing at least as a means of supplementing their income. This is not to say they were affluent by any means. Freelance writing could offer only a very precarious existence at best. In Australia writers could never attract anything like the large payments to the best-known of their contemporaries in Britain and America, and the depression hit them particularly hard. They had good reason to air the constant complaint that Australian writers were not properly recognised.

However the tenor of that complaint was changing. In 1872, Henry Kendall had grumbled that there was 'not the ghost of a chance' for those who aspired to join the 'colonial *literati*' to make a living outside journalism: so they 'join the Press, and in due time forget their

early aspirations and become plodding, satisfied newspaper hacks'.
He wanted more recognition, patronage and encouragement from
'that influential class in our midst who are lettered as well as leisured'.[7]
In 1899, Henry Lawson's complaint was that he was not earning
enough. The *Bulletin* was prepared to pay him 30 shillings per column,
but few other papers were, and he had earned only £700 in 12 years
of writing. His solution was blunter than Kendall's: if a young Australian writer could not escape overseas, he should shoot himself.[8]
Lawson soon afterwards left for London and disappointment. But
what is interesting about his outburst is a new professional concern
about the protection of the local literary product, and about how to
make writing pay. Kendall's desire had been for recognition from the
cultural establishment.

Artists were also becoming professional. There was more training
available for young artists, and it was of a reasonable standard.
Particularly at the National Gallery School in Melbourne in the
1880s, and among Julian Ashton's students in Sydney, a much greater
sense of an artistic community developed. They had a wider market
for their work, in the new illustrated press—again the *Bulletin* stands
out—and in the public galleries. Both writers and artists were forming
part of a new intellectual community, a professional 'Bohemia' in
which they could see themselves as men committed to their art. In
this way, through both their professionalism and their bohemianism,
they distinguished themselves from those educated middle-class laymen
who were committed to cultural improvement and had dominated
the cultural establishment since the gold rushes.

Accompanying the developing sense of professional identity was a
new attitude to the role of the artist and the purpose of art. The earlier
dominance of the layman or lay critic as cultural arbiter had led to a
utilitarian approach to art and literature. Art was seen as the servant
of society: it served morality, it educated the people, it could even
aid commerce.[9] Culture had become the great improver, the civiliser
of nations, and so art galleries and libraries had been built in industrial
Britain and materialistic Australia. John Ruskin, the epitome of the
gentlemanly intellectual all-rounder, had dominated the British cultural
establishment since the 1850s with his arguments about the moral
function of art.

This view of art began to be challenged in the 1870s in Britain with
the arrival of the 'aesthetic movement', proclaiming that art existed,
not for morality's sake but for art's sake. Whistler, flamboyant wit
and darling of the new aesthetic, argued for the independence of art
from any moral purpose:

Art should be independent of all clap-trap—should stand alone, and appeal to the artistic sense of eye or ear, without confounding this with emotions entirely foreign to it, as devotion, pity, love, patriotism, and the like.[10]

As the artist became professional, he claimed art as his province alone, not that of laymen or critics whom he increasingly portrayed as philistine boors. In time the moral earnestness of Ruskin was to give way to the sensuality, cosmopolitanism and exclusiveness of the aesthetes, but only after a struggle.

This difference of opinion came to a head in 1878, in a celebrated public clash between Ruskin and Whistler. Reviewing an exhibition of Whistler's work, Ruskin had attacked it savagely, writing of 'the ill-educated conceit of the artist', 'wilful imposture' and 'cockney impudence', and declaiming 'I never expected to hear a coxcomb ask two hundred guineas for flinging a pot of paint in the public's face'.[11] Whistler promptly sued him for libel, and turned the trial into a battle between artist and critic. During the trial Whistler argued that 'none but an artist can be a competent critic', and later satirised the Ruskin cultural 'scheme' in which 'the public, dragged from their beer to the British Museum, are to ... appreciate what the early Italians have done to elevate their thirsty souls'.[12] It was a sign of the times that Whistler won the case and was awarded a farthing damages.

Eleven years later, the same battle between critic and artist, between one generation's view of art and another's, was fought out in Australia, although with rather less showmanship. James Smith embodied the cultural evangelism of the immigrant generation. A trustee of the Melbourne Public Library and the National Gallery, an enthusiastic founder of cultural societies, a critic of art and literature, he was— it is hardly necessary to add—a follower of Ruskin. As a cultured layman proud of his wide intellectual interests, he was offended by the new values of the younger generation. And so, when he came to review for the *Argus* the famous 9 × 5 Exhibition of 'impressions' by Roberts, Conder, Streeton and others in 1889, his comments were scathing:

In an exhibition of paintings you naturally look for pictures; instead of which the impressionist presents you with a varied assortment of palettes. Of the 180 exhibits catalogued on the present occasion, something like four fifths are a pain to the eye. Some of them look like faded pictures seen through several mediums of thick gauze; others suggest that a paint-pot has been accidentally upset over a panel nine inches by five; others resemble the first essays of a small boy, who has just been apprenticed to a house-painter; whilst not a few are as distressing as the incoherent images which float through the mind of a dyspeptic dreamer.[13]

This review is often seen as evidence of the inability of the immigrant establishment, represented by Smith, to appreciate the 'real' Australia as portrayed by the Heidelberg School. In fact it was a repetition of Ruskin's attack on Whistler. When the artists concerned replied to Smith in letters to the *Argus*, they repeated arguments similar to those Whistler had used in court. They defended their 'impressions' against the charge that they lacked 'finish'; they found beauty in the commonplace, and questioned the ability of Smith, as a non-artist, to judge artistic merit: 'as it takes an artist to paint a picture, so also it takes one to appreciate it'.[14]

Later some of the new artists were to make the conscious effort to produce an 'Australian' art, with Roberts's and McCubbin's paintings of 'typical' bush life and Streeton's landscapes. The important thing is that the starting-point for this lay not in their Australian nationality, but in their interest in overseas trends (Impressionism in France but also as filtered through London) and in their stance as professional artists. Both provoked Smith. He condemned their 'Impressionism' as 'a craze of such ephemeral character as to be unworthy of serious attention', borrowing the judgement of W.P. Frith, R.A., who had been a witness for Ruskin. In response to the argument that only artists could fully appreciate art, he dismissed Roberts and company as 'a few young artists who have formed themselves into a Mutual Admiration Society'. In support of the layman, he cited the patronage of art by 'the Manchester cotton manufacturers' and 'the Birmingham steel-pen makers'.[15] It is unlikely that such examples convinced the artists.

The new writers associated with the *Bulletin* also openly rejected the old values of the British cultural establishment. Few could have been quite as irreverent at Ruskin's death in 1900 as A.G. Stephens of the *Bulletin*, who gaily debunked the 'superfluous veteran' as one who 'intellectually . . . does not count', and whose theories of art were 'imaginative gibberish'.[16] Irreverence provided the starting-point for the new image of Australia which the *Bulletin* writers helped create. The genial bohemianism, the scoffing at Victorian morality, the idealisation of the 'Common Man', the commitment to naturalism, were all aspects of a common revolt against received literary values. They were not initially distinctively Australian. Even the *Bulletin's* republicanism was based on an English radical tradition and Irish nationalism.[17] It had little to do with a sense of Australian identity or even the earlier Australian republican tradition derived from identification with America.

What came first was the revolt. As Archibald put it later: 'It was a Cant-ridden community . . . Socially, politically, all was a mean subservience to a spirit of snobbery and dependence . . . Sydney invited revolt from existing conditions, and the *Bulletin* was the organ of that revolt'.[18] Yet it should not be forgotten how much that revolt owed to the old cultural evangelism. The writers and their audiences were often the products of the Education Acts, the older generation's proudest achievement. The artists owed a debt to the public galleries and the associated art schools in which they trained. Even the young Norman Lindsay, the most irreverent of all, owed his introduction to art, and perhaps to sex too, to the Ballarat Art Gallery.[19] There were other continuities. *Plein air* painting, so closely identified with the Heidelberg School, had been preached by Buvelot; the *Bulletin* balladists owed much to Adam Lindsay Gordon; Henry Lawson was named after Kendall.

Their Bohemianism too owed something to a local tradition. In Sydney in the 1850s a loose literary circle had developed under the patronage of N.D. Stenhouse.[20] In Melbourne in the late 1860s, a rather self-conscious bohemianism had developed around Marcus Clarke, the Yorick Club and, when that became too respectable, the Bohemian Club. Clarke enjoyed looking back nostalgically: 'I fear we did not live virtuous lives . . . wicked and natural, and happy'.[21] From that bohemian outpost, he had praised Balzac, 'immortal Balzac', preached realism and, through his advocacy of a literature of everyday life, pleaded for an Australian literature. And yet, in all his attacks on established religion, his satires on local politics, his exposures of bourgeois respectability, his Gothic prose, even his experiments with marihuana, there remained a certain moral earnestness which bound him up with the values of his generation.[22]

The new bohemians of the 1890s were consciously hedonistic, and not so earnestly wicked. There was still something of the old style among the Melbourne group: Marshall Hall, for example, professor of music, poet and patron of the Heidelberg School, insisted on being seen in his pyjamas by Sunday church-goers.[23] Generally, however, the stress was on conviviality. It centred on the *Bulletin* office, bohemian clubs such as the Dawn and Dusk Club in Sydney and the Cannibal Club in Melbourne, and the various artists' camps where the new generation of painters discussed their work, smoked, talked, shared picnics and enthusiasms with their friends, and taught their students, usually girls conforming to the style of the 'New Woman'. In a letter to Roberts, Streeton reminisced about one of the camps:

> How we made sketches of the girls on the lawn. The lovely pure muslin, and gold, sweet grass-seeds and the motherly she-oak with its swing, spreading a quiet blessing over them all ... the silver dusk of night simplified the group of quiet happy boys and girls.[24]

Lionel Lindsay likened this happy life to 'pagan Greece, before Christianity came to throw its ominous shadow of melancholia and "purity" upon the blytheness of life.'[25]

There were also Artists Balls, Smoke Nights and, to raise money for friends, entertainments such as 'A Night in Bohemia' in the Sydney Town Hall.[26] When they could, they would act the part of bohemians in their dress—Roberts was noted for his crush hat and red cape—and furnish their studios exotically. Life was not easy for the writers and journalists especially during the depression: marriages broke up, Lawson turned to drink, Barcroft Boake rather dramatically hanged himself with his own stockwhip. But occasional poverty and uncertainty was all part of the irregular life they sought in bohemia.

Their sense of community tended to be exclusive and elitist. They shared Clarke's scorn for Philistines, but extended it to non-professionals and 'the public'. As artists they claimed for themselves, as we have seen, a higher appreciation of art. As professional artists, they demanded more say on artistic matters in the established art societies, which were dominated by amateurs and laymen intent on cultural improvement. The result was that in 1886 the younger professionals left the Victorian Academy of Art to form the Australian Artists' Association, and in 1895 a similar group split off from the Art Society of New South Wales to form the New South Wales Society of Artists. The names of the new societies were significant, for they implied the recognition of professional interests which needed protection. In both cases, Roberts led the walkout, and his followers included most of the important younger artists. As Streeton put it, they had mobilised 'for the sake of ART' against 'those old chaps'.[27] Later the splits were healed, but on the artists' conditions: the new Victorian Artists' Society, for example, ruled that non-exhibiting members 'shall not be entitled to vote ... on any matter affecting Art'.[28]

The Dawn and Dusk Club was also exclusive. Its membership included writers (Daley, Lawson, Brady, Bedford) and artists (Roberts, Mahony), but excluded 'the detestable Philistine', as one member put it, in order 'that soul may commune with soul alone'. Mocking the traditional criticism of the cultural possibilities of new societies, they included among their objectives 'one ... to establish a society for the

Being boys together: Smoke Night, Victorian Artists' Society, 1906, drawn by Percy Lindsay. From William Moore, Studio Sketches, *Melbourne, 1906, p. 20.*

erection of ancient ruins in Australia; another to form a fund for the
establishment of Australian Old Masters'.[29] They were also exclusive
in that they tended to be young single men, firmly rejecting middle
age and respectability; when they did get married it was often to the
sisters of their fellow bohemians.[30] In contrast, the older generation
of writers was often linked by marriage to the colonial gentry.[31]

France, Bohemia and the Bush

These then were the dimensions of the new generation's revolt:
professionalism, youthful hedonism, fellowship and a rejection of the
Victorian era's values. By the 1890s, 'Victorian' was already a dero-
gatory term.[32] Out of that revolt—almost as a by-product since the
same revolt was taking place in London—the new image of Australia
emerged. It was not seen then as being particularly nationalistic. The
rejection of the values of the British cultural establishment did not
necessarily involve the celebration of peculiarly Australian ones.
Indeed the revolt could take other directions altogether.

There was, for instance, an attraction towards France. As in Britain,
French realism in both literature and art was an important influence
on the younger generation. Paris was the new centre of the art world,
and French literature was considered by people such as A.G. Stephens
and Francis Adams as setting new standards for local writers. It went
deeper still. The *idea* of France appealed. As O'Dowd put it:

A wind hath spirited from ageing France
To our fresh hills the carpet of romance.[33]

Archibald, the greatest Francophile of all, changed his name from
John Feltham to Jules Francois, allegedly because of his 'inborn
objections to everything that sounded English'.[34] He dreamed of
establishing 'a "froggy" paper, utterly unlike anything under the
British flag, with . . . a column of smart local paragraphs written in
French'.[35] He left the Archibald Fountain as a memorial to French-
Australian friendship. Becke was another who Frenchified his name,
changing it from George Lewis to Louis. Sydney's bohemia liked to
eat at the Café Français and the Paris House restaurant ('oh! the
Bohemian orgies that were supposed to go on at Paris House!').[36]
Melbourne's equivalents were the Maison Dorée and Fasoli's. To the
British mind, France was traditionally associated with a rejection—
if only for a sordid weekend—of conventional values.

Another direction this rejection could take was towards the *idea* of bohemia. Melbourne had already been introduced to, and had re-coiled in shock from, 'a certain French picture . . . likely to suggest improper ideas'.[37] Lefebvre's stunning nude, *Chloe*, had proved too much for the National Gallery in 1882 and, despite a defence of the painting by McCubbin and others, it had ended up in Young and Jackson's Hotel. The new generation would continue to shock their more respectable elders by their open opposition to Victorian prudery. It should be remembered that this group of artists not only dabbled in 'impressionism' and created a new image of Australia, but they also introduced the nude into Australian settings. Indeed Roberts had been instrumental in having a life class established at the National Gallery school. There was a strand of naughtiness in bohemianism which culminated in Norman Lindsay's philosophy of art. He cele-brated sensuality and contrasted the creative bohemian with the philistine wowser.

A bohemian outlook could also lead towards a generalised political radicalism: republicanism, free thought and socialism of a sort found recruits among *Bulletin* writers. A series of 'progressive' causes were linked by the *Bulletin* and, later in the 1890s, by the emerging labour parties, and these were contrasted with prevailing conservative British values. But that radicalism, and the contrast, were themselves im-ported from Britain as part of the international urban culture. It is significant that labour parliamentarians were more likely to be recent immigrants and less likely to be native-born, than their non-labour colleagues, a point that is often lost in discussion of radical nationalism.[38] It is also worth noting that both bohemianism and radical republicanism were essentially urban, part of a world of artists' studios, cafes, bookshops, boarding houses and political meetings which could only exist in large cities such as Sydney or Melbourne.[39] Victor Daley acknowledged the allure of this world:

The town's confined, the country free—
Yet, spite of all, the town for me.[40]

In rejecting the values of the cultural establishment, the new genera-tion could turn to the idea of France, or the idea of bohemia. Most importantly, they could also be attracted to a cluster of symbols and principles which they associated with Australia: sunlight, wattle, the bush, the future, freedom, mateship and egalitarianism. This, like other images of Australia, was essentially artificial. It did not spring, in full bloom, from the Australian soil, but rather grew out of a set of attitudes to which the new generation had attached themselves and which provided a reference point for their revolt. They generally found this new Australia, which they thought of as the 'real' Australia, in the outback.

While this image of Australia was usually developed in the city, there were occasional forays into the bush to gather material. For his most consciously 'Australian' works—*Shearing the Rams, The Breakaway* and *The Golden Fleece*—Roberts visited sheep stations to make sketches, then finished the paintings in his city studio. His response was typically romanticised: 'If I had been a poet . . . I should have described the scattered flocks on sunlit plains and gum-covered ranges, the coming of spring, the gradual massing of the sheep towards the one centre, the woolshed'.[41] Henry Lawson too found what he had wanted on his trips, except that he had gone with a different set of expectations and in a season of drought:

> Further out may be the pleasant scenes of which our poets boast
> But I think the country's rather more inviting round the coast.
> Anyway, I'll stay at present at a boarding house in town
> Drinking beer and lemon squashes, taking baths and cooling down.[42]

The most ludicrous expedition was surely that undertaken by four self-styled bohemians associated with the Dawn and Dusk Club. One of them, George Taylor, a *Bulletin* artist, described it in his nostalgic *Those Were the Days*:

> It was decided that a real back-country adventure should be experienced. What was the good of posing as Australian artists or writers unless one had been 'there'. Harry Lawson got his 'local' color[sic] through personal experience, so it was up to the other Bohemian boys to do something in that line.

They took a train to Byrock, the first time any of them had been so far from Sydney. They waved wildly to any swagman they saw 'as if to a "brother of the track"' but ended up hiring a horse and buggy to carry their portmanteaus and other gear. On the road, they were soon depressed by the 'soul-destroying sameness', relieved only by 'dreams of city pleasures and delights', so they turned off the track to the Bogan River. On reaching it,

> It was only the work of a minute for Jessie to be unharnessed, and with four naked, joy-wild excitedly shouting Australians, to be trotting down to the welcome water to drink, to bathe and splash around with the very joy of living.
>
> Ah, it was worth while living in the back country to have such sport. 'City life holds no joys like these', said Artie. He was going to string some impromptu rhymes together, but thought better of it.

Oh, those were the days!

Time can never efface the joy times spent by the bank of that Bogan River. Gone were all thoughts of Gongolgan and Bourke . . . It was unanimously agreed to stay by that lovely river till it was time to go home.

Then they returned.

Back to Sydney! Back to Bohemian haunts; and four happy chaps brought back the 'local' color[sic] to tinge their story, verse and picture for ever more.[43]

Taylor's account of getting 'local' colour is a good illustration of just how self-conscious and artificial the process could be. The bush simply provided a frame on which to hang a set of preconceptions. At the same time it shows how the sense of freedom, comradeship and youthful spirits associated with the bush overlapped with the values which they infused into their bohemia. Thus, while it is possible to

Getting 'local colour' for a New South Wales Bookstall novel. From R. Wynn (et al.), The Late Alfred Cecil Rowlandson, *Sydney, 1922, p. 40.*

isolate the different directions rebellion could take, the various strands
—outback Australia, bohemia, even France—were in fact closely
interwoven. There were differences of emphasis, but men such as
Francis Adams and A.G. Stephens could quite comfortably combine
passionate attachments to France, the bush, radical politics, the artist
and Australia, all to some degree based on a rejection of dominant
British cultural values. Thus French literature and English aestheticism could both find a place in A.G. Stephens' vision of Australia:

> Verlaine's cult of Faded Things, extolling the hinted hue before the
> gross colour, finds a natural home in Australia,—in many aspects
> a land of Faded Things—of delicate purples, delicious greys, and
> dull, dreamy olives and ochres. Yet we have been content to let
> strangers foist upon us the English ideals of glaring green or staring
> red and orange ... This, though intelligent Englishmen themselves
> revolt against their tradition of crude colouring, and declare, like
> returning Morley Roberts, that ' ... the tint of grass after the
> soberer dull greys and greens and browns of Australia was extremely
> unpleasant to my eye. I thought the colour glaring, not to say
> inartistic ... ' To see the many-blossomed gum-tree moving in a
> breeze ... is to receive an aesthetic education ... In a word, let us
> look at our country ... through clear Australian eyes, not through
> bias-bleared English spectacles, and there is no more beautiful
> country in the world.[44]

Stephens shared the preference of Whistler and other aesthetes for
delicate tints rather than bright colours.

The connection between bohemian and bush values is also clear in
a group of paintings beginning with Roberts's *The Sunny South* (1887),
which portrayed naked Australian youth as part of a sunlit bush
landscape, with occasional *art nouveau* overtones. The whole effect
was one of freedom and healthy sensuality. Conder, McCubbin and
Long produced similar work. George Lambert could even turn Anzacs
into naked hedonists.[45] Will Ogilvie, a *Bulletin* balladist, dedicated a
volume of verse to *Fair Girls and Gray Horses*, while other poets
invested the bush with nymphs and satyrs. Henry Lawson could find
in mateship the virtues which others had found in bohemia:

> There were between us bonds of graft, of old times, of poverty, of
> vagabondage and sin, and in spite of all the right-thinking person
> may think, say or write, there was between us that sympathy which
> in our times and conditions is the strongest and perhaps the truest
> of all human qualities, the sympathy of drink. We were drinking
> mates together.[46]

Even the masculine exclusiveness of the bush ethos was repeated in the bohemianism of the 1890s. Women were as out of place in the Dawn and Dusk Club as they were in the shearing shed. George Taylor's emphasis on being 'Bohemian boys' together, for example, excluded all women except an artist's model, 'our sexless pal'.[47] For Arthur Jose, the romance of Sydney's bohemia was on the whole:

> devoid of feminine interest ... It was not that kind of romance. There were a few girls among the Boy Authors, but they were tolerated there mainly because they made tea and organized refreshments.

The only women writers who managed to penetrate that particular charmed circle were Louise Mack, who 'was on the whole taken as a joke by her fellow Boy Authors', and Amy Absell, who married the artist George Lambert and then 'absorbed her ambitions in her husband's'.[48]

One reason for this smothering sexism was that 'feminine' values were associated with the 'respectability' which the young bohemians condemned: they talked of Melbourne's literary circles as being 'obsessed with respectability, the respectability which they believed fervently to be of the ruling English type, for which Ada Cambridge wrote her polite and soothing novels'.[49] Another reason women were excluded was that their interest was assumed to be 'amateur' when the men were striving to protect their professional interests. Finally the 1890s generation joined in the idealisation of the 'masculinity' of 'The Coming Man', and helped forge his image: Streeton, for example, when he watched railway builders in the Blue Mountains, admired the 'big brown men ... toiling all the hot day', 'the big, stalwart men ... big and bronzed'.[50] There were women of this generation, notably Mary Gilmore and Barbara Baynton, who competed effectively as writers, but necessarily on the men's own ground. Women artists, although they actually outnumbered males at the National Gallery School, were not awarded the major prizes or scholarships, and generally failed to break into the professional bohemia of the period.[51] It is significant that at a time when women were making advances in politics and education, they were largely excluded from the newly professional artistic community of the 1890s. They had received more recognition in the earlier generation, and were to become prominent again after World War One.

The Real Australia

Thus this new intelligentsia carried into their image of the bush their

own urban bohemian values—their radicalism, their male comradeship, their belief in their own freedom from conventional restraints—
and presented it as the 'real' Australia. They also projected on to
their image of the bush their alienation from their urban environment:
they sought an escape from what the city represented. A few escaped
in other directions, Brady to sea, Becke to the islands, and found
there a similar freedom. Most chose the bush as an imaginative refuge.
The contrast between the cramping, foetid city and the wide open
spaces became a cliché for that generation: Paterson's 'Clancy of
the Overflow' was its most famous expression. In part it represented
a personal response to the poverty endured by many of the artists
and writers, the sort of life which, as Lawson put it, 'gives a man a
God-Almighty longing to break away and take to the Bush'.[52]

But it was more than this. The city could be identified with the values
of the older generation, their respectability, their philistinism, their
faith in progress which had turned sour in the depression. Even in
1885, Francis Adams's objection to Sydney had been that it was 'the
home-elect of the six-fingered and six-toed giant of British Philistinism'.[53] Later he would turn with relief to the bushman, his version
of 'The Coming Man', as Australia's saviour from the soft, debilitating
city. Paterson also contrasted Clancy, the drover, with the city:

> ... the hurrying people daunt me, and their pallid faces haunt me
> As they shoulder one another in their rush and nervous haste,
> With their eager eyes and greedy, and their stunted forms and
>   weedy,
> For townsfolk have no time to grow, they have no time to waste.[54]

It is important to note that this city-bush contrast was expressed
in very similar terms to those used by Kipling in depicting the relationship between the metropolis and the fringes of empire. Lawson resented
any comparison with Kipling. However they were writing for similar
audiences, and as a result had the same relationship to the dominant
literary culture and adopted similar literary forms. The cheap, popular
editions of the work of Lawson and others of his generation, published
and tirelessly promoted by the *Bulletin*, Angus and Robertson and,
later, the New South Wales Bookstall Company, were modelled on
the early Macmillan editions of Kipling.[55] The two writers also
espoused many of the same values, particularly in the identification
of their heroes of the wide frontier—Kipling's bearer of the 'white
man's burden', Lawson's 'real' Australian—with the cluster of ideas
embodied in 'The Coming Man'. Lawson's affinity with Kipling, and
his association of the 'real' Australian with 'The Coming Man', is

most explicit in a poem published in the *Bulletin* in 1892:

Ye landlords of the cities that are builded by the sea—
You toady 'Representative', you careless absentee—
I come, a scout from Borderland, to warn you of a change,
To tell you of the spirit that is roused beyond the range;
I come from where on western plains the lonely homesteads stand,
To tell you of the coming of the Natives of the Land!
>   Of the Land we're living in,
>   The Natives of the Land.
For Australian men are gathering—they are joining hand in hand
Don't you hear the battle cooey of the Natives of the Land?[56]

The attachment of Lawson and others of his generation to the bush-worker, as opposed to the older generation's preference for the squatter, was also parallelled in Kipling's idealisation of the 'Common Man' over the educated English gentleman.

Russel Ward has pointed out that the 'noble frontiersman' provided Western culture with a symbol of escape from urban, industrial civilisation, a romanticising of imperial expansion, and a focus for patriotic nationalist sentiment, especially in 'new' societies.[57] Ward himself was concerned with the third element, and argued that the nationalist image of the Australian bushman had a distinctively Australian inheritance in the nomadic bush-workers of the outback. However all three elements are so closely interwoven that the isolation of any one is distorting. We have already seen the contribution of urban bohemianism to the imagery of bush life. It must also be remembered that the bush-worker was an integral part of empire and, when he was ennobled as 'the Bushman' and his capacity for drunkenness and blasphemy forgotten, contributed much to imperial ideology. Even the London *Times* could 'value him as a part of the Empire . . . to leaven with his fine youthfulness our middle-aged civilization'.[58]

The imperial significance of the bush-worker rested on two points. Firstly the bush-worker, rather than the urban or agricultural worker, gave Australia its identity in the empire. The economic basis of empire was that the colonies provided a variety of raw materials for English industry. Australia's main contribution was wool. With that in mind, the suggestion could be made in 1849 that in the decoration for the new Houses of Parliament at Westminster, Australia should be represented by mines and sheep stations.[59] Australian shearers and squatters featured prominently in the literature of empire. Like the furhunter of Canada and the backwoodsman of the United States, they had been in the vanguard of white settlement of new frontiers: they had entered an alien landscape and made it profitable.

In the late nineteenth century the Australian economy was diversifying. From the imperial point of view the wool industry remained of special significance, and its drovers and shearers continued to contribute to the romance of empire. However, in the colonies, local manufacturing interests, particularly in Victoria, were increasingly influential in directing economic policy in their own interests. The idealisation of the bush-worker by Tom Roberts, A.B. Paterson and others was a reaffirmation that the wool industry was the 'real' basis of the Australian economy and of Australian prosperity, despite its imperial connections.

The second contribution that the bush-worker made to empire was in his role as 'The Coming Man' on whom the new imperialists pinned their hopes. The qualities which he was believed to display were the newly-respectable qualities of 'The Coming Man' on the fringe of empire: comradeship, self-confidence, generosity, restlessness, resourcefulness. It was to such men, 'the men who could shoot and ride' as Kipling put it, that the empire looked for its superior cannon fodder. So Australia chose contingents of 'Bushmen' to send off to the Boer War, and was thrilled when Chamberlain was impressed enough to ask for more.[60] In this light, bush-workers were respectable enough for a contingent of mounted shearers to be selected to lead the procession at the Federation ceremonies in 1901. They had the full approval of the conservative *Sydney Morning Herald* which praised the shearers as:

> men that could be sent anywhere to do anything, from shearing to soldiering—men who would give a good account of themselves in any company in the world ... fine-looking backblocks men with a certain freedom of bearing and suggestion of capability that was very effective.[61]

So when the professional writers and artists of the 1890s contributed to the idealisation of the bush-worker, they did so within a more general context of changing Western ideas, tastes and attitudes, which included new imperialism, Social Darwinism and the exalting of the common man, as well as the desire to create a nationalist symbol.

Much the same can be said about the image of the Australian landscape popularised by the *Bulletin* writers and the Heidelberg School artists. In terms of expressing what was distinctively Australian, the new generation dealt with little that was entirely new. The lost child, for example, almost a Jungian archetype in the Australian landscape, was used by McCubbin and Furphy, as it had been used earlier by Marcus Clarke and Henry Kingsley. Bushfire, flood and drought, pioneering, campfires, bush and station life, even the artistic problems of the gum tree, can all be found in the literature and art of both generations. Both were aware of the problems of 'local colour' and of the temptation to reduce Australian literature to conventional wattle and bushrangers, a temptation which a few writers in both generations managed to resist. Both generations realised that it was possible to be 'too' Australian, by unnaturally adding swagmen and gum trees at every opportunity.[62] Just as the younger generation owed institutional debts to their elders, they also owed much to their sketching-in of the possibilities for the writer and artist in Australia.

The differences between the generations in their depiction of landscape were essentially differences in taste. In terms of subject, for example, fashions had changed. Ruskin had turned the Swiss Alps into 'monuments of moral grandeur'[63] and Chevalier, Piguenit and von Guérard had done the same to the mountains of Tasmania and northern Victoria. By the time of the Heidelberg School, fashion demanded a more intimate approach to landscape, with gentler scenery and more attention to colour values, space and sunlight than to careful drawing, dramatic romanticism or heroic gloom. Similarly in poetry, Kendall's romanticism had attracted him to the eastern seaboard and fern-filled gullies; by the 1890s, fashion led Paterson towards sunlit plains and wide open spaces.

Changes in taste also demanded a different treatment of the landscape. By the 1890s, many critics were condemning one of the classic descriptions of the Australian landscape:

> What is the dominant note of Australian scenery? That which is the dominant note of Edgar Allan Poe's poetry—Weird Melancholy ... The Australian mountain forests are funereal, secret, stern. Their solitude is desolation. They seem to stifle, in their black gorges, a story of sullen despair ... The lonely horseman riding between the moonlight and the day sees vast shadows creeping across the shelterless and silent plains, hears strange noises in the primeval forest, where flourishes a vegetation long dead in other lands, and feels, despite his fortune, that the trim utilitarian civilisation which bred him shrinks into insignificance beside the contemptuous grandeur of forest and ranges coeval with an age in which European scientists have cradled his own race ... [64]

Marcus Clarke had written this in his preface to the poems of Adam Lindsay Gordon in 1876 but it had been adapted from descriptions of paintings by Buvelot and Chevalier which he had written earlier. From the 1890s on, this preface was continually held up as typical of a negative, alienated 'English' view of the Australian landscape, and compared unfavourably with the cheerful, sunlit vision of the 1890s generation. They professed to be seeing the landscape positively for the first time, because they saw it with 'clear Australian eyes', ignoring the fact that the settlers of the early nineteenth century also had a favourable image of the Australian landscape.[65]

A.G. Stephens was one of those to condemn Clarke's gloomy vision when he depicted Australia as a land of 'Faded Things' in his preface to *The Bulletin Story Book*.[66] Both men were conscious that they were writing prefaces to Australian literary landmarks; both men presented their images of Australia primarily in artistic terms; both, interestingly enough, had a literary commitment to naturalism. Yet the differences are stark, for the simple reason that Clarke conceived his vision within the conventions of late romanticism, with its fashionable gloominess, while Stephens conceived his within a framework of cheerful, *fin de siècle* bohemian aestheticism. Neither was more 'real', or more naturalistic, than the other: naturalism itself had its own artificial conventions. What had happened was that one standardised version of the Australian landscape had given way to another.

Making a Legend

From where, then, comes the legend that it was only in the 1890s that writers and artists first gave expression to the 'real' Australia, seeing it for the first time with 'Australian eyes' rather than with the eyes of an alienated exile? It was a common view after the Second World War, when many intellectuals sought to give the national identity a radical heritage. It was a common idea too in the 1920s, when national insularity sought a pure and uncorrupted Australian golden age. But the legend can be traced even further back, to the 'Bohemian Boys' themselves. They simply created their own.

After all, their commitment to naturalism required them to portray the 'real' Australia with the implication that all other versions of the landscape were artificially contrived. It was also a matter of self-interest. The *Bulletin* created its own legend as a sensible commercial enterprise: self-advertisement was part of the new journalism. For the writers and artists, it was in their professional interest to adopt and popularise a nationalist interpretation of Australian cultural development, to perpetuate the idea that the particular image of Australia which they had created was somehow purer, and more real, than any other. So they boosted each other as the only true inter-

Sir Arthur Streeton, Australian, 1867–1943, 'The Purple Noon's Transparent Might', 1896; Oil on canvas 121.9 × 121.9 cm. Purchased with the aid of a Government Grant, 1896, with its sunlit, blue-gold expanses, this painting was widely accepted as the ultimate expression of Australian sentiment.

preters of Australia. Victor Daley described Stephens in 1898 as

> . . . the blender of the pure
> Australian brand of literature.[67]

Later McCubbin could not 'imagine anything more typically Australian' than a painting of Streeton's, *The Purple Noon's Transparent Might*:

> this poem of light and heat . . . brings home to us so forcibly such a sense of boundless regions of pastures flecked with sheep and cattle, of the long rolling plains of the Never-Never, the bush-crowned hills, the purple seas of our continent. You could almost take this picture as a National Symbol.[68]

By 1905, Sydney Long was arguing that only artists who were Australian-born could produce a truly Australian art.[69]

In effect, Australian intellectuals were doing what Australian manufacturing interests were doing when they sought to protect local industry by tariffs, and advertised local products as superior to foreign imports. Once they were aware of themselves as a professional group, writers and artists began to make a claim for a sort of intellectual protectionism, seeking support for the local cultural industry. When faced with the argument that 'creative intellectual work' could easily be imported from Britain,[70] they retorted that the local product was superior, at least in Australian conditions. Joseph Furphy sub-titled his *Rigby's Romance* as *A 'Made in Australia' Novel*. In 1889, Victorian artists asked the Minister for Customs to impose a £10 duty on imported paintings. In 1910, one group formed an Australian Writers' and Artists' Union to protect their interests, but they were superseded by the Australian Journalists' Association. In 1912 writers and artists demanded tariff protection from imported magazines and novelettes to save 'the pioneers of culture' in Australia from 'semi-starvation'.[71] The irony was that the pastoral industry, which played such an important role in the national image developed by this generation, was always staunchly opposed to protectionism.

The link between economic self-interest, as a professional group, and their nationalist credentials as interpreters of Australia, is most explicit in E.J. Brady's account of Australian cultural development, written during the Great War:

> Once it was unfashionable to recognize Australian science, applaud Australian literary effort, or praise work of Australian artists.
> A persistent preference for the foreign article so discouraged local genius that it grew timid and deprecatory, or else fell a prey

to a melancholy which reacted upon all its aesthetic output . . .

Australian writers of my own generation have . . . loved our young country and realized her. In spite of social and monetary disadvantages, under which we all laboured, we have endeavoured, to the best of our abilities, to express our free and glorious motherland.

A few years ago a little group of writers and associate artists, who mostly found expression through the Sydney 'Bulletin', struck the first definite national note in Australian literary and artistic thought. Their influence has grown beyond expectation . . .

Literary and artistic genius of the next generation will not suffer the neglect and opposition which made life's highway more flinty to our feet . . . It is possible that a majority of them will be enabled to reap an adequate harvest from their life's efforts.[72]

As a spokesperson for his generation, Brady had impeccable credentials: a participant in the maritime strike, a balladist with the *Bulletin*, bushman and bohemian, he also had links with the next generation of nationalist writers who came into prominence after the Great War. His generation passed on to the next a national self-image, forged, they said, out of their Australianness, although in fact as we have seen there was little that was distinctive in it. It had already begun to sour.

7 Young, White, Happy and Wholesome

To cloud thy frank grey eyes,
No thought unworthy rise,
Clear as thy native skies
   Aye may they be.

                      Ethel Castilla, 'To an Australian Boy'[1]

Innocence in the outback. From the Lone Hand, *February, 1913, p. 271.*

On January 1, 1901, by Act of the British parliament, Australia was made a nation. The Commonwealth of Australia Constitution Bill had been passed at Westminster seven months earlier. Queen Victoria had signed it in time for the table she had used to be shipped to Sydney and set up in Centennial Park. There, the first Australian Governor-General, Lord Hopetoun, sat to sign his oath of allegiance to the Queen, and saw the new Commonwealth inaugurated, on the first day of the new century. As the form of the ceremonies implied, the sense of nationhood embedded in the new political entity and its constitution was a severely limited one. The competition of other loyalties was real.

The new Commonwealth was not sovereign: it had no power to declare war or peace, it could not make formal treaties with foreign powers and it had no diplomatic status abroad. The Head of State was the British monarch; the Governor-General, her representative, retained wide discretionary powers; Commonwealth law could be invalidated by legislation of the British parliament; the highest court of appeal was the Privy Council in London; the national anthem was England's. In 1901 few Australians felt such restrictions to be onerous. Most would probably have considered them as more symbolic than real, although even 75 years later many would see a Governor-General's use of his discretionary powers as legitimate. Most would have seen them as reflecting the vulnerability of the new Commonwealth, and its necessary dependence for its security on the British Navy. But most would also have seen it more positively, as reflecting a natural, wider loyalty to the empire. Race and blood ran deeper than nationality.

Other loyalties cut across the sense of nationhood. Federation represented less the birth of a nation and the culmination of patriotic feeling, than a readjustment of colonial relations, a somewhat shabby deal among the colonies based on deep suspicions and self-interested manoeuvring.[2] Commonwealth power was restricted to particular areas and firmly checked by the power of the states, which retained control over many of the more significant areas of government activity. The celebrations were affected by lingering colonial rivalries: they were less enthusiastic in Melbourne, because the Commonwealth was not being inaugurated there, and in Hobart, because no Tasmanian was included in the first cabinet. The procession was marred by another clash of loyalty: the Roman Catholic, Presbyterian and Wesleyan church hierarchies refused to take part after disputes about precedence.[3]

All the rhetoric about unity rang a little hollow, but the homogeneity of the new nation could not be denied, and was constantly remarked upon in the speeches and editorials which clogged the occasion. The Aborigines were a small enough minority now to be ignored, quite pointedly in the constitution itself, and there were no wide cultural divisions as in Canada or South Africa: the Irish at least spoke the same language, and could be included as part of the British or, as a few insisted, the 'Anglo-Celtic' race. In a society which dreaded the mixing of races as debilitating in the struggle for survival, in a society which was becoming more and more obsessive in its desire to protect the racial 'purity' of 'The Coming Man', the outlook in 1901 was promising. It could be proclaimed that the new nation was 98 per cent British, more British than any other dominion, some said more British than Britain itself. Of a total population of 3,773,801, as measured by the census in 1901, 77 per cent were Australian-born while 10 per cent were born in England and Wales, 3 per cent in Scotland and 5 per cent in Ireland. The largest non-British migrant groups were 1 per cent born in Germany and .8 per cent born in China. Most of the estimated 67,000 Aborigines were not counted at all.

The rhetoric of the occasion stressed this unity, and developed the theme of a twin identity, both Australian and British. The position of the 23 per cent of Australians who were Roman Catholic and of predominantly working-class Irish background remained ambiguous. For many of them, the empire was associated with oppression. Their twin identity, as taught in the Catholic school system, consisted of loyalty to Australia and to the (Irish) church. Other Catholics stressed their loyalty to empire and race, seeing no inconsistency with their Irish heritage. The majority of Australians identified with the government school tradition of Protestant God, British King and Anglo-Australian country, and they dominated the speech-making in proportion to their dominance of public life. Almost every reference to the new nation was tempered, qualified, checked by assurances that larger loyalties to empire remained.

The favourite images of nationhood were of an Australia reaching adulthood, joining the family of nations, cutting the painter, establishing a new branch of John Bull & Co. Kipling enhanced the occasion with a poem about 'The Young Queen'. The official invitations to the inauguration mixed several metaphors in an illustration of six white-robed maidens in the ship of state sailing a lotus-filled ocean towards the sun. The invitation to the opening of the first Commonwealth parliament was more straightforward, showing Britannia and Australia, her less martial counterpart, linked by an entwined grape-vine.[4] All of this imagery suggested the ambiguities of the Australian identity: a new status, a new independence, but only within the context of a continuing relationship with Britain.

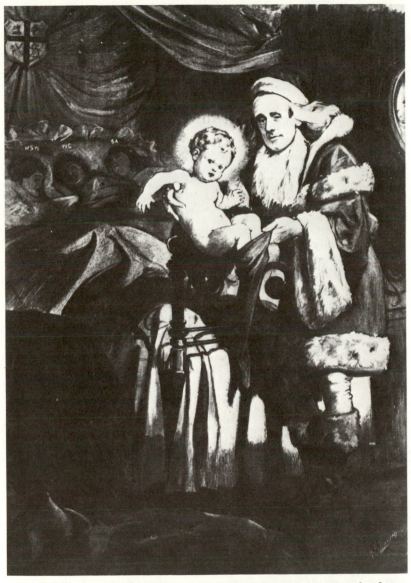

*Lord Hopetoun the first Governor-General presents a seasonal gift to
the sleeping States.*

*At the birth of the Commonwealth, the precise relationship between Australia,
the states and the mother country, as depicted in cartoons, was often confused
and at times open to misinterpretation. From* Melbourne Punch, *22 December,
1900.*

Despite the constraints on the new nation, and the lack of enthusiasm for federation, there was a great deal of talk about the need to foster Australian patriotic sentiment. Parents and teachers were told of their duty to instil into children a pride in Australia and all things Australian. The fetish for distinctively Australian motifs in popular art, literature, architecture and decor, which had been apparent in the 1880s, continued to gain strength. Aided and abetted by writers and artists more confident of their professional status, overt Australian patriotism was clearly a middle-class virtue. It had two basic impulses. Firstly, it was associated with the increasing significance of local manufacturing. Australians were being told to

Buy! Buy! Buy of your kindred!
To your own land be true.[5]

None was more enthusiastic in the celebration of Australiana than local companies advertising their products. By the turn of the century it was possible for patriotic Australians to buy Coo-ee cheese and tobacco, Boomerang brandy and explosives, Kangaroo-brand bicycles and dessicated potatoes.[6] Patriotism protected local manufacturers and their workers from outside competition. The second impulse was more overtly class-based: patriotism promoted national unity at a time when sections of the labour movement were increasingly militant and class-conscious.[7] National loyalties were encouraged by the middle class: class loyalties were condemned as divisive and un-Australian.

In 1901 these were the two ingredients of a new image being promoted in the interests of the national bourgeoisie. They set about identifying their interests with nationhood, and denying the existence of the deep class divisions within Australia which the more radical labour activists were discussing. They did this by stressing the idea that threats to Australia came from outside and that all groups had a common interest in the protection of Australia's innocence. Protection, not only of local labour and industry from foreign competition, but also of the nation generally from foreign aggression and assaults on its unity or its racial or moral purity became a dominant feature of Australian society.

It is striking how many of the major legislative achievements of the early parliaments were defensive and protective in their intent. The 'White Australia' policy—the first real issue dealt with by the new parliament—attracted almost unanimous approval. An Australian navy and a national system of compulsory military training were established. The 'New Protection' set out to protect and encourage local industry at the same time as it protected the living standards of workers. The living standards of Australian workers and their role in the system were also protected, consolidated and institutionalised by the arbitration system. Old age and invalid pensions protected particular groups, while even the maternity bonus could be seen as essential to national security.

One reason for this emphasis on defence and protection was the nature of the federation itself. More positive notions relating to the national identity—developing the nation's resources, industrial expansion, creating a better, more equal society, producing, developing and educating the 'New Man'—remained part of state rather than national politics. The Commonwealth powers were defensive and strictly limited but nevertheless the focus of public life had shifted towards federal parliament. The result was that the idea of nationhood was increasingly defined in terms of what it was being defended against rather than what it stood for.

Within the states, there was little debate about the direction society should take. With a few exceptions, state governments were concerned with ways and means rather than ends: their main function was to provide, administer and maintain parish pump services. In general, their one great commitment was a bipartisan one: development. The development ethos became an integral part of Australian nationhood. As manufacturing continued to expand, 'Australia Unlimited' became a national slogan, popularised by E.J. Brady's massive survey of Australian resources in 1918 and still celebrated in the *Sydney Morning Herald*'s annual survey of Australian development in the 1960s. Australia's first Commonwealth bank-notes, printed in 1913, included as national symbols illustrations of irrigation and coal-mining.[8]

There was wide agreement that it was the government's responsibility to provide much of the infrastructure for development, although private industry might reap the profit. An example was the establishment of B.H.P.'s steel-works at Newcastle in 1912, the biggest single step towards industrialisation. State and Commonwealth Labor governments disregarded the federal party platform and helped establish B.H.P.'s steel monopoly by contributing land, power, harbour facilities, government contracts and financial support from the new Commonwealth Bank.[9] With the growth of such large companies, enterprise, development, progress and growth were woven into the image of Australia. Apart from the commitment to development, Australia was identified with purity, innocence, wholesomeness, sanity, all of which were to be protected with an almost pathological obsession. All that was threatening, divisive, unhealthy, decadent, and impure was seen as being foreign. Nationhood, once it was made politically meaningful, began to look like paranoia.

Wholesome as the Wattle

Even in the 1890s, in the imagery of bush, clear skies and sunshine which was developed by the younger generation of writers and artists, there was something of an obsession with happy youth, health and wholesomeness. This was particularly true of Paterson's ballads and Streeton's paintings, and in the next few decades, their work was increasingly seen as the truest expression of the 'real' Australia—natural, cheerful and sane. The purity and sanity of Australia was contrasted with the decadence of Europe. In 1916, McCubbin warned native-born artists against visiting Paris, where they would be 'caught and dazzled by the fads and fashions of the extremists, rather than instructed by the honest methods of the true Artists'.[10] By the 1920s, Streeton, now knighted and home from Europe, was being portrayed as a bulwark of sanity and normality against the unhealthy decadence of foreign art movements. His art, according to the 1926 *Australian Encyclopaedia*, was 'purely wholesome', and could not blossom in 'foreign soil, so saturated with formulas'.[11] The encyclopaedia's editor, Arthur Jose, was concerned to dissociate Australia's bohemians from the *fin-de-siècle* decadence of Europe: 'Their whole spirit was healthily boyish, not adolescently revolutionary or boredly middle-aged'.[12]

This emphasis on wholesomeness in the national identity was not unique to Australia. It took up threads of an international interest, particularly strong in the United States, in physical fitness, mental health and eugenics. It was also related to the quest in many countries for 'National Efficiency', a movement which saw changes in the fields of health, education, industrial relations and slum clearance, leading to a more homogeneous, unified, 'decent' and productive population.[13] There were even occasional instances where the bohemians' interest in nudity sounded a little like the health reformer rather than the cheerful flouter of convention. A wide range of issues was linked to this concern for wholesomeness: from the need for more parks to temperance, from farm training for city youth to raising the age of consent, from defence to eugenics, racial purity and campaigns against venereal disease.[14] In Australia and elsewhere they were all associated with attempts to maintain the purity and personal efficiency of the race.

As well as the broad interest in 'National Efficiency', there was also a strong local tradition which had associated Australia with sunshine and good health: as early as the 1830s migrants had been attracted by the healthier, drier climate. So the 'wholesome' image of Australia was certainly not restricted to the bohemians of the 1890s. In 1890, Professor E.E. Morris condemned Marcus Clarke's 'weird melancholy' as the hangover of a 'fast life,' and was thankful that 'the great body of our nascent literature is cheerful and vigorous, as becomes the pioneer writers of a young and hopeful country'.[15] Six years later another critic argued that Australian literature was characterised by the 'sincerity' with which the 'wholesome pleasures' of 'this great wide land' were depicted.[16] Neither critic had the *Bulletin* writers in mind.

In the new century, the stress on wholesomeness became stronger. Maintaining the purity, virtue and moral soundness of youth was the set task of private, state and Catholic education systems, which were constantly emphasising to their charges the importance of 'keeping the race clean and fit and stalwart'.[17] Australians were congratulated on the 'moral sunlight'[18] of their social system, as opposed to the decadence of Europe. In 1907, C.E.W. Bean, journalist and later war historian, thought the Australian type was marked by 'personal cleanliness' and was 'pre-eminently a lover of the truth', qualities which were also Anglo-Saxon, but more pronounced in the Australian. Anyone who had the misfortune to have to live in a 'foreign' country would soon miss 'the indescribable frankness by which you can pick out an Anglo-Saxon face from a crowd of foreigners; and the cleanness which is no mere lick and a promise'.[19]

It was at this time that the wattle was promoted as a symbol of the sunshine, cheerfulness and wholesomeness in the national ethos, at least among a patriotic section of the middle class. Theirs was a conscious effort to inspire patriotic feeling, and imitated the Canadians' promotion of the maple leaf. Odes and songs to the wattle had been popular in the 1880s, and in 1890 a Wattle League had been set up in Adelaide as a women's off-shoot of the Australian Natives' Association. The members encouraged Australian literature and music, and wore sprigs of wattle conspicuously at their functions, but the organisation wilted and died. In 1899 the first Wattle Club was founded, and in 1909 a broad Wattle Day movement took root. The object of the Wattle Day Leagues was to encourage the display of patriotic feeling by promoting the wattle as the national floral emblem of Australia, and by celebrating Wattle Day, (on 1 August or 1 September) by planting it, wearing it, distributing it to the city poor and decorating statues with it. In 1910 New South Wales public schools began to celebrate Wattle Day, and in 1912 the wattle was incorporated into Australia's coat-of-arms.[20]

In 1913, the Labor Prime Minister, Andrew Fisher, opened the first Federal Wattle Day League Conference in Adelaide; unhappily he did not stay long enough to hear or act on the president's proposal that an 'Order of the Wattle Blossom' be created for outstanding non-political service to Australia. The speeches emphasised that the wattle was a natural, not a cultivated, flower, 'a radiator of sunshine' representing the golden ore of our mines, our golden grain, our golden opportunities and the golden hearts of Australians, a reference to a line of Lawson's.[21] Elsewhere it was said that the wattle stood for 'home, country, kindred, sunshine, and love—every instinct that the heart most deeply enshrines', and that the League's aim should be to 'make the Wattle synonymous with Australia's honour. Then any vandal who mutilates or destroys it will meet with the execration he deserves'.[22] Others pointed out that as well as being more beautiful than any other national emblem, it was also one of the world's most useful trees. A.J. Campbell, a botanist, did the rounds with a popular lecture entitled 'Wattle Time, or "Yellow-haired September"'; he was accompanied by optical lantern views of the varieties of wattle being displayed by young ladies in daringly Grecian robes, and occasionally by incidental organ music as well.[23]

After the Great War, wattle was planted at Gallipoli, and was made a feature of the decor at Government House. It continued as a symbol of sunshine and sanity. In 1938, K.R. Cramp, historian, inspector of schools and president of the Wattle League, was telling school children that 'On Wattle Day we remind ourselves that we are Australians, with a bright and healthy outlook on life, and a golden anticipation of a happy future': the wattle was 'a piece of solidified sunshine representing the cheerful spirit of a people that will not be downtrodden'.[24]

The Wattle Leagues tended to attract the sort of respectable nationalist bourgeoisie associated with the Australian Natives' Association but they were not the only devotees to the idea that Australia stood for sunshine, sanity and clean living. It was also characteristic, for example, of the New South Wales Bookstall Company which published the work of many of the *Bulletin* writers. The books were illustrated by Australian artists, in cheap popular editions, on the assumption that 'Australian readers . . . want the Australian outlook, the Australian sentiment; the sunny spirits of her roving sons and merry daughters'. The company was phenomenally successful: it began publishing in 1900 by paying Steele Rudd, who remained their most popular author, £500 cash for *Sandy's Selection*, and by 1920 had produced nearly 200 novels and sold more than four million copies.[25]

The stress on wholesomeness was also characteristic of the *Lone Hand*, a monthly offshoot of the *Bulletin*, set up in 1907 under the guiding hand of J.F. Archibald. There was still the old enthusiasm for France, with regular copy from two Parisian journalists, but the *Bulletin* announced its progeny as having 'no policy except the cultivation of an Australian sentiment . . . Its politics will be sunshine and good cooking, open air music and red umbrellas'.[26] The first issue proclaimed that the platform would be 'an Honest, Clean, White Australia . . . It will not worry about the people's politics, but will take a militant interest in the people's health'.[27] It thus took the fetish of wholesomeness to its logical conclusion, and the continuing war which it waged on food, drink and drug frauds was the nearest it came to having a political cause. It also contributed to the establishment of Arthur Streeton's art, summed up by *The Purple Noon's Transparent Might,* as the authorised image of national sentiment: it was 'absolutely sane . . . the interpretation of the patch of God's garment, made by that picture, is very much in accord with all our best conceptions of this good land'.[28]

Quite subtly, the bohemian image of the outback was reduced to wattle, sunshine and 'White Australia'. One result was that Henry Lawson's vision of the bush, and his personal degeneration, were increasingly seen as unrepresentative, too morbid to represent the young nation. In 1905, A.G. Stephens complained that Lawson's 'miserable broodings are far from depicting the cheerful courage of the men and women of the bush'.[29] Later he suggested that Lawson had an 'English personality', an 'alien temperament', and so always saw Australia 'through the distorting glass of his own moody mind . . . His womanish wail often needs a sturdy Australian backbone'.[30] Other critics argued that his poetry contained 'no inspiration for Australian youth' when in fact no country had 'more of the joy of life' than Australia.[31] Paterson on the other hand 'reflected so truly and cheerfully the spirit of adventurous youthfulness' with his 'straightforward, unmorbid, healthy' approach to bush life.[32] And so the bush and the bohemians were sobered up, made respectable and reinterpreted to stand for the new bourgeois virtues associated with the new nation, for the new ideals which needed protection.

Minerva and the Little Boy from Manly

A similar set of obsessions was a feature of the graphic image of

Australia, or of the ways in which the idea of Australia was conventionally depicted in cartoons and other illustrations. By the turn of the century, there were several possibilities in the black-and-white artist's repertoire. An obvious one was to depict Australia as a kangaroo, often in contrast to the British lion. Another, popular in the more radical press, was to portray Australia as a noble worker, but more often this figure appeared as a symbol of labour, competing with another stereotype, Mr Fat Man, a top-hatted boss bursting out of his waistcoat, who stood for capital. Far more popular than either of these were two other standard images, the classical convention of the idealised young woman, and the more recent invention of the little boy from Manly. By federation, both had been popular for some time, often representing individual colonies but also standing for Australia as a whole. Their popularity among cartoonists as symbols of Australia made them very powerful images for another two decades,

Australia as a young woman: when Prince Alfred visited Australia in 1868, Punch *turned Australia into Little Bo Peep. The importance of the wool industry in the Anglo-Australian relationship was clear. From* Punch, *25 January, 1868, p. 39.*

and for that reason they are worthy of closer examination.

The figure of a young woman was simply an adaptation of the scantily-clad allegorical convention that was used to represent any abstract ideal. A young feminine Australia was the equivalent of Britannia, Columbia or la France. Unlike them, she had no distinctive features, no breastplate or tricolour, although she was often drawn with blonde hair, as befitted the representative of the land of the wattle. Occasionally she appeared as a shepherdess. More often she gained distinctive features from the context in which she found herself. Firstly, she often had a particular relationship with Britannia or John Bull: there was a stress on the fact that she was the daughter, that she had parents, that she was growing up, approaching adulthood, about to flower into womanhood. Secondly, there was a distinctive stress on her remarkable beauty, but also on her innocence, her purity and her vulnerability. She often found herself in difficult situations, modestly blushing at vice, naively shocked at corruption, or in imminent danger of being raped.

The little boy from Manly displayed similar features. He first appeared in 1885 when, among the subscribers to the *Sydney Morning Herald*'s appeal on behalf of the Sudan contingent, there appeared 'a little boy at Manly' who had rather rashly sent in the contents of his money box for the cause. Livingstone Hopkins, 'Hop' of the *Bulletin*, seized the incident to create a new symbol. He used the little boy to replace the young women, the 'Minervas', whom he found 'difficult to acclimatize' and too feminine to represent the vigorous manliness of the colonies:

> A journalistic whim of the moment turned the 'Little Boy at Manly' to satirical account as typifying the well-meant impetuosity of a young colony in espousing a cause that was well able to take care of itself . . . and so filled a long-felt want.[33]

Previously, the Australian colonies had been represented by young currency lads and street urchins, but the little boy from Manly, appearing at a crucial period in the growth of the illustrated press, seemed to capture best what cartoonists wanted to say. For 30 years he was to be Australia's equivalent of England's John Bull and America's Brother Jonathan. He did not displace the young woman: she remained strong competition. Nor did the impetuosity last; he became more cautious and sometimes bemused but always independent and generous. On first appearance he was a particularly 'good' little boy ('Minerva' too was a dutiful daughter), dressed in Dickensian pantaloons, a floppy tie and frills. Norman Lindsay's version wore a

The first appearance of Hop's version of the Little Boy from Manly. From the
Bulletin, *4 April, 1885, p. 13.*

sailor suit, and others dressed as boy scouts. Although the little boy
from Manly did not survive the 1920s, Australia was still being portrayed as a little boy, often with the characteristics of Fatty Finn or
Ginger Meggs. Throughout he displayed the same two characteristics
as the young woman: he was young, growing up within a family
relationship with Britain, and he was reasonably innocent and very
vulnerable to any threats from an evil, outside world.

This image was flexible enough to suit both the main ruling groups,
although there was a difference in emphasis. Imperially-minded
pastoral interests stressed the need for the offspring to maintain
dependence on mother England. The manufacturers on the other
hand encouraged the youngster to break the maternal bonds and be
independent. As we shall see, they identified maturity with an industrialised economy, and promoted the view that industrialisation
was as inevitable as a child's growing-up. What both images left out
was class conflict which in the more radical press, was featured pro-

'Australia First'

*In cartoons by the Labor cartoonist, Claude Marquet, Australia was represented
by an idealised worker (the Coming Man?) while Mr Fat Man was a threat.
From the Australian Worker, 24 September, 1914.*

minently, particularly in cartoons which depicted the noble worker at odds with Mr Fat Man, the capitalist. The *Bulletin* had published such cartoons during the great strikes of the 1890s, but by 1917, when its radical sympathies had ossified into conservatism, labour was being depicted as fat, and capital as the underdog. It was testimony to the success with which the middle class had laid claim to the imagery of Australia.

8 Diggers and Heroes

> But, as the members of the Eureka Amalgamateds and others knew, the sometime kangaroo shooter was an extraordinary shot ... 'By goodness! but that was a marvellous shot!' cried the lieutenant from the periscope. 'You exploded the bomb in the poor beggar's hand'.
>
> Joseph Bowes, *The Young Anzacs*, 1917[1]

A key feature of the national paranoia about wholesomeness was the image of the digger. In the First World War, the national type faced, in the words of the *Official History*, 'the one trial that ... all humanity still recognises—the test of a great war'.[2] The digger emerged as the national hero. He held a special place in the national identity because he could be seen as the fulfilment of all the hopes that had been invested in 'The Coming Man', the ideal expression of the Australian 'type'. It was with a mixture of relief and pride that patriotic Australians could regard the national type as tested and not found wanting. With those credentials, the digger soon came to stand for all that was decent, wholesome and Australian. Not only did he embody Australianness, but he was its greatest protector.

Girded for Battle

Although the digger only conclusively proved himself at Gallipoli in 1915, his presence had been felt many years previously. In 1883, the Melbourne *Age* had announced that 'our men are splendid material for an army; very much above the average of the line in physique and intelligence'.[3] From then on the national type had been constantly summed up with an eye to his military potential. Soldiering prowess was the ultimate measure of worth by which 'The Coming Man' was judged in the heyday of European imperialism. And the superiority of the colonial soldier had been half-proved in the Boer War.

Yet there remained a nagging doubt. C.E.W. Bean who, as Official

War Historian, did more than anyone to turn the digger into a national legend, had summed up the character of the Australian type in 1907. The bush had 'hammered out of the old stock a new man'. The typical Australian took 'everything on its merits and nothing on authority'. He was utilitarian but clean, a very 'square' man who valued frankness highly, a man who owned no class distinctions. As for his potential as a soldier:

> The Australian is always fighting something. In the bush it is drought, fires, unbroken horses, and cattle; and not unfrequently strong men. Never was such a country for defending itself with its fists ... We look upon all this as very shocking and unruly in England nowadays; but there is no doubt that having to fight for himself gives a man pluck ... All this fighting with men and with nature, fierce as any warfare, has made of the Australian as fine a fighting man as exists.[4]

The only doubt was that he lacked the one quality which made a fighting man into an efficient soldier: discipline. He would always find it difficult to obey orders, and 'even when properly handled he is restless and suspicious of authority'. Here, in 1907, were all the features which Bean both as a war correspondent with the troops and later as their historian, was to note and to propagate as characteristic of the Anzacs.

Whether for the sake of empire or a 'White Australia', for the cause of King and Country or racial purity, Australians were being urged well before the war to be fit and ready for battle. Methodists for example sang hymns seeking protection from the 'alien host':

> God of battles, lend thy might
> Where e'er we fight Australia's foe.[5]

School children were being urged to emulate Nelson and Gordon, and to be ready to sacrifice themselves for empire. They were taught songs that prepared them for the test to come:

> Thy dormant days are ended,
> Thy hours of rest are run;
> Now rouse thee for a nation's work,
> And keep the Empire won!
> Beneath thy bright blue skies,
> Australia Fair, arise![6]

In 1895, Henry Lawson had looked forward to the day when 'the Star of the South shall rise—in the lurid clouds of War'. War was inevitable 'while blood is warm and the sons of men increase', and it was only in that supreme conflict that nations were born.[7] By 1916 W.M. Hughes, Labor Prime Minister and later to be closely identified with the troops as 'the Little Digger', was approving of the Great War for having prevented Australia 'from slipping into the abyss of degeneracy and from becoming flabby . . . War has purged us, war has saved us from physical and moral degeneracy and decay'.[8]

It was not just speeches and songs that prepared 'The Coming Man' for battle. Boys were drilled in school cadet corps, taught as boy scouts to 'Be Prepared', forced from 1911 to take part in compulsory military training. The role of women in preparing the nation for war was a secondary one: they were told to keep pure and produce as many children as possible. The test of a nation was not only the strength of its manhood, but also 'the purity of its young womanhood'.[9] Women could either symbolise national purity and wholesomeness, or be seen as a threat to it. The popularity of surf-bathing among women just prior to the war was thought on the one hand to promise 'much to improve the physique of the race'.[10] On the other hand, the Roman Catholic Archbishop Kelly saw mixed bathing as a threat to national purity: 'unless people are attracted by real womanly modesty and not by the indelicacies of the so-called up-to-date woman . . . we are not going to build up a good nation'.[11] During the war, the departing troops were warned of the threat posed by 'flighty' women, and were urged to 'Come back clean, to be the fathers of a pure-blooded and virile Australian race'.[12]

Fear of degeneracy also stemmed from the fact that the Australian birth-rate was falling at the turn of the century. A Royal Commission which examined the question in 1903 accused women of selfishness in putting their own 'pleasure' before the nation's need.[13] To safeguard white supremacy, to ensure a large and fit population able to resist aggression in the supreme test, Labor governments introduced such measures as maternity allowances in 1912—£5 'baby bonuses' paid to mothers on the birth of 'viable' children—and baby health clinics in New South Wales from 1914. Conservatives opposed such measures, some arguing their result would be a less fit race, unused to the harsh struggle for survival. But politicians on all sides accepted that any future war would be the ultimate test of the fibre of the new national type.

The result was that well before the outbreak of the Great War, the image of the Australian soldier was being sketched in. The national pride of a newly inaugurated nation demanded that he be a hero. And as a hero he was expected to display the conventionally heroic qualities of the day, the qualities of the idealised 'New Man', the boy scout, the Boys' Own Paper mixture of independence, manliness, honesty, curiosity, wholesomeness, a certain ordinariness and decency. It was inevitable that these qualities would be discovered in the digger at his baptism of fire. Even in August 1914, as the A.I.F. marched through Sydney, the *Sydney Morning Herald* commented on 'the fine physique of the men and soldierly bearing . . . All were young, active, and alert, born soldiers'. The paper congratulated the officers on the transformation they had brought to 'a heterogeneous crowd of ex-soldiers, bushmen, militia, athletes, and citizens'.[14]

With the landing at Gallipoli in April 1915, the ready-made myth was given a name, a time and a place. The tributes, expressing relief that the test of war had been passed, began to contribute to the legend. Given the imperial significance of 'The Coming Man', it was to be expected that the tributes would come not only from Australians but from British imperialists as well, and that they would be similar to the tributes given to, for example, the Canadian troops. They were part of the same breed, men 'bronzed with the suns of the Southern Cross and hardened by the snows of the northern star' as they had been described at Queen Victoria's jubilee in 1897.[15] The praise was not so much for them as Australians, but as representatives of the 'Coming Race'.

The famous British war correspondent, Ellis Ashmead-Bartlett, gave the first detailed account of the Australians in action. He wrote of the 'colonials, practical above all else', of 'this race of athletes', of their happiness that 'they had been tried for the first time and had not been found wanting'; these 'raw colonial troops . . . proved worthy

According to the Anzac Book *(1916), even the most effete gentleman could be transformed into the Coming Man.*

to fight side by side with the heroes of Mons, the Aisne, Ypres, and Neuve Chapelle'.[16] In 1916, John Masefield, the future poet laureate, described the inexperienced troops at Gallipoli as:

> the finest body of young men ever brought together in modern times. For physical beauty and nobility of bearing they surpassed any men I have ever seen; they walked and looked like the kings in old poems, and reminded me of the line in Shakespeare:
> 'Baited like eagles having lately bathed'.

With quotations from *The Song of Roland* and praise for the 'sheer naked manhood' of the Allies, he was helping turn Gallipoli into a legend.[17] The point is that he was not referring only to Australian troops, but to all those being tested for the first time.

The reaction in Australia was to accept these idealised heroic qualities as not only characteristic of the digger, but to see them as distinctive to Australians. Even here, the more imperially-minded, the Melbourne *Argus* for example, wrote of the Australians and Canadians distinguishing themselves at the same time, and praised 'the high patriotism and self-control of a ruling race' and 'the stirring story of duty manfully performed': 'Australia could not wish for a more inspiring scene in which to make her European debut as a fighting unit of the Empire'.[18] Among the more Kiplingesque imperialists, such sentiments were already a little dated. They were keener on the physique of 'The Coming Man' than on these more abstract qualities. Nationalists were equally admiring of his physique, but were inclined to see it as uniquely Australian. E.J. Brady prophesied:

> The breed that stormed and held the heights of Anzac will grow stronger and more self-reliant as their generations follow. The home-land suns that browned their burly frames will not cease to shine from out our blue Australian heavens; the home winds that filled their mighty lungs will not cease to blow, and there will be white Australian loaves and good Australian beef and butter to give them stamina.
> Their well-fed, well-developed bodies will house vigorous and intellectual minds. They will be just, powerful and humane.[19]

From such tributes it is clear that the qualities identified with the digger, as an archetypal Australian hero, were the conventionally admired ones. Although some attempted to establish that the Australian soldier was somehow different, the virtues attributed to him were often those claimed for the soldiers of other nations as well.[20] For some he stood for the duty and self-sacrifice of the British soldier;

for others, the independence, practicality, manliness and uncertain discipline of 'The Coming Man'. However, whatever characteristics the diggers were credited with, they returned to Australia as the upholders of what it meant to be Australian. It was through them that the Australian identity could be given a heroic, legendary core, and they offered themselves, and were used, as the custodians of nationhood.

Capturing the Legend

However the Australia to which the diggers returned in 1919 was not the one they had left. Two bitterly-fought conscription plebiscites, a prolonged general strike in New South Wales and growing war weariness in the last year had exposed deep divisions within the Australian community. In those struggles, each side strove to portray itself as representing the 'real' Australia, while the other was betraying national ideals. Conservatives, employers, the Protestant churches and the middle class generally saw anti-conscriptionists and strikers as traitors to the war effort, to the heroes at the front, to God, King and Country. The trade unions and the Irish saw the conscriptionists as prepared to throw away Australian lives in a war that was not Australia's own, and to betray Australia to imperialists and warmongers. As one anti-conscriptionist put it, the 'respectable' elements of society, although they declared themselves to be 'the moral backbone of the community', in fact had no connection 'with any of the vital elements in the life of Australia, and as far as they have an ideal at all, it is that of the English commercial middle class'.[21] Both sides in the conscription debate set out to woo the digger vote because of its symbolic impact, and although the soldiers' vote was surprisingly evenly split, the conscriptionists were to be more successful in capitalising on the digger legend and the patriotism associated with it. Their opponents were hereafter identified with disloyalty. The Labor Party had split. Hughes, 'the Little Digger', had joined the conservatives. The newly-formed Nationalist Party, with its carefully-chosen name, won a sweeping victory at the election of 1917.

As the war drew to a close, Herbert Brookes, the President of the Associated Chambers of Manufactures of Australia, made it clear that the returning digger could be identified with conservative business interests. Brookes had been an enthusiastic member of such conscriptionist organisations as the Universal Service League, the Australian Defensive League and the Citizens' Loyalist Committee. He now called for Australians to produce 'as much as it is possible to produce'; he wanted

> ONE GREAT NATIONAL PARTY IN AUSTRALIA, and we shall know then how to deal out their desserts to the disloyalist and sectarian traitor and Bolshevik in our midst. No longer shall a treacherous alien institution be permitted to sow the seeds of discord within our midst and preach disloyalty to the State in peace as in war. Then and not till then we shall have free industries, free men, and a free Australia. To this end let us dedicate our lives, and by doing so make Australia a fit country for the returned men who have risked their lives for us, for our Empire and for Civilisation.[22]

Brookes, a leading Protectionist, chairman of directors of Australian Paper Mills, a member of the Victorian Electricity Supply Board, the Federal Coal Board and the Federal Bureau of Commerce and Industry, embodied the development ethos of 'Australia Unlimited'.

To some extent this vision of Australia's future was in conflict with the older pastoral ethos which depicted the bush as the 'real' Australia. The association of Australia with development, particularly industrial development, was to become stronger. Gradually the idea that Australia should provide the raw materials for Britain's industry, was challenged by the argument that Australia should be industrially self-sufficient, and should manufacture for itself the goods which had previously been imported from Britain. It was a slow process, and by no means clear-cut. Both the pastoral and manufacturing sectors of the ruling class had important interests in common; this was recognised with the political fusion in 1909 of the Free-Traders and the Protectionists, and again in the Bruce-Page coalition government of the 1920s, led by Stanley Melbourne Bruce, an importer with some manufacturing interests, and Earle Christmas Grafton Page, the country doctor involved in farming. Nevertheless, the underlying differences meant that they developed different images of what it was to be Australian. In the 1920s in particular, there was competition between the two groups to mould the Anzac legend in their own image.

For C.E.W. Bean, the digger simply embodied the characteristics of the new national type which he had described in 1907 when writing for the *Sydney Morning Herald* and championing the pastoralists' Free Trade cause. He had argued for the beneficial influence of country life in building up the new race, comparing the 'sturdy little red-cheeked ruffian' of rural Australia with the 'poor little pale consumptive' of the cities.[23] The digger's superiority, like the national character itself, was the product of the bush and a rural-based economy. In the popular first volume of the *Official History*, which appeared in 1921,

Bean did his best to identify the digger with the bush:

> The bush still sets the standard of personal efficiency even in the
> Australian cities. The bushman is the hero of the Australian boy;
> the arts of the bush life are his ambition; his most cherished holidays
> are those spent with country relatives or in camping out. He learns
> something of half the arts of a soldier by the time he is ten years
> old ... The Australian was half a soldier before the war; indeed
> throughout the war ... the Australian soldier differed very little
> from the Australian who at home rides the station boundaries
> every week-day and sits of a Sunday round the stockyard fence.[24]

Bean argued that the bush life made men more independent and more
practical, and therefore diggers from the country were better soldiers
than those from the cities. Bean's own childhood had been spent in
the country at Bathurst, and later at an English school with a reputation for turning out men who served the empire.[25]

The explanation put forward in 1920 by the diggers' ex-commander,
Sir John Monash, was different. He agreed with Bean on the qualities
displayed by the Australian soldier: independent judgment, personal
dignity, manliness, practicality, adaptability, a readiness to learn. But
he thought the reasons were:

> The democratic institutions under which he was reared, the advanced
> system of education by which he was trained—teaching him how
> to think for himself and to apply what he had learnt to practical
> ends—the instinct of sport and adventure which is his national
> heritage, his pride in his young country, and the opportunity which
> came to him of creating a great national tradition.[26]

There was no mention of the bush. Monash was Melbourne-born
and educated, a businessman and engineer whose success as a general
rested on his organisational skills and his readiness to use mechanical
resources. In the 1920s, as chairman of the State Electricity Commission, he was closely identified with Victoria's industrial expansion.
For many, Monash was the archetypal digger. Other digger figures
were associated with city interests too. The Prime Minister, W.M.
Hughes, the 'Little Digger', was the member for Balmain and a staunch
Protectionist. C.J. Dennis turned Ginger Mick, a larrikin from the
Melbourne slums, into a Gallipoli hero, and *The Moods of Ginger
Mick* sold twice as well as the *Official History*.[27] The most powerful
digger image was that portrayed in the Sydney paper, *Smith's Weekly*,
for which Monash was 'The Greatest Digger of Them All'.[28] Founded
in 1919 by two of the new businessmen, (Sir) Joynton Smith, millionaire
Lord Mayor of Sydney, and Clyde Packer, a young journalist on the

way to becoming a newspaper mogul, *Smith's* styled itself as the
defender of the digger, whose stereotype became a white-collar city
worker with a larrikin streak. *Smith's* was ardently protectionist, its
platform being 'to strengthen Australia, to make it a self-contained
nation'. Indeed when it endorsed a policy as 'Australian', Australian
was a euphemism for protectionist.[29] In the stress placed on the antecedents of the Anzac, and in the manner in which the returned Anzac
was portrayed, vested interests were using the legend and remaking
the image along lines congenial to their own interests.

Discipline and the Digger

Both Bean and Monash noted the egalitarianism of the Australian
army, but it is significant that they both did so in the context of a
concern about discipline and control. When putting the case for a
democratic army, their hero was not only the common man, but also
the effective leader who could control him. Bean resolved his old
qualms about the discipline of the digger: there were no problems as
long as the officer was the right type, 'a man in every sense of the
word'. Diggers 'were readily controlled by anyone really competent
to teach them. They were hero-worshippers to the backbone'.[30] Later
he defined the ideal officer:

> Given courage and determination, the qualities most adapted for
> securing the best from Australians seemed to be in the main those
> implied in the English ideal of a gentleman ... the best type of
> Australian university man, with high, clear British ideals of honour
> and service, and the irresistible energy and resourcefulness which is
> latent in the best class of young Australian.[31]

Monash had a more 'modern' approach, although he was the older
man. He had discovered psychology, which was also being used by
manufacturers intent on improving efficiency in industry. For Monash,
leadership was 'psychology all along the line', a matter of boosting
morale and trying to 'deal with every task and every situation on the
basis of simple business propositions'.[32] The Australian soldier needed
careful handling:

> Psychologically, he was easy to lead but difficult to drive ... Taking
> him all in all, the Australian soldier was, when understood, not
> difficult to handle. But he required a sympathetic handling, which
> appealed to his intelligence and satisfied his instinct for a 'square
> deal' ... In short, the Australian Army is a proof that individualism

is the best and not the worst foundation upon which to build up collective discipline.[33]

It is worth adding that Bean was not always convinced of Monash's brilliance as a leader, considering him to have had 'an almost Napoleonic skill in transmitting the impression of his capacity'.[34]

The concern about military leadership came at a time when democracy itself was seen by many to be in need of leadership, not only in Australia but in other democratic societies as well. There was talk, particularly among those who saw themselves as natural leaders, that democracy had failed, that it could only produce politicians who were second-rate. Some turned to dictatorship as the solution. D.H. Lawrence, the English novelist who visited Australia in 1922, captured the flavour of local dissatisfaction with democracy in his would-be dictator, 'Kangaroo'. He believed only discipline, effective leadership and manliness could rescue Australia from the 'dead level' democracy of the 'masses'.[35] With the depression of the 1930s, there was still more talk in right-wing circles of the failure of democracy and a need for the 'discipline of competent masters' because 'the masses will not discipline themselves'.[36]

Others hoped to lead, persuade and educate the common man to make democracy more effective. Meredith Atkinson, an influential liberal intellectual, argued in 1915 that democracy had led to a more moral society, but had 'certainly caused some loss of national effectiveness, chiefly by dissipation of control and effective government amongst the mass'.[37] His solution was for intellectuals to provide leadership in such organisations as the Workers' Educational Association so the workforce could be educated to accept 'social efficiency' as an alternative to class struggle. Some remained disillusioned with the quality of Australian leadership: C.E.W. Bean was later to write that in the 1920s, 'in place of the leadership for which young Australia was crying and under which we could have achieved almost anything, we abandoned our youth to the mercy, too often, of political and industrial crooks, wreckers of every fine ideal with which young Australians had emerged'.[38]

The demand for effective leadership was related to the quest for 'National Efficiency', which linked industry, science and the state, and had been a feature of Progressivism in the United States, Fabianism in Britain, and in the 1920s, Fascism in Italy.[39] In Australia it coincided with the emergence of an Australian intellectual elite, university-educated, seeing themselves as providing the effective leadership which Australian democracy needed, so that the goals of 'National

Efficiency' and national development could be pursued. Symbolising the link between science, industry and development was the establishment in 1926 of the Council for Scientific and Industrial Research, later the C.S.I.R.O. Hughes had made the first moves towards it in 1916. He drew a rosy picture of future development:

> Science can make rural industries commercially profitable, making the desert bloom . . . Science can develop great mineral wealth . . . Science will lead the manufacturer into green pastures by solving for him problems that seemed insoluble. It will open up a thousand new avenues for capital and labour.[40]

The scientist, the engineer, the expert were replacing the common man as the hope of the world.

It was not only in science and industry that the new intellectuals offered their leadership. A new generation of writers set out to create an Australian culture. The circle around Vance and Nettie Palmer led the way, although few followed. Whereas the previous generation had been content to be professionals, this generation sought recognition as intellectual leaders. In 1930 Keith Hancock, the young historian, put the case for strong cultural leadership in his *Australia*, when he answered de Tocqueville's argument about the perpetual mediocrity of democratic society:

> under every form of society, it is always a minority which holds power. A minority which recognises true standards will know how to make them respected. If necessary, it will make them respected by overthrowing the majority. If democracy is essentially mediocre it will become decrepit and be thrust aside.[41]

Land Fit for Heroes

Through all this stalked the digger, returning home a hero, and claiming a special place in post-war Australia. Most of the troops returned, more or less successfully, to their pre-war lives. Some 40,000 committed themselves, with government aid, to the old rural ideal and became soldier settlers. About half of those eligible eventually joined the Returned Sailors' and Soldiers' Imperial League of Australia, founded in 1916. Acting in the interests of veterans and their dependents, the R.S.L. was determined to make the most of their new-found prestige, and encouraged the idea that the digger was the true defender and interpreter of what it meant to be Australian. The legend was protected, enshrined, sanctified. In 1921 the word 'Anzac'

was protected by an act of parliament, which forbad its use as a title
or for commercial purposes. Between 1921 and 1927, all states made
Anzac Day a statutory holiday, although it had been celebrated since
1916. At first it had been seen as an occasion when returned men
would 'meet each other, and with thrilling reminiscences tell of the
brave old days when Australia's sons fought for freedom and
honour'.[42] In time it developed a common form of observance,
complete with a semi-religious ritual, liturgy and hymnal, perhaps
filling a spiritual need in a secularised society. With government
encouragement, war memorials sprang up in most towns and suburbs,
usually depicting the digger conforming to a classical ideal, although
a few in mining areas, such as Broken Hill and Lithgow, used the heroic
conventions of socialist realism.

From the start, the image of the digger developed a split personality.
In *The Anzac Book* of 1916, a sort of A.I.F. school magazine edited
by Bean from contributions written by the troops, the digger is portrayed as an ideal type on the one hand and, with self-mocking humour,
as an unkempt larrikin on the other. Both images stuck. Anzac Day
itself developed a schizophrenic quality, with solemn rituals and
services in the morning, and boozy celebrations, brawls and ostentatious games of two-up afterwards. *Smith's Weekly* encouraged the
larrikin view, developing a populist disrespect for pomposity, authority
and red-tape.

On the other hand the idealisation of the Anzac could go so far as
to remove any resemblance to Australian soldiers. All that was noble
and admirable came to be attributed to the Anzac. This included the
continuing obsession with masculinity. When it was suggested that
the focal point of the Sydney War Memorial (built in 1934) should
be a female figure representing Australia, the ensuing outcry led to
its replacement by a naked male warrior. The Anzac became the
reincarnation of the classical Greek. In 1939 one Gallipoli veteran
pictured him as a Greek warrior.[43] The Australian War Memorial
quoted Pericles' funeral oration in its guide and took it as its motto.
The qualities of the Australian soldier were set out in the Hall of
Memory: Coolness, Control, Audacity, Endurance, Decision, Comradeship, Ancestry, Patriotism, Chivalry, Loyalty, Resource, Candour,
Devotion, Curiosity, Independence.[44] By 1945, A.G. Butler, who
worked with Bean on the *Official History*, had gone even further.
The digger stood for freedom, comradeship, tolerance and the innate
worth of man. Thus many qualified as 'good Diggers': Billy Hughes,
Hereward the Wake, Shakespeare, Florence Nightingale, Leonidas
the Spartan.

The Canadian 'Mounties' have been accepted as exhibiting authentic Digger attributes . . . Caius Marius was a dinkum Digger . . . In his outlook on life, St Paul himself was a Digger; and he followed in the footsteps of a greater than he.[45]

It is interesting how the conventional virtues had altered over the years but, like the *Bulletin's* 'real' Australian, the definition of the digger could be spread so wide as to become meaningless.

Politically the digger legend had a definite influence, however schizophrenic the actual image was. The R.S.L. was given direct access to cabinet, an intimacy no other pressure group enjoyed. Theoretically, in a party sense, the R.S.L. was non-political, maintaining close links with the party in power. Politicians on both sides sought to parade their war records and R.S.L. badges. However the R.S.L.'s political interest went far beyond the bread and butter concerns of its members. Many returned servicemen saw themselves as having given Australia its nationhood in the war, and as defending that nationhood in peace. They were naturally interested in defence as an issue, but this extended to a conservative, defensive attitude to the preservation of 'nationhood' as *they* defined it. In this way, among the most vocal section of returned servicemen, the digger legend contributed much to the defensiveness which continued to mark the idea of a pure and wholesome Australia throughout this period.

Returned servicemen provided the impetus for the various secret armies that existed in the 1920s and 1930s to defend the 'nation' against 'subversion', committing the digger legend to the defence of the established order. The New Guard of the 1930s, standing for 'sane' government and the 'suppression of any disloyal and immoral elements in Governmental, industrial and social circles',[46] was best-known for the simple reason that it was not secret. Its predecessors remained secret, but were better organised and more influential. They relied on the maintenance of close informal contacts among ex-officers in business and the professions, men who were ever ready to organise strike-breaking or to step in to maintain 'law and order' wherever they saw the need or opportunity.[47]

The digger was identified with open attacks on 'disloyal' elements. These could include trade unionists, pacifists, the Irish, anyone considered not to have been whole-heartedly behind the effort to smash the Germans. Most virulent were the attacks on 'Bolshevism'. After the Russian revolution of 1917, conservatives were depicting communists, and radicals generally, as foreign, subversive and un-Australian, contrasting their stereotype of the scruffy, fanatical, excessively foreign, bomb-throwing 'Bolshie' with the right-thinking

Anzac hero. Some Australians had remained in Europe after the war to fight with the White Russian forces against the Red Army. In Australia there were riots among ex-servicemen directed against trade unionists and 'Bolshevism', and communists were refused entry to the R.S.L. In Brisbane in 1919, an R.S.L. 'Anti-Bolshevik Committee' organised a 2000 strong 'Army to Fight Bolshevism' to take on the 'disloyal' anti-conscriptionist Labor government. In 1921 in Sydney, ex-servicemen attacked a May Day meeting in the Domain, and the R.S.L. organised a counter-demonstration the following week: 'It's Our Flag! Our Diggers Fought For It! Our Women Worked For It! The Bolsheviks Would Pull It Down!'.[48]

These demonstrations of digger 'loyalty' and the outbreaks of hostility towards 'Bolshevism' were simply the most visible signs of deeper social divisions. The political function of the digger image was much more pervasive than the occasional bashing of a Bolshie. It effectively divided the working class into the deserving (the loyal returning heroes) and the undeserving (the bulk of the working class,

'Could you oblige me with a match'
The Little Boy from Manly meets the Red Menace. From the Bulletin, *1 May, 1919, p. 5.*

including many ex-servicemen, who rejected the empty gesture of putting the digger on a pedestal). Not that the deserving were always rewarded. Some returned men were shabbily treated by their pre-war employers. Many had difficulty finding jobs and readjusting to civilian life. Others would never escape the appalling physical mutilation which served as a constant reminder of the barbarity of the Great War. There were emotional exposés of the plight of the returned digger, and demands that he be adequately rewarded, but their effect was to obscure the fact that other groups were in equal need of social justice. The presence of the deserving digger meant that the working class generally could be seen as selfish and disloyal. So long as the digger suffered, so long as he was inadequately rewarded, what right had others to object? The legitimate national responsibilities were soldier settlements and repatriation hospitals. Demands for more radical change were not only unnecessary but treacherous. The workingman's paradise had been made over into the land fit only for heroes.

9 Growing Up

It is time *now* for Young Australia to become Adult, to accept the responsibilities and duties of being Adult, of being civilized; of becoming a fully-cultured nation—self-supporting, if need be, in matters of culture.

P.R. Stephensen, 1936.[1]

The idea that Australia was young, white, happy and wholesome, and in constant need of protection, had been established before the Great War. The digger legend intensified the obsession with virile youth and defensiveness, but it would have climaxed in the 1920s in any case. Never was Australia's innocence and purity protected with more zeal. The same trend towards safe, isolationist conservatism appeared elsewhere. In the United States, Warren Harding had won the 1920 election promising 'a return to normalcy', while his successor, Calvin Coolidge, declared that America needed no importations, 'industrial, intellectual, or political'.[2] In Britain, Stanley Baldwin came to power standing for 'Safety First'. They all represented a shift away from welfare, reform and idealism, towards 'safe' business principles and, at times, hysterical anti-communism. Australia's Stanley Melbourne Bruce, Prime Minister from 1923 to 1929, fitted the same pattern. He claimed to be just 'a plain businessman and a plain soldier'; the *Australasian Manufacturer* was thankful that he was 'a very average person, and that is the secret of his success . . . There is safety in mediocrity'.[3]

Inoculating Australia

For Bruce, and for respectable opinion generally, Australia had to be protected for the benefit of British civilisation. The 'White Australia' policy effectively kept out the 'Yellow Peril,' and remained a fundamental principle of Australianness. Other threats to Australia's purity and to Anglo-Australian sentiment were also portrayed as being

essentially alien, originating outside Australia. Almost any threat to
the social order was attributed to Russian Bolshevism or Irish Sinn
Feinism, and the solution was to keep such threats out. Bruce attempted
to break the Seamen's strike by amending the Immigration Restric-
tion Act so that the leaders, Tom Walsh and Jack Johnson, could be
deported as undesirable immigrants. The High Court decided that,
since they had lived in Australia for 32 and 15 years respectively,
they were Australian and not foreign subversives. Censorship was also
increased to preserve Australia from the foreign evils of Sinn Fein
pamphlets and communist works. In 1921, Hughes extended the
Customs Act to prohibit literature expressing a 'seditious intention'
against established government. By 1929 over 200 political (mostly
communist) works had been prohibited, including the *Communist
Manifesto*. 'Obscene' literature too was of increasing interest to
Customs: *Ulysses* was banned in 1929, and by 1936, the 5000 Prohibited Publications included *Moll Flanders, Brave New World* and
Down and Out in Paris and London.[4] Most Western countries increased
censorship in these years, although only Spain and Ireland were more
enthusiastic than Australia.

The view of a wholesome Australia beset by foreign evils was
encouraged by the Spanish influenza epidemic which raged throughout
1919. The virus, probably introduced by returning troops, had killed
12,000 Australians before it was beaten. Inevitably disease became a
popular metaphor for those seeking to depict communism as an evil
foreign influence attacking the healthy but vulnerable Australian body
politic. It also helped lead to the establishment of the Commonwealth Department of Health, with its Director-to-be dreaming of
'leading this young nation of ours to a paradise of physical perfection'.[5] But the concern about health had sprung from the earlier
stress on keeping Australia healthy and wholesome, and also from
admiration for the success of American Progressivism in this field.
Stringent quarantine regulations had been worked out in 1907–08,
and it is significant that in other pre-war defensive measures, such as
the citizens forces and cadet corps, health care and physical training
played an important part. State agricultural bureaus also concentrated
on ridding Australia of foreign pests and disease, and preventing the
introduction of others.

The obsession with racial purity was as strong as ever. *Smith's
Weekly* could refer to the few Italian migrants as 'that greasy flood of
Mediterranean scum that seeks to defile and debase Australia', and
regularly referred to 'dirty Dago Pests'.[6] A bigger threat, at least for
British and Australian manufacturing and commercial interests, was

'The Jazz arrives at Dingo Flats'

Jazz brought new heights of sophistication to Dingo Flat, but it also had a clearly deleterious effect on local morals. From Aussie, *15 October, 1920, p. 25.*

'Americanisation'. Despite high tariffs, imports from America continued to increase and reached 25 per cent of Australia's total in 1926–27. Hollywood was blamed for increasing vulgarity. Jazz, doubly evil because it was black as well as American, was seen as leading to immorality. American comics were seducing Australian children.[7]

Writers and artists reinforced this idea that Australia was besieged by foreign evils: many agreed with Louis Esson, the playwright, who wrote in the *Bulletin* that 'Art, unlike science, is . . . the expression of the personality of a race and country'.[8] Some drew the conclusion that therefore Australian culture had to be cheerful and wholesome. Some sought tariff protection for Australian writers and artists to suppress the 'tipping of mental rubbish from foreign countries into our Commonwealth that is as yet clean and mentally healthy'. Syndicated comics and radio programmes from overseas, particularly America, represented an 'infection of the Australian mind by a mental plague no less serious than cholera morbus in its sociological effects'.[9] The Minister for Customs did not want to see the 'prostitution of the people by offensive films' from America.[10] The *Bulletin* wanted 'clean films and home-grown actors';[11] others supported 'all Australian Pictures—showing the brightest and best side of Australian life'.[12] When Australia's own products, such as Norman Lindsay's titillating novels satirising country town morality, or films of the convict past such as *For The Term of His Natural Life*, did not portray Australia as impeccably wholesome, there was an outcry. Returning from Europe, Will Ashton declared that modern art was foreign, incomprehensible rubbish: Australian art was 'eminently sane, honest, and thorough'.[13] Australian writers too were praised for their sanity. They could 'appreciate the sunny beauty of their surroundings', unlike the melancholic and remorseful exiles who, in depicting the gum tree as grotesque, had betrayed some 'Freudian complex'.[14] Even D.H. Lawrence was misinterpreted in an Australian review of *Kangaroo*: 'a very beautiful book . . . full of the sunshine and flowers of Australia'.[15] In fact, Lawrence was critical of the vacancy and meaningless cheerfulness of Australian democracy.

The protection of the purity of Australian nationhood continued to be associated with the protection of manufacturing. The Customs Tariff Act of 1921 saw the triumph of tariff protection for Australian industry. Business interests made much of national sentiment. An Australian Industries Protection League was formed in 1919, and set out 'to create a national sentiment in favour of Australian-made goods'.[16] In 1924 the 'Australian-Made' Preference League was formed. Based on 'sane and practical patriotism', it set out to encourage the consumer to exercise 'a little practical patriotism' in buying 'Australian-Made' goods: 'it is at once good patriotism and good business to support the industries of his country'.[17] It supported the Great White Train, a travelling exhibition of Australian-made goods which in 1925 covered over 4000 miles and visited 90 New South Wales country towns, as an 'Ambassador of Nationhood' which 'planted the seed of a national sentiment that will yield its harvest in the progress, prosperity, and security of Australia'.[18] The Australian Natives' Association pursued the same ends. Its three objectives in the 1920s were 'White Australia', support for the Made in Australia Movement, and constitutional reform which would facilitate commercial and industrial development. According to its treasurer, James Hume Cook, businessman, politician and author of *Australian Fairy Tales*, the A.N.A.'s 'demand for a clean, wholesome nation found practical expression in the support the Association gave towards eradicating "Miner's complaint", and the still more effective work it has done—and is doing—in connection with the "red plague, syphilis"'.[19]

Throughout the 1920s, in a great range of fields, the dominant image was of Australia—clean, chaste, young, sane and wholesome—being assailed by external evils. Immigration, defence, tariff protection, communism, censorship, cultural growth, industrial development, were all dominated by the same imagery, of disease, of flood, of war. In an evil world, only Australia with her British inheritance was safe. And in safety, Australians could listen to the compliments of an advertising executive, Lord Burnham, in 1927, as he spoke on radio of 'the quality of her clear, cheerful sunniness, which ought to make Australians all sun-angels . . . No children on earth were of finer and more cheerful growth than the Australians'.[20]

Innocence and Maturity

In the 1930s, important aspects of this image began to be questioned. Isolation from Europe had been seen in the 1920s as a virtue, protecting Australia from the decadence, war and morbidity of Europe. In 1923 Lionel Lindsay had welcomed isolation, as offering

> escape from all the revolutionary manias of a rotted world; all the patent art theories in which are exposed, stark and coverless, the degeneration of the creative instinct in art; all that base egotism, brother of the Revolution, which strikes in envious hate, upwards, at everything most noble in man's past achievement.[21]

'Spirit of Australia and her golden wattle attendants'
The wattle still had pride of place at the 1938 sesquicentennial Public School
Children's Festival at the Sydney Cricket Ground.

By the late 1930s, many thought isolation had led to Australia's
backwardness, insularity and lack of sophistication. In the 1920s
youth had been a great virtue. In 1923, the *Vision* school of writers
had set out 'to vindicate the possession of Youth . . . by responding
to all other expressions of Youth, and by rejecting all that is hiero-
glyphic, or weary and depressed'.[22] They called for 'reaffirmation of
vitality, the sunlit quality'.[23] In the 1930s there was more talk about
'maturity', about the need for Australia to 'grow up'. A new image
was being formed.

Much of the confidence which was publicly expressed in Australia's
unlimited development in the 1920s was shattered by the depression
of the 1930s. So exaggerated had been the expectations of the 1920s
that the geographer, T. Griffith Taylor, had been ostracised because
he had dared to suggest Australia could not carry a population of
more than sixty million. By 1939 a common expectation was that
Australia's population would begin to decline in the foreseeable
future. The Australian parliament moved to Canberra in 1927, an
appropriately rural setting for the set speeches about developing the
land; by the 1930s there was already talk of abandoning the new
capital.[24] In 1933 national unity took a beating when Western Australia voted by a two-to-one majority to secede from the Commonwealth. There was discussion of 'Australia's National Decline' and
many conservatives were convinced that Australian democracy had
failed.[25]

When Australia celebrated its sesquicentenary in 1938, there was little of the confidence or enthusiasm of the centennial celebrations of 1888. Inter-state rivalry was still strong enough to confine the celebrations largely to New South Wales. Victoria and South Australia preferred to concentrate on their own centenaries in 1934 and 1936. A national sense of inferiority was still strong enough for attempts to be made to play down Australia's convict origins. Aborigines protested that what was being celebrated was a white invasion of their land and the cautiously sympathetic press reaction suggested that even the confident racism of earlier years was beginning to recede. Some trade unions organised alternative celebrations but they were largely ignored.

If anything the depression intensified the paranoia and isolationism of the 1920s. Ingrained racism meant that the financial crisis itself could be seen as the work of Jewish financiers. Others blamed British bankers, seeing Britain itself as 'foreign' and therefore threatening. Indeed anti-British feeling was so strong that the use of bodyline bowling by the English test cricket side in 1932 had repercussions at government level. The government continued to protect Australia's innocence. Its censorship of 'obscene' and 'subversive' foreign literature peaked in 1936. The government attempted to prevent the entry of a British woman, Mrs Freer, because she might break up 'a perfectly good Australian marriage',[26] and of a Czech lecturer, Egon Kisch, because he was believed to be a communist. Both attempts were unsuccessful. In Kalgoorlie in 1934, racial feeling was still strong enough for several men to be killed in riots between Australian-born workers and southern European immigrants.

Those concerned about Australian culture could become hysterical. J.S. MacDonald, the Director of the National Gallery of Victoria, attacked 'modern' art as 'the work of perverts' and entirely 'foreign to this relatively happiest of countries'.[27] In 1936, the influential publisher, P.R. Stephensen, argued for the virtues of Australia 'being the only whiteman's continent, *the only isolated continent*', and demanded the 'de-Pommification' and 'un-Yankeefying' of Australian culture.[28] The Fellowship of Australian Writers formed a 'Cultural Defence Committee', with Stephensen as Chairman, and proceeded to condemn newspapers, radio and film for propagating 'a set of cultural ideas which are entirely and literally foreign to Australian sentiment and British-Australian traditions'.[29] Shortly afterwards, Rex Ingamells, the Adelaide poet, formed the Jindyworobak movement, which sought to 'free Australian art from whatever alien influences trammel it', breaking away completely from the spirit of

English culture, and turning instead to purer 'environmental values' and Aboriginal culture, 'something initially far-removed from the engaging and controlling factors of modern European life'.[30] Whether to protect public taste or the possibilities of an Australian culture, the common reaction was to keep 'alien' influences out.

Nevertheless, in those years before the Second World War, important changes were taking place. Recovery from the depression was slow—by 1935, 18 per cent were still unemployed—but Australian 'big business' emerged stronger, more efficient and more influential, while many small businesses went to the wall. Development, which before the depression was an ideal that applied to both primary and secondary industry, was now increasingly identified with powerful technocrats such as Essington Lewis, the general manager of B.H.P., an engineer and a nationalist, determined to promote growth and technology at any cost. Symbolically, in 1938, a Hall of Manufactures was erected by the New South Wales government at that bastion of primary industry, the Royal Agricultural Society's Sydney Showground.[31]

At the same time there were signs of a wider cultural life. The A.B.C., founded in 1932, was building up its orchestras, sponsoring concerts by overseas artists and promoting discussion of the arts. Kirsova and Borovansky established ballet companies. A trickle of refugees from Europe began to make a cultural contribution. In 1938 the Contemporary Art Society was formed, and in 1939 the Melbourne *Herald's* exhibition of Modern Art, sponsored by Sir Keith Murdoch, another big businessman, helped widen the Australian public's acceptance of modern art. The admiration of innocence for its own sake began to pall. There was a conscious effort to give Australia a more sophisticated image, and 'high' culture became one of the measures of sophistication.

This could even filter through to a popular magazine such as *Man*, 'The Australian Magazine for Men', founded in 1936. Its readers were supposed to be city sophisticates, with interests in men's fashion, French wines, ballet, cars, modern art, cocktail recipes, theatre and—of course—women. *Man* condemned the old image of Australia found in the 'traditional Lawson-Patterson[sic] jingle'. To *Man* it was a false image:

> drab pictures of bark huts and hopeless ageing men and illiterate kiddies . . . it is half a century old . . . Nobody says, 'We have cities as well as the country, and even so, all our country is not red sand and broken fences and hopeless, teeth-grinding women'.
>
> Lawson is not big enough to be our national poet . . . nor is

Patterson[sic] or any other last-century jingler who tickles the fancy but hides the whole and wholesome truth.[32]

Whereas Lawson had earlier been criticised for not being cheerful enough, in the 1930s there was more concern about his crudity and lack of sophistication. P.R. Stephensen preferred the work of Elioth Gruner, 'a sophisticated painter', to the 'garishness' of Streeton.[33] He thought the *Bulletin* of the 1890s had 'encouraged crude literature' by presenting 'a larrikin view of Australian life', and demanded a more 'mature' literature.[34] Another critic thought that the problem with the *Bulletin* was that 'It hadn't grown up'.[35] For Miles Franklin, it was time writers shifted their attention from bushrangers, drovers and diggers, and turned instead to 'the population in the cities . . . the successors of the hard-toiling pioneers, the men and women who now have the amenities of urban life and labour-saving devices, including smaller families'.[36]

The Second World War exposed other 'crudities'. Australia's alleged lack of sophistication seemed to be highlighted by the American troops who arrived after 1941. The government was on the defensive when it apologised to the Americans because Australia lacked many of the consumer items which were taken for granted in the United States, and promised that Australians were willing to learn to appreciate coca-cola and the jitterbug if the Americans were willing to teach.[37] The Jindyworobak writers attacked a different aspect of the same problem when they published their anthology *Poets at War*. They hoped it would help dispel the 'cartoonists' myth' that the Australian serviceman was an unsophisticated oaf interested only in booze, two-up, women, brawling, bludging and going Absent Without Leave—although the editor also had to apologise that one poem was included without the permission of the author who, 'having been A.W.L. for some months', was impossible to contact.[38]

Industrialists and Intellectuals

The renewed cultural vitality of the late 1930s, and the desire for sophistication and cultural 'maturity', were closely linked to the new industrialism, although the connection was not always obvious. It was quite explicit when the *Australia National Journal* was founded in 1939, one of a number of new 'national' magazines established in this period, only to be crippled by the outbreak of war. Edited by Sydney Ure Smith and backed by Charles Lloyd Jones, the retailer, it aimed to 'give expression to our progress in Art, Architecture and Industry', with no effort spared 'to produce a high-class journal, and one which Australians can be proud to send abroad, or present to overseas visitors'. Opposite a frontispiece of the new Prime Minister, R.G. Menzies, 'A man of vision, strength and understanding', the editor explained that 'the peaceful isolation which we enjoyed for so many years has gone ... As a nation we realise we must stand on our own feet in order to help Britain and ourselves. In every way this continent must be developed'. He hoped that the journal 'should quickly become a vehicle for all forms of expression in the Arts and Industry ... and form a practical link between them'. This the journal proceeded to do by featuring 'personalities' in industry, politics and the arts, reporting developments in both areas and publishing essays on the relationship between industry and the arts: Norman Lindsay, for example, contributed an article on 'Commerce and Culture'.[39]

It was in the interests of the manufacturing sector, as it grew more powerful, to promote an image of Australia which could compete with the old rural myth. It had encouraged a view of Australia in which the 'real' Australia was the bush, and the pastoral industry in particular. This had promoted the links between Britain and Australia. In the 1930s England was still commonly called 'Home', the bush-worker was still seen as 'typically Australian', Australia still rode on the sheep's back and a preferential tariff for British manufactures was still government policy.

But the challenge was there. Between 1933 and 1947, the percentage of the labour force employed in primary industry dropped from 24 per cent to 18 per cent while in secondary industry it rose from 19 per cent to 28 per cent. Manufacturers were now determined not simply to convince Australians to buy Australian, but to transform the whole economy by giving it a heavy industrial base. The image of Australia as an industrial nation was part of an ideological offensive. Companies such as B.H.P. had established that their own position was central to the Australian economy and were looking to markets outside the traditional trading relationship with Britain. Despite the fact that industrialisation was dependent on British capital, it was in the interests of local manufacturers to break down the dependence on British imports and the old Anglo-Australian provincialism. They encouraged a view of Australia which stressed industrial progress, cultural 'maturity' and urban sophistication, all with the inference that the Australian economy should be self-contained. Consistent with this view, Lewis and other industrialists led a defence lobby which decried Australia's reliance on the British Navy, and argued that Australia should develop an aircraft industry of its own. When war did break out, Lewis became Director-General of Munitions. In their defence lobbying, in their conception of Australia's industrial future, and in their image of a strong, independent Australia, the new industrialists were putting a nationalist view in opposition to the pro-British attitudes of other conservatives. During the war, their nationalism was more in accord with that of Labor, and they gained a more central role in policy-making under war-time Labor governments.

A new, more confident image of Australia was in the interests of Australian industry; but it was also in the interests of the United States. In competing with Britain for world markets, American interests were intent on breaking into the empire trade arrangements so favourable to Britain. American diplomats in Australia naturally sought to encourage nationalist trends, siding with 'those who think as Australians' against 'those Australians who still think colonially'. They argued that the Australian 'type' was quite distinct from the British model, and had been greatly influenced in its development by 'American civilization'. They mocked the Anglophile attitudes of the Melbourne establishment, 'a group of economic royalists who sit in the midst of their comfortable possessions, fear, and look out upon a world that they do not understand and which is repugnant to them'.[40] American interests could readily prefer the more nationalistic Labor Party to the conservative U.A.P. and Menzies who, according to one diplomat, had 'something of the Uriah Heep in his make-up that is rather disgusting'.[41]

Americans also took an active interest in the stimulation of Australian intellectual life in the 1930s. American money, in the form of Carnegie grants, was responsible for the foundation of the Australian Council for Educational Research in 1930, for research grants allowing young graduates to study in the U.S.A., and for the influential Munn-Pitt report into the state of Australian public libraries in 1935.[42] Also important was the American writer, C. Hartley Grattan, who consolidated his links with the nationalist intelligentsia when he was in Australia as a Carnegie Research Fellow in 1936–38. He exhorted intellectuals to take a more decisive role in forming public opinion, criticised the 'crown colony psychology' of Australia's political leaders, and argued that 'The future of Australia rests with the manufacturing industries'. In the establishment of a greater Australian independence from Britain—economically, politically, intellectually—lay the hope of a closer relationship between Australia and the United States: Grattan was 'quite confident that as Australia becomes more mature, less "colonial" and "dependent", the cultural borrowings between the two countries will multiply'.[43] The development of an independent Australian intelligentsia was an important step towards this.

However, while the broad connection between greater cultural vitality in the late 1930s, industrial expansion and the restructuring of the image of Australia is clear, its actual mechanics are more complex. Nationalist intellectuals played an important part in the creation of an image of Australia as independent and 'mature', but they were by no means the mere mouth-pieces for economic interests. They themselves were an increasingly powerful interest group. Their perception of themselves, as a class, was changing in two directions. Firstly they developed the idea of 'maturity' which they associated with a self-contained, urban manufacturing society and a more complex, sophisticated and vital cultural life. Many writers since then have dated Australia's 'coming of age' in that decade after the depression.[44] But what they also referred to was their own 'coming of age', the development of a more central role for the university-based intelligentsia within Australian society. What they described as the 'maturity' of Australia was often simply the recognition given to their own self-importance. As a group they were most influential in the 1940s when, along with the new industrialists, they were co-opted into the government's decision-making machinery. Their importance was recognised in the large-scale recruitment of university graduates to the public service, in the planning for post-war reconstruction, in the importance given to adult education in the 1940s, and in the expansion of research facilities. This trend had already begun in the late 1930s, when 'maturity' became the new virtue, replacing the pre-depression celebration of Australia's 'youthfulness'.

The concern with 'maturity' was partly the logic of the metaphor which portrayed Australia as a child growing up. But the idea of the 'mature', well-rounded personality was also central to the popular psychology which was increasingly influential throughout the West in the 1930s, and to the development of ideas about civics and citizenship in democracy. It was also a common metaphor for economic self-sufficiency in other developing countries, and other nations found themselves 'coming of age' at the same time. So Australia was not alone in 1936 when P.R. Stephensen put out his call for 'Young Australia to become Adult' and to be 'self-supporting, if need be, in matters of culture'.[45] A year later, Adrian Lawlor, the artist and an outspoken modernist, thought Australia was 'due for a kick in the pants . . . due for cultural, as well as industrial, development'.[46] Will Lawson, editor of the Fellowship of Australian Writers' annual, saw 'many signs of maturity';[47] by 1939 Frank Dalby Davison was writing

'Australia is growing and hardening towards maturity at a swift rate, and this development is reflected in the work of our authors'.[48] Some—particularly Grattan—saw maturity largely in terms of breaking away from British parental influence while others thought it came with a mother's encouragement. A. Grenfell Price, for example, geographer, historian, educationalist and, for a time, a U.A.P. member of parliament, saw it in this light when he published *Australia Comes of Age* in 1945. Mainly concerned with the 'Growth to Nationhood' in foreign policy, he constantly stressed Australia's obligation to both Britain and the U.S.A., and his conclusion was:

> By 1944 Australia . . . had come of age with the plaudits of a generous Motherland. She had asserted her Dominion independence. She had proclaimed her intention of administering her own little Empire . . . On the whole the Australian people could be proud of their growth to maturity . . . under British guidance and protection, they had developed a continent; in that continent they had built up a prosperous community with high standards of life.[49]

At the same time that intellectuals were seeing themselves as more central to a maturing Australian community, they were also for the first time predominantly dissident, seeing themselves as outside the dominant culture, rejecting conventional values and critical of the government. That they were both more central and more dissident is not as paradoxical as it seems. Their dissidence was not the self-conscious bohemianism of the late nineteenth century; nor were they simply democracy's natural leaders, as some had seen themselves in the 1920s. They were more likely now to see their role as forming, moulding and redirecting public opinion. They were dissident on two levels. As an interest group, they were active in attacking government policy when they thought it displayed provincialism or anti-intellectualism and they became involved in lobbying, anti-censorship committees, and the newly-formed Council for Civil Liberties.[50] At another level, they asserted a claim to be the interpreters of nationhood. Academic interest in Australian history and literature increased markedly in the late 1930s. From that position they condemned trends in Australian life or government policy which did not fit their image of a mature society. The case they put forward could range from support of the 'mature' economy which the industrialists envisaged to an anti-capitalist critique. The Communist Party of Australia, at its strongest in the 1940s, engaged the energies of many radical intellectuals. At both extremes the intellectuals claimed to stand for an essential Australia which was not fully expressed in present circumstances or policies.

This view of an Australian essence vitiated by a layer of false values took various forms. A.D. Hope's poem, 'Australia', published in 1939, attacked the:

> vast parasite robber state
> where second-hand Europeans pullulate
> timidly on the edge of alien shores,

and hoped to find, in the 'real' Australia rather than in Europe,

> some spirit which escapes
> the learned doubt, the chatter of cultured apes
> which is called civilization over there.

Meanjin, the influential cultural journal which began in 1940, also gave expression to the view of a mature, central ethos hidden at the time under a superficial materialism and provincialism. Its 'Crisis Issue' in 1942, when Australia seemed threatened by Japan, referred to 'strong, vital forces ... hidden underneath our social framework'. Vance Palmer wrote:

> If Australia had no more character than could be seen on its surface, it would be annihilated ... But there is an Australia of the spirit, submerged and not very articulate, that is quite different from these bubbles of old-world imperialism. Born of the lean loins of the country itself ... it has developed a toughness all its own. Sardonic, idealist, tongue-tied perhaps, it is the Australia of all who truly belong here. When you are away, it takes on a human image, an image that emerges, brown and steady-eyed from the background of dun cliffs, treed bushlands, and tawny plains ... it has something to contribute to the world ... in ideas for the creation of that egalitarian democracy that will have to be the basis of all civilized societies in the future ... I believe we will survive ... sounder than we went in, surer of our essential character, adults in a wider world than the one we lived in hitherto.[51]

The demands of 'total war', the need to define war aims, and the planning for post-war reconstruction, all encouraged a reassertion of democracy and nationalism. The belief that the post-war world would have to be more equal, and that socialism, very loosely defined, was part of Australia's future, was a common one. During the war, the 'national character' was described in terms of democracy, egalitarianism and social justice. This was the positive image opposed to the authoritarian Nazi or the barbaric 'Jap'. The old Australian 'type' was given renewed vitality. One group of intellectuals traced an egalitarian and collectivist heritage for him as Palmer did, through the radical writers of the 1890s: Henry Lawson, Bernard O'Dowd, Joseph Furphy. For Miles Franklin, writing in 1944, Furphy's *Such is Life* was 'the touchstone for the Australian literary intelligentsia because, by his feeling for it, any literary Australian betrays whether he lives in a state of Australian grace or in one of mental colonialism'.[52] The national type was given a history which was radical and nationalist, in which Eureka, the strikes of the 1890s, and the rise of the Labor Party were interpreted as expressions of the true Australian ethos. Ned Kelly, too, was canonised in Douglas Stewart's verse play in 1942, Sidney Nolan's first Kelly series of paintings in 1945–47, and the Borovansky ballet, 'The Outlaw', in 1951.[53]

This idea of the national character was to continue to attract radical intellectuals after the war. As in the 1890s, the nationalism, the radicalism, the interest in 'the Common Man', were tinged with sexism which emerged, not only from the male environment of war-time, but also from post-war university life which was dominated by a lively group of ex-servicemen on government allowances. It is interesting that women artists and, to a lesser extent, women writers, who had been particularly active between the wars, were again pushed into the background, as in the 1890s.[54] Intellectuals continued to espouse the radicalism of the national type in their proposals for post-war reconstruction, in the pages of *Meanjin* and *Overland*, both Melbourne journals, and in 'radical nationalist' histories: those of Brian Fitzpatrick, who was writing pre-war, and Robin Gollan, Ian Turner and Russel Ward, who at some time were all members of the Communist Party. The last great re-statement of the character of the Australian type was Russel Ward's *Australian Legend* in 1958. Ward traced the origins of the type through the common man's response to the bush, through convicts, outback workers, gold diggers, trade unions and the *Bulletin*. Their academic nationalism parallelled the literary nationalism of the 1890s, and there was a similar claim to be seeing Australian history and literature for the first time through Australian eyes.

The National Type at Bondi Beach

However, for some years previously the idea of a national type had been losing meaning. The last popular addition to the type was the cult of the Bondi lifesaver, which was particularly strong in the late 1930s. The beaches were enormously popular, and the lifesaver's prestige was enhanced in February 1938 when, in a mass rescue at

Bondi, lifesavers saved 200 lives. It was, the *Daily Telegraph* said, a 'tribute to their manhood';[55] the comment of an American observer, that 'There are no men in the world like your lifesavers', was much-quoted afterwards.[56] Between the wars, surfing had become a 'national pastime', and Foster's Lager advertisements could talk about 'The love of the sun and sea on our bodies' as being part of the 'National Heritage'.[57] Surf Life-Saving Clubs, first established just prior to the Great War, had rapidly expanded, developing not only rescue methods but also all the elaborate rituals of the surf carnival, and the military associations of drill, discipline, march-pasts, equipment inspections and voluntary sacrifice.

Significantly, during the sesquicentenary celebrations of 1938, just a week before the Bondi rescue, a phalanx of lifesavers had rounded off the 'March to Nationhood' pageant.[58] Although the hot Martin Place asphalt ruined the effect somewhat—spectators had to provide them with newspapers to stand on—they were filling the same role that the shearers had filled in 1901, and the diggers after Gallipoli. Increasingly the lifesaver appeared as symbolic of Australia in coffee table accounts of the nation, alongside the more traditional sheep, drovers and gum trees. During the Royal Tour of 1954, one of the treats prepared for the young Queen Elizabeth was a surf carnival, with a mass march-past of virile lifesavers. In 1956, by which time there were 186 clubs in Australia, the surf lifesaving movement was being described as

> truly Australian in spirit. Its character savors [sic] of sun-drenched sand and a free and boisterous surf. In it we see democracy function as it was meant to. There are no barriers of creed, class, or color[sic]. All these things are forgotten in the wonderful spirit of humanitarian mateship.[59]

In the lifesaver, Australians could once again identify nationhood with an ideal type of manhood. Women were generally excluded from lifesaving clubs and although some women's clubs were set up in response, the role of women in the image was to beautify Australia's beaches rather than to make them safe. In 1980 women were admitted to the clubs, but by then the movement was not attracting enough males.

Although most aspects of the lifesaver conformed to the traditional Australian 'type'—the 'sun-bronzed' physique, the masculinity, the cult of mateship, the military associations, the hedonism and wholesomeness of the beach—there were important differences. Unlike the bushman and Bean's version of the digger, the lifesaver was identified

'This colour picture aptly symbolises the Australian Surf Life Saver'. The *national type as depicted by* The History of the Bondi Surf Bathers' Life Saving Club 1906–1956, *Sydney, 1956, p. 23.*

with the city rather than the bush, and particularly with Sydney. And although he could be admired for the conventional virtues—courage, coolness, initiative, the voluntary sacrifice of leisure time for community service—his image was less malleable, less directly political, than the image of the bushman or the digger.

Other traditional types were being over-worked. We have already seen that the digger, as the embodiment of nationhood, had been idealised beyond recognition. The bushman was being given a specifically socialist heritage. Both communists and conservative Catholics had been claiming the gold-diggers at Eureka and Ned Kelly for themselves, the communists interpreting the Australian character as rebellious, the Catholics interpreting it as essentially Irish.[60] The national type was also losing its identity in the search for sophistication, because it had always been the antithesis of urban pretensions and decadence. In the crises of depression and war, the old confidence in the Australian type faltered.

More importantly, the war helped discredit the whole idea of a national type. It was uncomfortably close to Nazi ideas about the Aryan master race. Throughout the West, eugenicist and Social Darwinist ideas were being undermined, and environment rather than heredity, nurture rather than nature, was beginning to predominate in the social sciences. The dominance of the United States too caused problems because, given the racial heterogeneity of its population, it was difficult to isolate an American 'type'. Prior to the war, Americans had readily given detailed assessments of the Australian type,[61] but significantly in 1942 an American authority on Australia, C. Hartley Grattan, condemned any talk about an Australian 'race'. He criticised W.M. Hughes for the comment that 'we have a race, hardy, virile, resourceful, courageous', and a professor of physiology for discussing 'Factors in the Development of an Australian Race'.[62] The time had come for an entirely new concept to make its appearance.

10 Everyman and his Holden

The Australian Way of Life
as seen by Her Majesty the Queen
can be yours . . .
as the Modern Emigrant.
Slogan in Australia House, London, 1954[1]

During the 1940s, the basis of the Australian identity changed. The idea of a racial or national type, a fundamental part of what it meant to be Australian since the early nineteenth century, was replaced by a new concept, 'the Australian way of life'. Although only invented, it seems, in the 1940s,[2] the term proved so popular that by 1950 a columnist could complain that she was 'sick and tired of hearing people bleating about The Australian Way of Life'.[3] Not that she deterred anyone: in 1953 alone, three significant general surveys of Australia appeared, one called *The Australian Way of Life*, and the other two containing essays on the subject where similar books before the war might have included chapters titled 'The Australian Type'.[4] Throughout the 1950s, the new concept was central to any discussion of Australian society.

Selling a Way of Life

The idea of a 'Way of Life' fulfilled both general Western needs and more specific Australian ones. George Caiger's *The Australian Way of Life*, published under the auspices of the Australian Institute of International Affairs, was the first volume to appear in a UNESCO 'Way of Life Series' which later included such titles as *The South African Way of Life, The Pakistani Way of Life* and *The Norwegian Way of Life*. They represented a broad shift in Western thought which was closely related to a new Cold War outlook. In that Cold War context, Australia was becoming an important bulwark of 'freedom'. Australia's racial identity became less important than its alliance with the United States in the Cold War.

As a concept, a 'way of life' was more effective in defending the status quo than 'the national character' or 'the national type', which radicals had actually been associating with social change. The Cold War defensiveness inherent in the concept was spelled out in the introduction to another of the 1953 analyses of Australian society, W.V. Aughterson's *Taking Stock*, which suggested that 'our way of life in Australia is a miracle for this kind of world, and . . . the danger lies in thinking of it as "natural" and likely to endure without a passionate determination on our part to preserve and defend it'.[5] Similarly, in 1951, when the Commemorative book celebrating the fiftieth anniversary of the Commonwealth dealt with 'The Australian Way of Life', it stressed stability and congratulated Australians on their lack of a revolutionary heritage.[6]

The defensiveness was partly a continuation of the obsessions of the 1920s, but then the stress had been on the purity of Australia, the foreignness of Bolshevism, and the fact that it undermined a British civilisation. Now, with the greater strength of the Communist Party within Australia and the dissidence of many intellectuals, the Cold War outlook encouraged the pursuit of internal ideological warfare. As in other Western countries, fear of the external threat posed by 'Russian expansionism' gave it added impact. Thus in 1949, the Institute of Public Affairs, which helped formulate Liberal Party policy, inserted full-page newspaper advertisements stating: 'It is the communist influence within the Labour Party that is lowering production. This dangerous influence must be eradicated if the Australian way of life is to survive'.[7] 'The Australian Way of Life' was what was 'at stake' in the Cold War, and was used by conservatives against internal as well as external opposition.

The concept of 'the Australian Way of Life' was central to another issue that dominated the 1950s—immigration. The large-scale post-war assisted immigration begun by the Chifley government and continued under Menzies was the product of earlier 'populate or perish' fears, the Japanese threat during the war and the decision to industrialise Australia. What distinguished this from earlier immigration schemes was not only its size and effectiveness—between 1947 and 1964 more migrants were added to the population than in the 80 years after 1860[8]—but also the fact that a large proportion of migrants were not British. In this context, 'the Australian Way of Life' again played a crucial role.

In the 1920s, non-British immigration, like communism, was essentially an external threat; 'undesirable' migrants were kept out by the 'White Australia' policy, while British immigrants were exhorted to 'live up to your British tradition and aspire to emulate the Australian spirit of Anzac'.[9] Now, however, the non-British immigrant was a problem to be dealt with within Australia, and 'the Australian Way of Life' provided the basis for government policy. Assimilation, required of both migrants and Aborigines throughout the 1950s, assumed a common, homogeneous Australian way of life which would be threatened unless outsiders conformed to it. Successive ministers for immigration made the same point. In 1945, Labor's Arthur Calwell thought it 'economically unsound to bring migrants to the country until there is ... proper housing and other social amenities to help them fit themselves quickly into the Australian way of life'.[10] In 1950, the Liberals' Harold Holt stressed that 'We can only achieve our goal through migration if our newcomers quickly become Australian in outlook and way of life'.[11] In 1957, in John O'Grady's very successful novel, *They're a Weird Mob*, migrants were told

> There are far too many New Australians in this country who are still mentally living in their homelands, who mix with people of their own nationality, and try to retain their own language and customs ... Cut it out. There is no better way of life in the world than that of the Australian.[12]

In this way the concept was used to discriminate against migrants in Australia. Since it was never really defined, and often was simply a formula for expressing a general prejudice against outsiders and a distaste for non-conformity, all migrants could be criticised for failing to adopt 'the Australian Way of Life'. It not only denied the possibility that the cultural traditions of migrants might enrich Australian life, but also denied the existence of different 'ways of life' among Australians themselves. Cultural differences were an affront to a society which demanded social uniformity, if not equality. 'The Australian Way of Life' proved a useful tool of intolerance because it was so vague a notion, but it was rare for an Australian to point out how meaningless it was. One who did was Elizabeth Webb, a Brisbane journalist and commentator, who wrote:

> When it comes to The Australian Way of Life every foreigner I have met is completely at sea. To quote one—'What is this Way of Life? No one yet tells me what this is! Yet always they tell me I must adopt it ... perhaps I begin to behave like you behave in pubs. I drink beer until I am stupid. Or learn to "put in the boot" and bash the other fellow with a bottle ... Is this the way of life I must learn? Thank you. No. I stay a bloody Reffo!'[13]

The idea that 'the Australian Way of Life' might in fact only boil down to beer and gambling disturbed some writers. They wanted to define its true essence, but they simply repeated the vague rhetoric of Cold War politics. George Johnston, for example, argued that 'the beer-swilling spectacle in any Sydney pub ten minutes before closing time' was not 'a true or even partly true picture of the Australian way of life', but he could only define its essence as 'something which for all its uneasiness and confusion seems to talk of true democracy of the spirit'.[14] Another article on the subject explained that 'the Australian way of life' was 'something much deeper than words can depict', that it embodied some 'inner principle' which, although difficult to define, was related to 'the freedom, the security, the justice and the individualism of life in this sunburned, muscular continent'.[15]

Although the stated definitions were vague and contrived—like earlier definitions of the Australian 'type'—it did not matter because what was important was not the meaning of the term but the way in which it was used. It provided a mental bulwark against communism, against change, against cultural diversity; it could call forth a common emotional response to the Cold War and to immigration, in defence of stability and homogeneity. In this, it was more effective than the concept of an Australian 'type', as a 1955 Australian News and Information Bureau pamphlet implied, when it reinforced the idea that Australia was united and classless:

> What is a 'typical Australian'? Even few Australians agree on this point, for the development of the land has brought with it a great diversity of occupation and outlook. Many Australians have a distinctive accent; many have not. Many conform to the popular overseas picture of the tall, lean, sun-tanned stockman; but more spend their lives in the crowded cities. Yet throughout this wide-ranging land, where outback station and city night-club are equally part of the social fabric, and where opal gouger, crocodile hunter, city clerk and atomic scientist are all members of its community, one language prevails; and its people are united in customs, character and tradition. Few are so rich that they need not work; none so poor that he cannot enjoy recreation.[16]

It is significant that egalitarianism, seen by left-wing writers as a radical impulse in the national 'type', is here presented as merely another factor which makes for cultural unity.

Again, although it lacked definition, the image of 'the Australian Way of Life' was closely related to the image of Australia as a sophisticated, urban, industrialised, consumer society. This suited the needs of an Australian manufacturing sector which was increasingly aligning itself with the United States, and which had been strengthened in the industrial expansion promoted by the war. Whereas the Australian 'type' had been seen as an extension of the British 'type', and Britain had set the standard against which the developing Australian character was measured, it was the United States which provided the standard against which Australia, and other Western nations, measured their 'way of life'. After all, 'the American Way of Life' was the original, the most glamorous, the best publicised. Hollywood and, after 1956, television had seen to that.

The break with Britain among conservatives was quite sudden. In 1953, one of the older generation, F.W. Eggleston, could still write of Australia as 'a British community . . . following the English way of life . . . England is "Home"'.[17] At the same time another observer of Australian life was remarking that the habit of calling Britain 'Home' was dying fast.[18] Brian Fitzpatrick thought the habit had died during the Second World War.[19] Its death, however, did not signify the leap towards a confident national independence for which many radicals yearned. For many conservatives, economic, cultural and military dependence on Britain was replaced by similar dependence on America, and the concept of 'the Australian Way of Life' simply disguised the switch. Australian conservatism was impressively un-sentimental about its change of allegiance, despite the Anglophile rhetoric of Menzies. In 1958, at a time when both radicals and old conservatives were critical of American influences, a Gallup Poll found that only 29 per cent of voters thought that 'the United States is influencing our Australian way of life too much', and these were more likely to be Labor than Liberal voters.[20] Typical of this new conserva-tism was Donald Horne, who saw anti-Americanism as the bad feeling of a deluded Left and a 'mindless', sentimental Right. For him, 'Australia was the first country in the contemporary world to be saved by the Americans' and he looked forward to a 'quite massive relationship with America'.[21] While his republicanism would have been too iconoclastic for many in the 1950s, his shift of outlook to-wards America was common. There were even suggestions that Australia should become the fifty-first state.

A second feature of the 'Australian Way of Life' which tied it to the manufacturing sector was its urban character. The national 'type' eulogised in the past had been a rural 'type' but the 'Way of Life' was undeniably urban, or rather suburban. The city had lost the pejorative connotations it had had in the past, when it was viewed as a festering sore corrupting and debilitating the national type. Now suburbia was an ideal. In 1951, the Commonwealth celebrated its jubilee with an article on 'the Australian Way of Life' written by a refugee:

> What the Australian cherishes most is a home of his own, a garden where he can potter, and a motor car ... as soon as he can buy a house and a garden he ... moves to the suburbs. This accounts for the enormous size of Australian cities—and also for the overwhelmingly middle-class outlook and way of life.
>
> A person who owns a house, a garden, a car and has a fair job is rarely an extremist or a revolutionary.[22]

Not only was 'the Australian Way of Life' specifically urban; it was also increasingly identified with Sydney. Before the phrase was commonly used, Sydney had been seen as exceptional rather than representative. Bohemians had left Sydney to find their 'real' Australia. Lawson described Sydney as

> She, of Australian cities
> The least Australian of all!
> Greedy, luxurious, corrupting
> Her sisters one by one.[23]

In the 1930s, Thomas Wood had expected to find Sydney 'the centre of Australian thought', but instead found it 'worlds apart from ... the men who plough and shear and mine—and keep Australia going ... Sydney lives its own life: a city life with city interests and city pleasures, and Australia may go hang'.[24] By the 1950s however, Sydney was seen as 'the most "Australian" of Australian cities', although (or because) it was also considered the most American.[25] Constantly writers on 'the Australian Way of Life' would refer to Sydney to describe what was typically Australian. Increasingly, in books about Australia, photographs of Sydney—Bondi, Manly, busy Pitt Street, cosmopolitan King's Cross, the Bridge, the Harbour— were challenging the familiar iconography of outback Australia—the homestead, the sheep, the lonely gum and the proud Aborigine. In 1953, for example, Caiger's *The Australian Way of Life* had as its frontispiece 'A Sydney Street Scene', and contained seven photographs of rural scenes, six of Sydney, two each of Newcastle and Canberra, one each of Adelaide and Perth, and none at all of Melbourne. Melbourne was the centre of attention when the Olympic Games were held there in 1956, but its glory was momentary. By the 1970s the Sydney Opera House had become easily the most popular symbol of Australia, both here and overseas.

For the manufacturing sector, the most important feature of 'the Australian Way of Life' was its identification with consumerism. It was no coincidence that the Official Commemorative Book for the Commonwealth Jubilee in 1951 should illustrate its article on 'the Australian Way of Life' with photographs of the major city department stores. The familiar picture of suburban family life, with its focus on home and garden, and on a catalogue of family possessions such as refrigerators, washing machines, radiogrammes, television sets and, of course, the family car, was the basis of post-war affluence and the vast new consumer economy which the manufacturers and governments encouraged. Home ownership in Sydney rose from 40 per cent in 1947 to 60 per cent in 1954 (when homes were easier to buy than ever before or since), and to 71 per cent in 1961.[26] An Australian white goods industry expanded rapidly after the war so that the household appliances which had been luxuries before the war were now available to almost everyone. In 1949–50, Australia produced 31,638 washing machines, 150,878 refrigerators and 1070 petrol lawn mowers; ten years later the figures were 201,873; 237,328 and 246,721 respectively.[27] And then there was 'Australia's own car', Australia's own in the sense that all the capital investment involved was Australian and only the profits went to America. The first Holden was produced in 1948. The Labor Prime Minister, Ben Chifley, was photographed next to it but, appropriately, Essington Lewis was invited to buy it.[28] Lewis more than anyone was identified with Australia's industrialisation. By 1962 one million more Holdens had been sold, and in 10 years car ownership had increased from one for every nine people to one per $3\frac{1}{2}$.[29] It was all accompanied by advertising campaigns structured around the imagery of 'the Australian Way of Life'.

Both major political parties encouraged this manufacturing boom and the consumerism which went with it, although the Liberals more successfully identified with it. In 1949, the last year of the Labor government, a Liberal Party think-tank, chaired by the large retailer, G.J. Coles, demanded for Australia 'the American attitude of mind ... leaders who can bring the nation to a new way of life'.[30] Fifteen years of Menzies' government later, they looked back with some satisfaction at 'improvements' in 'the Australian way of life':

> democratisation of the motor car with its side effects of road congestion, numerous, immaculate petrol stations and modern-architectured motels ... multiplication of modern, attractively designed factories ... houses comprehensively equipped with the labour-saving and entertainment-giving 'gadgets'.[31]

As late as 1977, one of Malcolm Fraser's academic advisers, David Kemp, explained the A.L.P.'s failure to win office as due to its association 'with what are still perceived as significant threats to the Australian way of life'.[32]

The role of women in this vision of Australia was two-edged. On the one hand they were central to the new identity, in a way they had not been to the old Australian type. They, more than men, were conceived by the advertisers as the great consumers, dominating family, home and garden, and the consumer economy was structured around them. In 1947, for example, the *Argus* Women's Magazine had told its readers that 'the American Way of Life is Easy for the Housewife', and described how

> Big New York stores trade exclusively in household gadgets. Seven and eight floors are devoted solely to them.

The reporter hoped 'to interest manufacturers here and get into production small labour-saving devices for the Australian house-wife'.[33] For the next two decades women were inveigled into buying small labour-saving devices and persuading their husbands to buy larger ones.

However this role was a very restrictive one. Men had many outlets in 'the Australian Way of Life', as workers, fathers, sportsmen, beer-drinkers, home handymen. Women were part of it only as full-time housewives and mothers. The variety of experience which women could have outside family life was denied, yet in 1961 a quarter of factory workers were women, and a third of females over 15 were not married.[34] Women had at last been given a role in the dominant image of Australia, but it was one that worked to keep them in their place.

The image needed to be fairly static, but it also embraced two great symbols of development which caught the imagination of Australians in the 1950s and 1960s. One was the Snowy Mountains Scheme, a major government enterprise set up in the late 1940s. It reflected the changing balance of the economy: its main purpose was to generate electricity for Canberra and for industry in the cities, while a secondary feature was irrigation farther west. The idea of migrants from many countries contributing to this great national enterprise seems to have had particular appeal to many Australians. In fact their work in the snow and mud was providing power for suburban washing machines. The scheme added to the exuberant self-confidence of the development ethos. George Johnston later described its impact on a thinly-disguised version of himself:

> The yellow tractors against the glaring drifts of snow, the beards and mackinaws, the polyglot babble of smoke-hazed mess huts, the tingling atmosphere of a collective excitement; these as much as the

sheer audacity of the concept had a profound effect upon Meredith
. . . 'It's like coming to an oasis in a desert, when you've been thirsting
for something of promise, something to believe in. It's magnificent,
darling! It's exciting! It's the only *visionary* thing I've seen since
I've been back in this bloody country . . . I'm going down *there* to
work . . . then write it as a novel. It could be the greatest bloody
novel ever. It *could*, Cress. It's the most fabulous theme. It's got
everything. *Everything!*'[35]

The other acknowledged symbol of development was Canberra. As
one government adviser put it in 1965, Australians should be encouraged to look on the city 'as a place where growth and development are being initiated, not only in local projects but in national
policies'.[36] Itself a monument, Canberra was also a city of monuments,
and as each one rose up, as rural peace gave way to the suburb beautiful,
the changing image of Australia was put on record. The Australian
War Memorial, designed in the 1920s under C.E.W. Bean's inspiration, but postponed in the depression, was opened in 1941. It continued to be extended until 1970, paying tribute to the lingering
significance of the digger legend. The Australian National University
was established in 1946, reflecting that period's heightened respect
for the intelligentsia. In 1954, it was time to recognise Australia's
place in Cold War politics: when the Australian-American monument
was built it was situated between the Department of Defence office
blocks. In the same year a Senate Committee recommended the
establishment of a National Capital Development Commission which,
when it was established in 1958, turned Canberra into the fastest
growing city in Australia. Here was the suburban ideal made manifest.
Ironically it was based on leasehold rather than freehold principles:
even the most suburban of dreams could not be consummated through
private ownership, and even Menzies recognised it. Planning was
centred on the car, the family, the garden and a uniformly middle-
class life-style—'the Australian Way of Life' in all its glory. Filling
the lake in the early 1960s was like providing one gigantic backyard
swimming pool. But that ideal began to pall. The 1960s and the
1970s saw efforts to develop a more sophisticated cultural identity,
and cultural monuments, such as the National Library, the Civic
theatre complex, the School of Music and the National Gallery began
to appear.

New Images

The appearance of monuments to culture in Canberra as well as in most other Australian cities reflected yet another change in what it meant to be Australian. The expression 'the Australian Way of Life' began to fall into disuse, although it still remained popular in letters to the editor from older Australians concerned about the 'rising tide' of permissiveness or the failure of migrants to conform. Left-wing intellectuals had never been happy with the concept. They had made use of it in criticising American influence in Australia: Rupert Lockwood for example had condemned American investment and cultural imperialism with a flourish which a virulent anti-communist would have been proud of, writing 'The whole Australian way of life is at stake, all our finest traditions—and even our very existence'.[37] But that was a matter of fighting an enemy with his own weapons. In general the Left concentrated on convincing themselves of a natural egalitarianism and collectivism in the 'national character' or the 'typical Australian', and on combating Americanisation with a revival of bush ballads, Lawson and Tom Roberts's shearers, who replaced Paterson and Streeton's landscapes as the touchstone of Australianism. Occasionally they had qualms. Ian Turner was disturbed by 'a contradiction between what has been accepted as the Australian character, and the sort of society we now live in'.[38] Robin Boyd, although hardly a radical, observed 'The Wild Colonial Boy is selling used cars'.[39] The Australian 'type', it seemed, had become ensnared by 'the Australian Way of Life'. Some of the most bitter critiques of Australian society appeared in the 'Godzone' series in *Meanjin* in the mid-1960s. Alan Ashbolt asked *Meanjin* readers to

Behold the man—the Australian man of today—on Sunday mornings in the suburbs, when the high-decibel drone of the motor-mower is calling the faithful to worship. A block of land, a brick veneer, and a motor-mower beside him in the wilderness—what more does he want to sustain him, except a Holden to polish, a beer with the boys, marital sex on Saturday nights, a few furtive adulteries, an occasional gamble on the horses or the lottery, the tribal rituals of football, the flickering shadows in his lounge room of cops and robbers, goodies and baddies, guys and dolls.

He too asked what had become of the Wild Colonial Boy.[40] There was less and less to sustain the 1940s idea that Australians were naturally radical or rebellious. Melbourne historians such as Geoffrey Serle and Ian Turner asked similar questions. Another contributor suggested intellectuals seemed to share a common 'alienation from the way of life of ordinary Australians'.[41]

This critique of the suburban way of life was not the only reason that it fell from grace as the dominant image of Australia. In the late 1960s, Australia's participation in the Vietnam War, and the spread of an international dissident youth culture—with its protest songs, student movements and counter-culture—provided another focus for dissatisfaction with 'the Australian Way of Life'. It could now be identified with an older generation which, in the view of their children, had sold out to consumerism. The 1966 election, fought largely on Vietnam, produced a record majority for the Liberals, who had made use of traditional fears of Asia, of communism and of internal subversion. But later elections showed an increasing division in the voting patterns of the generations. If intellectuals felt alienated from 'the Australian Way of Life', so did the younger generation of university-educated opinion-makers.

By the 1970s they had become the new generation of academics and social critics. Many of them identified with the New Left and were critical, not only of Australian society, but more importantly of the way in which the 'Old Left' had promulgated their myths about the 'Australian character'. Humphrey McQueen, for example, was arguing in 1970 that Ward, Serle and Turner had got it wrong: the 'Australian character' was never egalitarian or collectivist, but petty bourgeois, and it was forged, not by a worthy nationalism, but by a jingoistic and vicious racism.[42] At the same time, the Women's Movement was beginning to point to both the restrictiveness of the role of women in 'the Australian Way of Life', and also the sexism inherent in the 'Old Left's' view of the 'real' Australian. Anne Summers's *Damned Whores and God's Police*, published in 1975, was particularly influential in reassessing the place of women in cherished Australian myths. Some began to wonder whether the concern with national identity among intellectuals in Australia was an evasion of the need to confront social and sexual divisions within Australian society. But so far, it seems, this view has had little effect on more popular notions of what it means to be Australian.

Through the 1960s another change was taking place which had more effect on popular attitudes. Gradually the racial exclusiveness and intolerance associated with 'the Australian Way of Life' showed signs of weakening. In Aboriginal policy, in theory at least, 'integration' replaced 'assimilation', and although official attitudes to 'Our Aborigines' remained paternalistic, they at least allowed for the maintenance of the sort of cultural identity which Aborigines themselves were developing. The same change of outlook, from 'assimilation' to 'integration', could be seen in official attitudes towards migrants in Australia. 'Pluralism' was a convenient way of coping with the refusal of minority groups to accept 'the Australian Way of Life' as their own.

In addition, strict adherence to the 'White Australia' policy was quietly replaced by a policy which admitted a small number of non-Europeans in the late 1960s. But it was only in the 1970s, particularly under the Whitlam governments of 1972–75, that Australians recognised the fact that they lived in a 'multi-cultural' society, to such an extent that 'multi-culturalism' itself could become something of a fad. The 'White Australia' policy was formally abandoned and 'self-determination' became the new stated policy on migrants and Aborigines. Ethnic radio and, by 1980, ethnic television recognised the existence of more than one culture within Australia, although the attitudes of some conservative politicians suggest that they see such initiatives as a means of exerting more effective social control over minority groups.

By the early 1970s, Australia was being promoted as a pluralistic, tolerant, multi-cultural society, although it did not reflect any real improvement in the position of Aborigines and migrants, most of whom remained on the lower rungs of the socio-economic ladder. This image coincided—somewhat paradoxically—with what Whitlam referred to as the 'new nationalism'. Like Whitlam himself, it was closely identified with the arts. In particular, Australian drama and film had expanded considerably just prior to the Whitlam years. Whitlam built on this with an election policy for the arts which deliberately set out to 'help develop a national identity through artistic expression and to project Australia's image in other countries by means of the arts'.[43] In 1974, an election rally in the Sydney Opera House had the support of such cultural figures as Patrick White (newly awarded his Nobel Prize), Manning Clark and Bobby Limb.

The 'new nationalism' was never clearly spelled out, but it related to a general pride in Australian achievement, particularly cultural achievement, and an increasing disquiet at the extent of foreign investment in Australia. From the mid-1960s, the founding of a Fellowship of First Fleeters, the expansion of the National Trust's role and the appearance of native shrubs in suburban gardens had all heralded a new confidence in being Australian. In 1979, even the New South Wales Higher School Certificate succumbed, and Australian History became an acceptable subject for 17-year-olds. (It had been taught in other states at that level for some time.) Intellectuals no longer felt themselves to be quite so alienated: when the Australia Council was established in 1973 as the government's cultural entrepreneur, many of the 'Godzone' contributors were associated with it.

From the late 1960s the Australian identity was increasingly associated with the arts. Bruce Petty illustration for the Australian Council for the Arts Annual Report *1973, p. 29.*

For Geoffrey Serle, in his cultural history of Australia published in the same year, we had finally arrived at 'mature nationhood'.[44]

The irony was that, although many of the plays, novels and films produced in the 1970s were intensely critical of aspects of Australian life, they were absorbed by the 'new nationalism' and applauded for their Australianness. Thus the film, *The Chant of Jimmy Blacksmith*, was an indictment of Australian racism and a critical success at Cannes; its overall impact was to induce pride in the local film industry rather than shame at the treatment of Aborigines. Similarly, the figure of the 'Ocker' originated as a satire on Australian boorishness, but became an affectionate tribute to the national identity and ended up as the most effective way of selling cigarettes to children.

What should we be Singing in the Eighties?

On the edge of the 1980s, a new image of Australia is developing. There have been many attempts to define the Australian identity and there will no doubt be many more, although each will claim to be revealing it for the first time. Thus David Armstrong, Director of the Australian Bicentennial Authority, sees the aim of the 1988 celebrations as being 'to find a national identity'.[45] It will be no more meaningful than any of the other attempts. It will, however, adjust to new economic realities. The old commitments to egalitarianism have disappeared; pluralism has produced not a more tolerant society, but a more unequal one. A new economic orthodoxy is beginning to operate in favour of export industries; no end is offered to high unemployment; welfare is cut and education and the taxation system are restructured to favour the haves over the have-nots. The future is tied, not to pastoral, or agricultural, or manufacturing industry, but to mining, a sector of the economy which, because it is capital-intensive and largely foreign-controlled, promises only to exacerbate inequalities. It is tied, not to the cities, but to the outback, not to the south-east, but to the north and west.

In 1980, a convoy of trucks, escorted by a substantial force of police, stormed up the highway from Perth, driving through all resistance, in order to set up a drilling rig for an American company on Aboriginal land at Noonkanbah. Just as irresistibly, and with the same corporate and government backing, a new image of Australia will emerge, rich in resources, selling herself cheaply to the world. One of the most recent efforts at inventing Australia, Geoffrey Dutton's *Patterns of Australia*, was commissioned by Mobil Oil; Utah supports the Australian Opera; the Australian Mining Industry sponsored a television series on Ned Kelly; MacDonald's Hamburgers advertise their commitment to young Australians, Mount Isa Mines their recreation of 'the Australian Way of Life' in their mining towns. Mining companies and multi-national corporations will be central to the formation of a new Australian identity. It all goes to explain the symbolism of the new parliament house being built in Canberra: it will be dug into a hill, with the rather sad look about it of a disused quarry.

Further Reading

General

Barnes, J. (ed) *The Writer in Australia: A Collection of Literary Documents 1856 to 1964*, Melbourne, 1969.

Clark, C.M.H. *A History of Australia*, Melbourne, 1962-

Hancock, W.K. *Australia*, London, 1930.

Inglis, K.S. *The Australian Colonists: An Exploration of Social History 1788–1870*, Melbourne, 1974.

McQueen, H. *A New Britannia: An Argument Concerning the Social Origins of Australian Radicalism and Nationalism*, Melbourne, 1970.

Serle, G. *From Deserts the Prophets Come: The Creative Spirit in Australia 1788–1972*, Melbourne, 1973.

Smith, B. *Australian Painting 1788–1970*, Melbourne, 1971.

Summers, A. *Damned Whores and God's Police: The Colonization of Women in Australia*, Melbourne, 1975.

Turner, I. (ed) *The Australian Dream: A Collection of Anticipations about Australia from Captain Cook to the Present Day*, Melbourne, 1968.

Ward, R. *The Australian Legend*, Melbourne, 1966.

Before 1850

Clarke, F.G. *The Land of Contrarieties: British Attitudes to the Australian Colonies, 1828–1855*, Melbourne, 1977.

Conlon, A. '"Mine is a Sad yet True Story": Convict Narratives 1818–1850', *Journal of the Royal Australian Historical Society,* 55/1 (March 1969), pp. 43–82.

Dixson, M. *The Real Matilda: Women and Identity in Australia 1788 to 1975*, Melbourne, 1976.

Gollan, R. 'Nationalism and Politics in Australia before 1855', *Australian Journal of Politics and History*, 1/1 (November 1955).

Harris, A. *Settlers and Convicts*, Melbourne, 1964 (1st ed London, 1847).

McLachlan, N.D. '"The Future America": Some Bicentennial Reflections', *Historical Studies*, 17/68 (April 1977).

Moorehead, A. *The Fatal Impact: An Account of the Invasion of the Pacific 1767–1840*, London, 1966.

Proudfoot, H.B. 'Botany Bay, Kew, and the Picturesque: Early Conceptions of the Australian Landscape', *Journal of the Royal Australian Historical Society*, 65/1 (June 1979).

Roe, M. *Quest for Authority in Eastern Australia 1835–1851*, Melbourne, 1965.

Smith, B. *European Vision and the South Pacific 1768–1850: A Study in the History of Art and Ideas*, Oxford, 1969.

Sturma, M. 'Eye of the Beholder: The Stereotype of Women Convicts, 1788–1852', *Labour History*, 34 (May 1978).

Ward, R. and Macnab, K. 'The Nature and Nurture of the First Generation of Native-born Australians', *Historical Studies*, 9/39 (November 1962).

1851–1914
Blackton, C.S. 'Australian Nationality and Nativism: The Australian Natives' Association 1885–1901', *Journal of Modern History*, 30/1 (March 1958).
Blackton, C.S. 'Australian Nationality and Nationalism, 1850–1900', *Historical Studies*, 9/36 (May 1961).
Cole, D. '"The Crimson Thread of Kinship": Ethnic Ideas in Australia, 1870–1914', *Historical Studies*, 14/56 (April 1971).
Cole, D. 'The Problem of "Nationalism" and "Imperialism" in British Settlement Colonies', *Journal of British Studies*, 10/2 (May 1971).
Connolly, C.N. 'Class, Birthplace, Loyalty: Australian Attitudes to the Boer War', *Historical Studies*, 18/71 (October 1978).
Cozzolino, M. *Symbols of Australia*, Melbourne, 1980.
Davison, G. 'Sydney and the Bush: An Urban Context for the Australian Legend', *Historical Studies*, 18/71 (October 1978).
Denholm, D. *The Colonial Australians*, London, 1979.
Gollan, R. *Radical and Working Class Politics: A Study of Eastern Australia, 1850–1910*, Melbourne, 1960.
Grimshaw, C. 'Australian Nationalism and the Imperial Connection, 1900–1914', *Australian Journal of Politics and History*, 3/2 (May 1958).
Hirst, J.B. 'The Pioneer Legend', *Historical Studies*, 18/71 (October 1978).
Lansbury, C. *Arcady in Australia: the Evocation of Australia in Nineteenth-Century English Literature*, Melbourne, 1970.
Mandle, W.F. 'Cricket and Australian Nationalism in the Nineteenth Century', *Journal of the Royal Australian Historical Society*, 59/4 (December 1973).
Markus, A. *Fear and Hatred: Purifying Australia and California 1850–1901*, Sydney, 1979.
Mayne, A. 'City Back-Slums in the Land of Promise: Some Aspects of the 1876 Report on Overcrowding in Sydney', *Labour History*, 38 (May 1980).
Palmer, V. *The Legend of the Nineties*, Melbourne, 1954.
Penny, B.R. 'The Australian Debate on the Boer War', *Historical Studies*, 56 (April 1971).
Phillips, A.A. *The Australian Tradition: Studies in a Colonial Culture*, Melbourne, 1958.
Rickard, J. 'National Character and the "Typical Australian": An Alternative to Russel Ward', *Journal of Australian Studies*, 4 (June 1979).
Roe, M. 'An Historical Survey of Australian Nationalism', *Victorian Historical Magazine*, 42/4 (November 1971).
Souter, G. *Lion and Kangaroo: The Initiation of Australia, 1901–1919*, Sydney, 1976.
Walker, R.B. 'Bushranging in Fact and Legend', *Historical Studies*, 11/42 (May 1964).
Wallace-Crabbe, C. (ed), *The Australian Nationalists: Modern Critical Essays*, Melbourne, 1971.
Ward, R. 'Two Kinds of Australian Patriotism', *Victorian Historical Magazine*, 41/1 (February 1970).
Ward, R. and Roe, M. 'The Australian Legend: An Exchange', *Meanjin*, 21/3 (1962).

After 1914
Bean, C.E.W. 'Sidelights of the War on Australian Character', *Journal of the Royal Australian Historical Society*, 13/4 (1927).

Connell, R.W. 'Images of Australia', *Quadrant*, 52 (March 1968).

Docker, J. *Australian Cultural Elites: Intellectual Traditions in Sydney and Melbourne*, Sydney, 1974.

Gammage, B. *The Broken Years: Australian Soldiers in the Great War*, Canberra, 1974.

Gordon, R. (ed), *The Australian New Left: Critical Essays and Strategy*, Melbourne, 1970.

Harris, M. *Ockers*, Adelaide, 1974.

Inglis, K.S. 'The Anzac Tradition', *Meanjin*, 24/1 (1965).

Inglis, K.S. 'The Australians at Gallipoli', *Historical Studies*, 14/54–55 (April and October 1970).

McLachlan, N. 'Nationalism and the Divisive Digger: Three Comments', *Meanjin*, 24/3 (1965).

McQueen, H. 'From Gallipoli to Petrov: The Dialectic of Class Consciousness and National Consciousness in Australia 1915–1955', *Historian*, 25 (October 1973).

Mandle, W.F. *Going it Alone: Australian National Identity in the Twentieth Century*, Melbourne, 1978.

Robson, L.L. (ed), *Australia and the Great War 1914–18*, Melbourne, 1969.

Roe, M. 'Comments on the Digger Tradition', *Meanjin*, 24/3 (1965).

Rowse, T. *Australian Liberalism and National Character*, Melbourne, 1978.

Serle, G. 'The Digger Tradition and Australian Nationalism', *Meanjin*, 24/2 (1965).

Spearritt, P. and Walker, D. (eds), *Australian Popular Culture*, Sydney, 1979.

Turner, I. 'Australian Nationalism and Australian History', *Journal of Australian Studies*, 4 (June 1979).

Walker, D. *Dream and Disillusion: A Search for Australian Cultural Identity*, Canberra, 1976.

White, R. '"Combating Cultural Aggression": Australian Opposition to Americanisation', *Meanjin*, 39/3 (October 1980).

White, R. '"The Australian Way of Life"', *Historical Studies*, 18/73 (October 1979).

Endnotes

Chapter 1 Terra Australis Incognita

1. Annie Raine Ellis (ed), *The Early Diary of Frances Burney 1768–1778*, London, 1907, vol. I, p. 291.
2. C.M.H. Clark, *A History of Australia*, Melbourne, 1962, vol. I, pp. 3–38; Kenneth McIntyre, *The Secret Discovery of Australia: Portuguese Ventures 200 Years Before Captain Cook*, Adelaide, 1977.
3. William Dampier, *A New Voyage Round the World*, 3rd ed, London, 1698, vol. I, pp. 463–67.
4. William Dampier, *A Voyage to New Holland*, 2nd ed, London, 1729, p. 102.
5. *Ibid.*, p. 122.
6. William Dampier, *A New Voyage Round the World*, p. 468.
7. *Ibid.*
8. Cited in Bernard Smith, *European Vision and the South Pacific 1768–1850: A Study in the History of Art and Ideas*, Oxford, 1969, p. 8.
9. William Dampier, *A New Voyage Round the World*, dedication.
10. James Edward Smith, *A Specimen of the Botany of New Holland*, London, 1793, vol. I, p. 2.
11. James Edward Smith, *A Selection of the Correspondence of Linnaeus and other naturalists*, London, 1821, vol. I, p. 231. Ellis to Linnaeus, 19 August 1768.
12. *Ibid.*, p. 263. Ellis to Linnaeus, 16 July 1771.
13. J.C. Beaglehole (ed), *The Journals of Captain James Cook on his Voyages of Discovery*, Cambridge, 1955, vol. I, p. 397.
14. *Ibid.*, p. 310.
15. Cited in Joseph Banks and Daniel Solander, *Illustrations of Australian Plants Collected in 1770 During Captain Cook's Voyage round the World in H.M.S. Endeavour*, London, 1905 (by order of the trustees of the British Museum), Introduction.
16. James Edward Smith, *A Specimen of the Botany of New Holland*, vol. I, p. 9.
17. J.C. Beaglehole (ed), *The Endeavour Journal of Joseph Banks 1768–1771*, Sydney, 1962, vol. II, p. 72.
18. *Ibid.*, pp. 119–21.
19. *Ibid.*, p. 84.
20. *Ibid.*, p. 94.
21. Coral Lansbury, *Arcady in Australia: The Evocation of Australia in Nineteenth-Century English Literature*, Melbourne, 1970, p. 5.
22. Broadside cited in G.C. Ingleton, *True Patriots All*, Sydney, 1952, p. 17.

23. A.O. Lovejoy, *The Great Chain of Being: A Study in the History of an Idea*, Cambridge, Mass., 1964, pp. 233–36.
24. Cited in Alan Moorehead, *The Fatal Impact: An Account of the Invasion of the Pacific 1767–1840*, London, 1966, p. 115.
25. George Shaw, *The Zoology of New Holland*, London, 1794, vol. I, p. 2.
26. Cited in Bernard Smith, *European Vision and the South Pacific 1768–1850*, p. 251.
27. Peter Cunningham, *Two Years in New South Wales*, London, 1827, vol. II, p. 39.
28. Robert Brown, *Prodromus Florae Novae Hollandiae et Insulae Van Diemen*, London, 1810, edited by W.T. Stearn, Weinheim, Germany, 1960, p. xxxiv.
29. Cited in Bernard Smith, *European Vision and the South Pacific 1768–1850*, p. 170.
30. Peter Stanbury, *Australian Animals: Who Discovered Them?* Sydney, 1978, p. 62.
31. Cited in Bernard Smith, *European Vision and the South Pacific 1768–1850*, p. 170.
32. *Ibid.*, pp. 169–73; F.G. Clarke, *The Land of Contrarieties: British Attitudes to the Australian Colonies, 1828–1855*, Melbourne, 1977, pp. 154–56.
33. J.C. Beaglehole (ed), *The Endeavour Journal of Joseph Banks 1768–1771*, vol. II, p. 125.
34. *Ibid.*, p. 130.
35. J.C. Beaglehole (ed), *The Journals of Captain James Cook on his Voyages of Discovery*, vol. I, p. 399.
36. *Ibid.*, p. 359.
37. John Hawkesworth, *An Account of the Voyages undertaken by Order of His Present Majesty for Making Discoveries in the Southern Hemisphere*, London, 1773, vol. I, p. vii.
38. Bernard Smith, *European Vision and the South Pacific 1768–1850*, p. 22.
39. Annie Raine Ellis (ed), *The Early Diary of Frances Burney 1768–1778*, vol. I, p. 337.
40. George Barrington, *A Voyage to Botany Bay with a Description of the Country, manners, Customes, Religion, &c. of the Natives*, London, 1796? p. 117.
41. Charles Pickering, *The Races of Man: and their Geographical Distribution*, Philadelphia, 1848, p. 137.
42. Coral Lansbury, *Arcady in Australia*, p. 5.
43. J.C. Beaglehole (ed), *The Endeavour Journal of Joseph Banks 1768–1771*, vol. I, p. 300.
44. Bernard Smith, *European Vision and the South Pacific 1768–1850*, pp. 165–66, 201–02.
45. Cited *ibid.*, pp. 130–31.
46. Alan Moorehead, *The Fatal Impact*, p. 80.

Chapter 2   Hell Upon Earth

1. Cited in T. Crofton Croker (ed), *Memoirs of Joseph Holt, General of the Irish Rebels, in 1798*, London, 1838, vol. II, p. iii.
2. Cited in Coral Lansbury, *Arcady in Australia*, pp. 10–11, 16.
3. Cited in F.G. Clarke, *The Land of Contrarieties*, pp. 155, 170.
4. Coral Lansbury, *Arcady in Australia*, pp. 7–12.

5. T. Crofton Croker (ed), *Memoirs of Joseph Holt*, vol. II, p. 219.
6. *Take Your Choice: or, the Difference between Virtue and Vice*, London, 1805, frontispiece.
7. Charles Dickens, *Hard Times for These Times*, Penguin, 1969, (1st ed 1854), p. 90.
8. *Ibid.*, pp. 179–81.
9. Elizabeth Mavor, *The Ladies of Llangollen: A Study in Romantic Friendship*, Penguin, 1973, p. 149.
10. George Loveless, *The Victims of Whiggery. A Statement of the Persecutions experienced by the Dorchester Labourers*, 8th ed, London, 1838, p. 22; F.G. Clarke, *The Land of Contrarieties*, pp. 8–9.
11. George Loveless, *The Victims of Whiggery*, p. 23.
12. T. Crofton Croker (ed), *Memoirs of Joseph Holt*, vol. II, p. 220.
13. Cited in G.C. Ingleton, *True Patriots All*, p. 221.
14. Cited *ibid.*, p. 213.
15. Anne Conlon, '"Mine is a Sad yet True Story": Convict Narratives 1818–1850', *Journal of the Royal Australian Historical Society*, 55(1), March 1969, pp. 43–82.
16. London, 1825? broadsheet in British Museum.
17. Ikey Solomons, *The Life and Exploits of Ikey Solomons, Swindler, Forger, Fencer, and Brothel-Keeper*, London, n.d., pp. 2–4.
18. Peter Cunningham, *Two Years in New South Wales*, vol. I, pp. 15–16.
19. Charles Dickens, *Great Expectations*, London, 1861, vol. I, p. 3; vol. III, pp. 7, 23.
20. Thomas Hardy, *The Hand of Ethelberta*, Penguin, 1978, (1st ed 1876), p. 343.
21. Cited in F.G. Clarke, *The Land of Contrarieties*, p. 30.
22. John Turnbull, *A Voyage Round the World in the Years 1800, 1801, 1802, 1803, and 1804*, London, 1805, vol. III, pp. 182–84.
23. J.C. Byrne, *Twelve Years' Wanderings in the British Colonies from 1835 to 1847*, London, 1848, vol. I, p. 238.
24. Cited in F.G. Clarke, *The Land of Contrarieties*, p. 33.
25. Anne Summers, *Damned Whores and God's Police: The Colonization of Women in Australia*, Penguin, 1975, pp. 267ff.; Michael Sturma, 'Eye of the Beholder: The Stereotype of Women Convicts, 1788–1852', *Labour History*, no. 34, May 1978.
26. R.H.W. Reece, *Aborigines and Colonists: Aborigines and Colonial Society in New South Wales in the 1830s and 1840s*, Sydney, 1974, p. 31.
27. F.G. Clarke, *The Land of Contrarieties*, pp. 30–31.
28. J.C. Byrne, *Twelve Years' Wanderings in the British Colonies from 1835 to 1847*, vol. I, pp. 228–29.
29. *Ibid.*, p. 223.
30. Michael Sturma, 'Eye of the Beholder: The Stereotype of Women Convicts, 1788–1852', p. 10.
31. Richard Whately, *Thoughts on Secondary Punishments*, London, 1832, p. 164. See also A.G.L. Shaw, *Convicts and the Colonies: A Study of Penal Transportation from Great Britain and Ireland to Australia and Other Parts of the British Empire*, London, 1966, pp. 266ff.
32. Cited in C.M.H. Clark (ed), *Select Documents in Australian History 1788–1850*, Sydney, 1950. p. 154.
33. Richard Whately, *Thoughts on Secondary Punishments*, pp. 83, 204.
34. *Edinburgh Review*, January 1850, p. 54.
35. Cited in C.M.H. Clark (ed), *Select Documents in Australian History 1788–1850*, p. 434.

36. Cited *ibid.*, pp. 154–55.
37. John Dunmore Lang, *An Historical and Statistical Account of New South Wales both as a penal Settlement and as a British Colony*, London, 1834, vol. II, p. 236. See also C.M.H. Clark, *A History of Australia*, Melbourne, 1968, vol. II, p. 321.
38. A.H. Chisholm (ed), *The Secrets of Alexander Harris 'Religio Christi'*, Sydney, 1961, p. 135.
39. F.G. Clarke, *The Land of Contrarieties*, p. 31.
40. W.C. Wentworth, *Australasia. A Poem*, London, 1823, pp. ix, 15–18.
41. Peter Cunningham, *Two Years in New South Wales*, vol. I, p. 9; vol. II, pp. 53–63.
42. Richard Whately, *Thoughts on Secondary Punishments*, p. 82.
43. John Dunmore Lang, *Freedom and Independence for the Golden Lands of Australia*, London, 1852, pp. 306, 309.
44. J.C. Byrne, *Twelve Years' Wanderings in the British Colonies from 1835 to 1847*, vol. I, p. 228.
45. John Dunmore Lang, *Freedom and Independence for the Golden Lands of Australia*, pp. 309–10.
46. George Arnold Wood, 'Convicts', *Journal of the Royal Australian Historical Society*, 8(4), 1922, p. 187. See also R.M. Crawford, '*A Bit of a Rebel': The Life and Work of George Arnold Wood*, Sydney, 1975, pp. 334ff.
47. A.G.L. Shaw, *Convicts and the Colonies*, p. 146.
48. Coral Lansbury, *Arcady in Australia*, p. 22.
49. G.C. Ingleton, *True Patriots All*, p. 269.

Chapter 3   A Workingman's Paradise?

1. A.B. Paterson (ed), *Old Bush Songs*, 5th ed, Sydney, 1926, pp. 77–78.
2. Russel Ward, *The Australian Legend*, Melbourne, 1966, p. 15; R.B. Madgwick, *Immigration into Eastern Australia 1788–1851*, Sydney, 1969, pp. 219–25.
3. Bernard Smith, *European Vision and the South Pacific 1768–1850*, p. 133.
4. *Ibid.*, p. 134.
5. *Ibid.*, p. 133.
6. W.J. Turner (ed), *British Commonwealth and Empire*, London, 1943, p. 80.
7. Peter Cunningham, *Two Years in New South Wales*, vol. I, p. 132. See also Helen Baker Proudfoot, 'Botany Bay, Kew, and the Picturesque: Early Conceptions of the Australian Landscape', *Journal of the Royal Australian Historical Society*, 65(1), June 1979, pp. 30–45.
8. Cited in Kathleen Fitzpatrick (ed), *Australian Explorers*, London, 1958, p. 138.
9. Cited in F.G. Clarke, *The Land of Contrarieties*, p. 5.
10. L.L. Robson, *The Convict Settlers of Australia: An Enquiry into the Origins and Character of the Convicts transported to New South Wales and Van Diemen's Land 1787–1852*, Melbourne, 1965, pp. 154–55.
11. Cited in F.G. Clarke, *The Land of Contrarieties*, p. 18.
12. James Loveless *et al.*, *A Narrative of the Sufferings of Jas. Loveless, Jas. Brine, and Thomas & John Standfield*, London, 1838, pp. 13–14.
13. David Mackenzie, *The Emigrant's Guide: or Ten years Practical Experience in Australia*, London, 1845, pp. 20–23.
14. Richard Whately, *Thoughts on Secondary Punishments*, p. 203.

15. Cited in K.S. Inglis, *The Australian Colonists: An Exploration of Social History 1788–1870*, Melbourne, 1974, p. 5.
16. *Ibid.*, pp. 4–6.
17. Cited in H. Reynolds, '"That Hated Stain": The Aftermath of Transportation in Tasmania', *Historical Studies*, 14(53), October 1969, p. 28.
18. E.J. Hobsbawm, *Industry and Empire*, Penguin, 1969, p. 113.
19. *Edinburgh Review*, January 1850, p. 60.
20. A.G.L. Shaw, 'British Attitudes to the Colonies. ca. 1820–1850', *Journal of British Studies*, IX(1), November 1969. Margaret Kiddle, 'Caroline Chisholm and Charles Dickens', *Historical Studies*, 3(10), July 1945, p. 86.
21. G.J. Abbott, 'The Emigration to Valparaiso in 1843', *Labour History*, no. 19, November 1970, p. 2.
22. F.G. Clarke, *The Land of Contrarieties*, p. 89.
23. *Ibid.*, pp. 80–81; R.W. Connell and T.H. Irving, *Class Structure in Australian History*, Melbourne, 1980, p. 115.
24. W.C. Wentworth, *Australasia. A Poem*, p. 14.
25. W.C. Wentworth, *A Statistical, Historical, and Political Description of the Colony of New South Wales, and its dependent Settlements in Van Diemen's Land*, London, 1819, pp. 88–89.
26. John Dunmore Lang, *An Historical and Statistical Account of New South Wales*, p. 36.
27. Cited in Ian Turner (ed), *The Australian Dream: A Collection of Anticipations about Australia from Captain Cook to the Present Day*, Melbourne, 1968, p. 21.
28. Caroline Chisholm, *Prospectus of a Work to be Entitled 'Voluntary Information from the people of New South Wales'*, Sydney, 1845. See also Mary Hoban, *Fifty-One Pieces of Wedding Cake: A Biography of Caroline Chisholm*, Kilmore, Victoria, 1973, p. 166.
29. Caroline Chisholm, *Comfort for the Poor! Meat Three Times a Day!! Voluntary Information from the People of New South Wales Collected in that Colony by Mrs Chisholm in 1845–6*, London, 1847, p. 11.
30. *Edinburgh Review*, January 1850, p. 54.
31. Cited in F.G. Clarke, *The Land of Contrarieties*, pp. 135, 141.
32. Cited in Clarence Karr, 'Mythology vs. Reality: The Success of Free Selection in New South Wales', *Journal of the Royal Australian Historical Society*, 60(3), September 1974, p. 199.
33. Peter Cunningham, *Two Years in New South Wales*, vol. I, pp. 3–10.
34. George Loveless, *The Victims of Whiggery*, p. 26. See also A. James Hammerton, *Emigrant Gentlewomen: Genteel Poverty and Female Emigration, 1830–1914*, London, 1979, p. 61.
35. George Loveless, *The Victims of Whiggery*, p. 23.
36. John Dunmore Lang, *An Historical and Statistical Account of New South Wales*, vol. II, pp. 194–219.
37. Samuel Butler, *The Hand-Book for Australian Emigrants; being a Descriptive History of Australia*, Glasgow, 1839, p. 94.
38. Charles Cozens, *Adventures of a Guardsman*, London, 1848, pp. 227–33.
39. J.C. Byrne, *Emigrant's Guide to New South Wales Proper, Australia Felix, and South Australia*, 8th ed, London, 1848, p. 4. See also R.W. Connell and T.H. Irving, *Class Structure in Australian History*, pp. 42–43.
40. Anthony Trollope, *Australia and New Zealand*, London, 1873, vol. I, p. 168.
41. Cited in F.G. Clarke, *The Land of Contrarieties*, p. 135.
42. Raymond Williams, *Culture and Society 1780–1950*, Penguin, 1961, pp. 99ff.

43. Charles Dickens, *The Personal History of David Copperfield*, Penguin, 1966 (1st ed 1850), p. 798.
44. Henry Kingsley, *The Hillyars and the Burtons: A Story of Two Families*, Boston, 1865, p. 14.
45. Werner P. Friederich, *Australia in Western Imaginative Prose Writings 1600–1900: An Anthology and A History of Literature*, Chapel Hill, 1967, pp. 66–135; Coral Lansbury, *Arcady in Australia, passim;* John Douglas Pringle, *On Second Thoughts: Australian Essays*, Sydney, 1971, pp. 126–33.
46. Charles Kingsley, *Alton Locke, Tailor and Poet: An Autobiography*, London, 1850.
47. Henry Kingsley, *The Hillyars and the Burtons*, p. 354.
48. Henry Kingsley, *The Recollections of Geoffrey Hamlyn*, Cambridge, 1860, pp. 256, 293.
49. James Backhouse, *A Narrative of a Visit to the Australian Colonies*, London, 1843, pp. 559–60.
50. Cited in F.G. Clarke, *The Land of Contrarieties*, p. 97.
51. E.J Hobsbawm, *Industry and Empire*, p. 84.
52. Cited in C.M.H. Clark (ed), *Select Documents in Australian History 1788–1850*, pp. 194–95.
53. *Van Diemen's Land Monthly Magazine*, November 1835, p. 115.
54. Cited in F.G. Clarke, *The Land of Contrarieties*, p. 186.
55. Henry Parkes, *Fifty Years in the Making of Australian History*, London, 1892, p. 2. See also G.C. Ingleton, *True Patriots All*, p. 230.
56. Cited in J.P. Priestley, *Victoria's Heyday*, Penguin, 1974, p. 18.
57. Cited in George Nadel, *Australia's Colonial Culture: Ideas, Men and Institutions in Mid-Nineteenth Century Eastern Australia*, Sydney, 1957, p. 67.
58. Cited in J.N. Molony and T.J. McKenna, '"All that Glisters"', *Labour History*, no. 32, May 1977, p. 39.
59. H. Mortimer Franklyn, *A Glance at Australia in 1880: or, Food from the South*, Melbourne, 1881, pp. 36, 166.
60. *Sydney Morning Herald*, 26 January 1888, p. 6.
61. T.A. Coghlan, *The Wealth and Progress of New South Wales 1893*, Sydney, 1893, pp. 547, 770–95.
62. G.J. Abbott, 'The Emigration to Valparaiso in 1843', p. 8.
63. A.B. Paterson, *Old Bush Songs*, pp. 77–78.
64. Egon Kisch, *Australian Landfall*, London, 1937, p. 211. See also Marie de Lepervanche, 'Australian Immigrants, 1788–1940: Desired and Unwanted', in E.L. Wheelwright and Ken Buckley, *Essays in the Political Economy of Australian Capitalism*, Sydney, 1975, vol. I, pp. 82–86.
65. Henry Lawson, 'Faces in the Street'.
66. William Lane, *The Workingman's Paradise: An Australian Labour Novel*, Sydney, 1948, p. ii.
67. Cited in Max Kelly, 'Picturesque and Pestilential: The Sydney Slum Observed 1860–1900', in Max Kelly (ed), *Nineteenth-Century Sydney: Essays in Urban History*, Sydney, 1978, p. 66.
68. *Ibid.*
69. *Ibid.*, p. 74; Michael Cannon, *Life in the Cities*, Melbourne, 1975, pp. 264–66.
70. David Clark, '"Worse than Physic": Sydney's Water Supply 1788–1888', in Max Kelly (ed), *Nineteenth-Century Sydney*, p. 64.
71. E.J. Hobsbawm, *Industry and Empire*, pp. 74–117.
72. Michael Cannon, *Life in the Cities*, p. 251.

73. G.C. Mundy, *Our Antipodes*, 3rd ed, London, 1855, pp. 547–48.
74. John Niland, 'The Birth of the Movement for an Eight Hour Working Day in New South Wales', *Australian Journal of Politics and History*, XIV(1), April 1968, p. 77; Michael Cannon, *Life in the Cities*, pp. 250f.
75. *Ibid.*, p. 252.
76. *Ibid.*, p. 272.
77. *Ibid.*, p. 277.
78. Alan Mayne, 'City Back-Slums in the Land of Promise: Some Aspects of the 1876 Report on Overcrowding in Sydney', *Labour History*, no. 38, May 1980, p. 26.
79. H. Mortimer Franklyn, *A Glance at Australia in 1880*, p. 8.
80. Cited in Alan Mayne, 'City Back-Slums in the Land of Promise', p. 38.
81. R.E.N. Twopeny, *Town Life in Australia*, London, 1883, p. 36.
82. Caroline Chisholm, *Comfort for the Poor! Meat Three Times a Day!!*
83. Anthony Trollope, *Australia and New Zealand*, vol. I, pp. 166–67.
84. John Niland, 'The Birth of the Movement for an Eight Hour Working Day in New South Wales', p. 78.
85. Michael Cannon, *Life in the Cities*, p. 271.
86. Nat Gould, *Town and Bush: Stray Notes on Australia*, London, 1896, p. 201; John Rickard, *Class and Politics: New South Wales, Victoria and the Early Commonwealth, 1890–1910*, Canberra, 1976, pp. 300–03.
87. R.E.N. Twopeny, *Town Life in Australia*, pp. 36–37.
88. Graeme Davison, *The Rise and Fall of Marvellous Melbourne*, Melbourne, 1979, p. 184.
89. R.E.N. Twopeny, *Town Life in Australia*, p. 95.
90. R.W. Connell, 'Images of Australia', *Quadrant*, no. 52, XII(2), March-April 1968, p. 10.

Chapter 4   Another America

1. W.H. Hudspeth, 'Leaves from the Diary of a Van Diemen's Land Official', (G.T.W.B. Boyes), *Royal Society of Tasmania, Papers and Proceedings*, 1946, p. 49.
2. Peter Burroughs, *Britain and Australia 1831–1855: A Study in Imperial Relations and Crown Lands Administration*, Oxford, 1967, Appendix II. See also F.K. Crowley, 'The British Contribution to the Australian Population: 1860–1919', *University Studies in History and Economics*, 11(2), July 1954, pp. 57–58.
3. Anthony Trollope, *Australia and New Zealand*, p. 2.
4. Cited in N.D. McLachlan, '"The Future America": Some Bicentennial Reflections', *Historical Studies*, 17(68), April 1977, p. 372.
5. *Ibid.*, pp. 361, 367; Alan Frost, '"As it were another America": English Ideas of the First Settlement in New South Wales at the End of the Eighteenth Century', *Eighteenth Century Studies*, 7, 1973–74, p. 255; F.G. Clarke, *The Land of Contrarieties*, p. 53; *Alan Moorehead, *The Fatal Impact*, p. 166; Max O'Rell (L.P. Blouet), *John Bull and Co.*, London, 1894, p. 71; Frank Cowan, *Australia: A Charcoal-Sketch*, Greensburg, Pa., 1886, p. 34.
6. George Francis Train, *Young America Abroad in Europe, Asia, and Australia*, London, 1857, pp. 10–12; Mark Twain, *Following the Equator: A Journey around the World*, New York, 1897, pp. 129–30; Frank Cowan, *Australia: A Charcoal-Sketch*, p. 34; V.S. Clark, *The Labour Movement in Australasia*, New York, 1906, pp. vii, 14–15.

7. Charles Dilke, *Greater Britain*, London, 1885, p. 379.
8. James Anthony Froude, *Oceania or England and her Colonies*, London, 1886, cited in A.L. McLeod (ed) *The Pattern of Australian Culture*, Ithaca, N.Y., 1963, p. 128.
9. E.C. Booth, *Another England: Life, Living, Homes, and Homemakers in Victoria*, London, 1869.
10. Edward Kinglake, *The Australian at Home: Notes and Anecdotes of Life in the Antipodes*, London, 1891, cited in Sidney J. Baker, *The Australian Language*, Sydney, 1978, p. 398.
11. A.G. Austin (ed) *The Webbs' Australian Diary 1898*, Melbourne, 1965, p. 115.
12. E.g. Peter Cunningham, *Two Years in New South Wales*, vol. II, p. 67.
13. Cited in N.D. McLachlan, '"The Future America": Some Bicentennial Reflections', p. 381.
14. Cited in Michael Cannon, *Life in the Cities*, p. 11.
15. Anthony Trollope, *Australia and New Zealand*, vol. II, pp. 38, 253–54.
16. E.g. *ibid.*, vol. I, p. 474.
17. N.D. McLachlan, '"The Future America": Some Bicentennial Reflections', p. 381; L.G. Churchward, *Australia and America 1788–1972: An Alternative History*, Sydney, 1979, pp. 65–67.
18. Glen Lewis, 'Australian Nationalism and the Queensland Tariff Debate', *Journal of the Royal Australian Historical Society*, 62(3), December 1976, p. 169.
19. N.D. McLachlan, '"The Future America": Some Bicentennial Reflections', p. 382.
20. R.E.N. Twopeny, *Town Life in Australia*, p. 65.
21. Cited in Hugh and Pauline Massingham (eds) *The Englishman Abroad*, London, 1962, pp. 179–80.
22. George Loveless, *The Victims of Whiggery*, p. 26.
23. David Mackenzie, *The Emigrant's Guide*, p. 23.
24. Cited in Ian Turner (ed) *The Australian Dream*, p. 101.
25. Cited *ibid.*, p. 102.
26. Alan Frost, '"As it were another America"', p. 256.
27. N.D. McLachlan, '"The Future America": Some Bicentennial Reflections', p. 375.
28. Michael Roe, *Quest for Authority in Eastern Australia 1835–1851*, Melbourne, 1965, pp. 81–83; K.S. Inglis, *The Australian Colonists*, p. 47.
29. Robin Gollan, 'Nationalism and Politics in Australia before 1855', *Australian Journal of Politics and History*, 1(1), November 1955, pp. 41–42.
30. Cited in N.D. McLachlan, '"The Future America": Some Bicentennial Reflections', p. 368.
31. *Ibid.*, p. 370.
32. Ruth Knight, *Illiberal Liberal: Robert Lowe in New South Wales 1842–1850*, Melbourne, 1966, p. 224.
33. John Dunmore Lang, *Freedom and Independence for the Golden Lands of Australia*, pp. 60–61.
34. D.P. Crook, *American Democracy in English Politics 1815–1850*, Oxford, 1965, pp. 166ff.
35. C.M.H. Clark, *A History of Australia*, vol. III, pp. 193–95; John W. Cell, *British Colonial Administration in the Mid-Nineteenth Century: The Policy-Making Process*, New Haven, 1970, pp. 88ff.
36. E.K. Silvester (ed) *Speeches in the Legislative Council of New South Wales on the Second Reading of the Bill for Framing a New Constitution*

for the Colony, Sydney, 1853, pp. 26, 35.
37. John Bright, *Speeches on Parliamentary Reform*, London, 1867, pp. 6, 34.
38. Robert Lowe, *Speeches and Letters on Reform*, London, 1867, pp. 53, 88, 148, 153.
39. Earl Grey, *Parliamentary Government Considered with Reference to a Reform of Parliament. An Essay*, London, 1858, p. 214.
40. Cited in F.G. Clarke, *The Land of Contrarieties*, p. 151.
41. C.M.H. Clark, *A History of Australia*, vol. IV, p. 54.
42. Geoffrey Serle, *The Golden Age: A History of the Colony of Victoria, 1851–1861*, Melbourne, 1963, pp. 169, 176, 181.
43. Cited in Charles Carrington, *Rudyard Kipling: His Life and Work*, London, 1955, p. 398.
44. E.J. Hobsbawm, *Industry and Empire*, p. 125.
45. P. Bradley (ed) Alexis de Tocqueville, *Democracy in America*, New York, 1953, vol. II, pp. 48, 56, 217, 259, 263.
46. Richard White, '"Combating Cultural Aggression": Australian Opposition to Americanisation', *Meanjin*, 39(3), October 1980, pp. 275–80.
47. R.H. Super (ed), *The Complete Prose Works of Matthew Arnold*, University of Michigan, 1960–77, vol. XI, pp. 17–18.
48. E.T. Cook and Alexander Wedderburn (eds), *The Works of John Ruskin*, London, 1903–12, vol. XXVII, p. 170.
49. John Barnes (ed), *The Writer in Australia: A Collection of Literary Documents 1856 to 1964*, Melbourne, 1969, p. v.
50. Cited in Bernard Smith (ed), *Documents on Art and Taste in Australia: The Colonial Period*, Melbourne, 1975, p. 248. See also K.S. Inglis, *The Australian Colonists*, p. 274.
51. Geoffrey Serle, *From Deserts the Prophets Come: The Creative Spirit in Australia 1788–1972*, Melbourne, 1973, pp. 55, 130; R.M. Crawford, *An Australian Perspective*, Melbourne, 1960, p. 53.
52. Cited in John Barnes (ed), *The Writer in Australia*, pp. 9ff.
53. Cited in Michael Wilding (ed), *The Portable Marcus Clarke*, Brisbane, 1976, p. 637.
54. Cited in John Barnes (ed), *The Writer in Australia*, p. 60.
55. Cited in Bernard Smith (ed), *Documents on Art and Taste in Australia*, p. 249.
56. John Barnes (ed), *The Writer in Australia*, p. 19.
57. *Van Diemen's Land Monthly Magazine*, November 1835, pp. 112–13.
58. Cited in Geoffrey Serle, *From Deserts the Prophets Come*, p. 54.
59. Cf. George Nadel, *Australia's Colonial Culture*, p. 34.
60. *Ibid.*, pp. 1, 35.
61. Cited *ibid.*, p. 41.
62. Cited in John Niland, 'The Birth of the Movement for an Eight Hour Working Day in New South Wales', p. 81.
63. J.H. Buckley, *The Victorian Temper: A Study in Literary Culture*, London, 1966, p. 154.
64. Cited in Michael Roe, *Quest for Authority in Eastern Australia*, p. 151.
65. *Van Diemen's Land Monthly Magazine*, November 1835, p. 113.
66. Cited in Michael Roe, *Quest for Authority in Eastern Australia*, p. 151. See also George Nadel, *Australia's Colonial Culture*, p. 272.
67. Cited in Geoffrey Serle, *The Golden Age*, p. 351.
68. *Age*, 12 February 1856, p. 2.
69. Vance Palmer, *The Legend of the Nineties*, Melbourne, 1963, p. 26.
70. David Mackenzie, *The Emigrant's Guide*, pp. 41, 147.

71. Michael Cannon, *Life in the Cities*, p. 258. See also Michael Roe, *Quest for Authority in Eastern Australia*, p. 186; Geoffrey Serle, *From Deserts the Prophets Come*, p. 25.
72. Anthony Trollope, *Australia and New Zealand*, vol. I, p. 484.

Chapter 5   The National Type

1. Cited in Ian Turner (ed), *The Australian Dream*, p. 130.
2. Rolf Boldrewood, 'The Australian Native-Born Type', in his *In Bad Company and Other Stories*, London, 1901, pp. 357–58.
3. Steven P. Shortus, '"Colonial Nationalism": New South Welsh Identity in the mid-1880s', *Journal of the Royal Australian Historical Society*, 59(1), March 1973; Peter Spearritt, 'New South Wales—The Non-Existent State?', *Meanjin*, 39(2), June 1980, p. 139.
4. *Oxford English Dictionary*.
5. J.H. Buckley, *The Victorian Temper*, p. 155. See also Bernard Smith, *European Vision and the South Pacific 1768–1850*, pp. 151ff.
6. Cited in D.J. Mulvaney, 'The Australian Aborigines, 1606–1929: Opinion and Fieldwork', *Historical Studies: Selected Articles*, Melbourne, 1964, pp. 20–21. See also H.N. Nelson, 'The Missionaries and the Aborigines in the Port Phillip District', *Historical Studies*, 12(45), October 1965, p. 58.
7. George Combe, *Lectures on Phrenology*, London, 1839, pp. 172, 215. See also T.M. Parsinen, 'Popular Science and Society: The Phrenology Movement in Early Victorian Britain', *Journal of Social History*, Fall 1974, p. 1.
8. Charles Pickering, *The Races of Man: and their Geographical Distribution*, Philadelphia, 1848, p. 137.
9. R.H.W. Reece, *Aborigines and Colonists*, pp. 87–94; F.G. Clarke, *The Land of Contrarieties*, p. 118.
10. H. Reynolds (ed), *Aborigines and Settlers: The Australian Experience 1788–1939*, Melbourne 1972, p. 114.
11. Cited in D.J. Mulvaney, 'The Australian Aborigines, 1606–1929: Opinion and Fieldwork', p. 28.
12. J.C. Byrne, *Twelve Years Wanderings in the British Colonies*, vol. I, p. 240.
13. John Turnbull, *A Voyage Round the World in the Years 1800, 1801, 1802, 1803, and 1804*, vol I, p. 47. See also Russel Ward and Ken Macnab, 'The Nature and Nurture of the First Generation of Native-Born Australians', *Historical Studies*, 9(39), November 1962, p. 291.
14. Peter Cunningham, *Two Years in New South Wales*, vol. II, pp. 53–56.
15. *Edinburgh Review*, January 1850, p. 61.
16. Cited in Christine Bolt, *Victorian Attitudes to Race*, London, 1971, p. 1.
17. Thomas Woolnoth, *Facts and Faces: or the Mutual Connexion between Linear and Mental Portraiture Morally Considered, and Pictorially Illustrated*, London, 1852, p. 228.
18. Henry Kingsley, *The Recollections of Geoffrey Hamlyn*, London, 1859, vol. I, pp. 288–90.
19. *Ibid.*, pp. 293–95.
20. Cited in James Laver, *The Age of Optimism: Manners and Morals 1848–1914*, London, 1966, pp. 126–28.
21. Charles Darwin, *The Origin of Species by Means of Natural Selection,*

or The Preservation of Favoured Races in the Struggle for Life, London, 1892 (1st ed 1859), p. 402.

22. P.D. Marchant, 'Social Darwinism', *Australian Journal of Politics and History*, 3(1), November 1957; Richard Hofstadter, *Social Darwinism in American Thought 1860–1915*, Philadelphia, 1945, p. 174.
23. Charles Darwin, *The Origin of Species*, p. 80.
24. Ann Mozley, 'Evolution and the Climate of Opinion in Australia, 1840–76', *Victorian Studies*, X(4), June 1967, pp. 425–30.
25. Cited in K.S. Inglis, *The Australian Colonists*, p. 166.
26. Cited in D.J. Mulvaney, 'The Australian Aborigines, 1606–1929: Opinion and Fieldwork', p. 21.
27. Thomas Major, *Leaves from a Squatter's Notebook*, Sydney, 1900, pp. 194, 165.
28. Geoffrey Serle, *The Rush to be Rich: A History of the Colony of Victoria 1883–1889*, Melbourne, 1971, pp. 229–30; C.M.H. Clark (ed), *Select Documents in Australian History 1851–1900*, Sydney, 1955, p. 810.
29. Cited in W.F. Mandle, 'Cricket and Australian Nationalism in the Nineteenth Century', *Journal of the Royal Australian Historical Society*, 59(4), December 1973, pp. 234ff.
30. 'Will the Anglo-Australian Race Degenerate?', *Victorian Review*, I, November 1879, pp. 122–23.
31. Cited in J. Foster Fraser, *Australia: The Making of a Nation*, London, 1910, pp. 54–55.
32. Cited in Douglas Cole, '"The Crimson Thread of Kinship": Ethnic Ideas in Australia, 1870–1914', *Historical Studies*, 14(56), April 1971, p. 515.
33. Cited in James Laver, *The Age of Optimism*, p. 230.
34. Elizabeth Lee (ed), *Britain over the Sea: A Reader for Schools*, London, 1901, p. xlv.
35. Cited in W.F. Mandle, 'Cricket and Australian Nationalism in the Nineteenth Century', pp. 236–37.
36. Henry Parkes, *Fifty Years in the Making of Australian History*, p. 640; James F. Hogan, 'The Coming Australian', *Victorian Review*, III, November 1880, p. 103.
37. C.M.H. Clark, *A History of Australia*, vol. IV, pp. 393–94.
38. John Ruskin, *The Crown of Wild Olive*, London, 1886, p. 122.
39. Cited in S.G. Firth, 'Social Values in the New South Wales Primary School 1880–1914: An Analysis of School Texts', *Melbourne Studies in Education 1970*, Melbourne, 1970, p. 154.
40. Cited in Geoffrey Serle, *The Rush to be Rich*, p. 199.
41. Cited in Frank Crowley (ed), *A New History of Australia*, Melbourne, 1974, p. 271.
42. Geoffrey Serle, *The Rush to be Rich*, pp. 231ff. See also K.S. Inglis, *The Australian Colonists*, p. 99.
43. C.M.H. Clark, *Select Documents in Australian History 1851–1900*, p. 787.
44. J.F. Daniell, 'The Jubilee of Melbourne', in Douglas Sladen (ed), *A Century of Australian Song*, London, 1888, p. 121.
45. W.M. Hughes, 'The Story of Australia and New Zealand in the Twentieth Century', in F.H. Hooper (ed), *These Eventful Years: The Twentieth Century in the Making*, New York, 1924, vol. II, p. 291.
46. Anthony Trollope, *Australia and New Zealand*, vol. I, p. 480.
47. Michael Davitt, *Life and Progress in Australasia*, London, 1898, p. 118.
48. Cited in Ian Turner (ed), *The Australian Dream*, p. 268.

49. P.R. Cole, 'The Development of an Australian Social Type', *Journal of the Royal Australian Historical Society*, XVIII(2), 1932, p. 54.
50. Michael Davitt, *Life and Progress in Australasia*, p. 120.
51. Henry Ling Roth, 'The Influence of Climate and Soil on the Development of the Anglo-Australian Race', *Victorian Review*, October 1880, p. 849.
52. W.F. Mandle, 'Cricket and Australian Nationalism in the Nineteenth Century', p. 234.
53. *Victorian Review*, III, November 1880, pp. 103, 106.
54. *Ibid.*, p. 106.
55. Cited in Charles Carrington, *Rudyard Kipling: His Life and Work*, pp. 130, 258, 180.
56. E.W. Hornung, *A Bride from the Bush*, London, 1890, p. 107.
57. *Daily Telegraph*, 2 January 1901, p. 14.
58. Frank Wilkinson, *Australia at the Front: A Colonial View of the Boer War*, London, 1901, p. 10.
59. Charles Carrington, *Rudyard Kipling: His Life and Work*, pp. 307–19.
60. R.C. Thompson, 'The Labor Party and Australian Imperialism in the Pacific, 1901–1919', *Labour History*, 23, November 1972, p. 28.
61. C.M.H. Clark, *Select Documents in Australian History, 1851–1900*, pp. 800–01.
62. C.H. Pearson, *National Life and Character. A Forecast*, London, 1893, p. 84.
63. Cited in Russel Ward, *A Nation for a Continent: The History of Australia 1901–1975*, Melbourne, 1977, p. 67. See also Richard Broome, 'The Australian Reaction to Jack Johnson, Black Pugilist, 1907–09', in Richard Cashman and Michael McKernan (ed), *The Making of Modern Sporting History*, Brisbane, 1979, p. 343.
64. Cited in Richard Jebb, *Studies in Colonial Nationalism*, London, 1905, p. 212.
65. Douglas Cole, '"The Crimson Thread of Kinship"', p. 512.
66. Bruce Mansfield, *Australian Democrat: The Career of Edward William O'Sullivan 1846–1910*, Sydney, 1965, p. 263.
67. Douglas Cole, '"The Crimson Thread of Kinship"', pp. 516–17.
68. Cited in Richard Hofstadter, *Social Darwinism in American Thought, 1860–1915*, p. 155.
69. G.R. Searle (ed), *Arnold White, Efficiency and Empire*, Brighton, 1973, pp. xii–xiv.
70. Cited in Charles Carrington, *Rudyard Kipling: His Life and Work*, p. 268.
71. Henry Lawson, 'Australian Engineers'.
72. *Young Australia: An Illustrated Annual for Boys throughout the English-Speaking World*, London, vol. 7, 1899.
73. Edwin J. Brady, *Australia Unlimited*, Melbourne, 1918, p. 64.

Chapter 6 Bohemians and the Bush

1. Cited in George A. Taylor, *'Those were the Days': Being Reminiscences of Australian Artists and Writers*, Sydney, 1918, p. 9.
2. R.H. Croll, *Smike to Bulldog: Letters from Sir Arthur Streeton to Tom Roberts*, London, 1946, p. 128.
3. E.J. Hobsbawm, *Industry and Empire*, p. 157.
4. Charles Carrington, *Rudyard Kipling: His Life and Work*, p. 212.
5. *Ibid.*, pp. 166–67.
6. *Victorian Census*, 1891, 1901; *N.S.W. Census*, 1891, 1901; *Common-*

wealth Census, 1911; Great Britain Central Statistical Office, *Annual Abstract of Statistics*, 1912. See also Graeme Davison, 'Sydney and the Bush: An Urban Context for the Australian Legend', *Historical Studies*, 18(71), October 1978, p. 193.

7. Henry Kendall, 'Men of Letters in New South Wales', in *Punch Staff Papers*, Sydney, 1872, pp. 229–30.

8. Henry Lawson, '"Pursuing Literature" in Australia', in Cecil Mann, *The Stories of Henry Lawson*, 3rd series, Sydney, 1964, pp. 402–04.

9. John Steegman, *Victorian Taste: A Study of the Arts and Architecture from 1830 to 1870*, Nelson, London, 1970, pp. 142–46, 282.

10. J.A.M. Whistler, *The Gentle Art of Making Enemies*, London, 1892, p. 128. See also Raymond Williams, *Culture and Society*, p. 172.

11. Cited in J.A.M. Whistler, *The Gentle Art of Making Enemies*, p. 1.

12. *Ibid.*, pp. 6, 32–33.

13. Bernard Smith (ed), *Documents on Art and Taste in Australia*, p. 203.

14. *Ibid.*, p. 207.

15. *Ibid.*, pp. 204, 209.

16. A.G. Stephens, *The Red Pagan*, Sydney, 1904, pp. 19–21.

17. Graeme Davison, 'Sydney and the Bush', p. 199; C.N. Connolly, 'Class, Birthplace, Loyalty: Australian Attitudes to the Boer War', *Historical Studies*, 18(71), October 1978, p. 230.

18. Cited in Ian Turner, 'The Social Setting', in Geoffrey Dutton (ed), *The Literature of Australia*, Penguin, 1976, p. 35.

19. Bernard Smith, *Australian Painting 1788–1970*, Melbourne, 1971, p. 109.

20. Ann Mari Williams, *The Stenhouse Circle: Literary Life in Mid-Nineteenth Century Sydney*, Melbourne, 1979.

21. Michael Wilding (ed), *The Portable Marcus Clarke*, p. 668.

22. *Ibid.*, p. xi.

23. Arthur W. Jose, *The Romantic Nineties*, Sydney, 1933, pp. 41–42.

24. Bernard Smith (ed), *Documents on Art and Taste in Australia,* p. 253.

25. Cited in Bernard Smith, *Australian Painting*, p. 104.

26. George A. Taylor, '*Those were the Days*', pp. 47ff; Graeme Davison, 'Sydney and the Bush', pp. 206–08.

27. R.H. Croll (ed), *Smike to Bulldog*, p. 13.

28. Victorian Artists' Society, *Memorandum and Articles of Association*, Melbourne, 1895, p. 13. See also Art Society of New South Wales, *15th Annual Report*, 1895, p. 3.

29. George A. Taylor, '*Those were the Days*', pp. 10–12.

30. Randolph Bedford, *Naught to Thirty-Three*, Sydney, 1944, p. 288.

31. David Denholm, *The Colonial Australians*, London, 1979, pp. 151–53.

32. J.H. Buckley, *The Victorian Temper*, p. 2.

33. Cited in Arthur W. Jose, *The Romantic Nineties*, p. 43.

34. *Ibid.*, p. 52.

35. J.F. Archibald, 'The Genesis of "The Bulletin"', *Lone Hand*, June 1907, p. 166.

36. Arthur W. Jose, *The Romantic Nineties*, p. 26. See also George A. Taylor, '*Those were the Days*', p. 113.

37. Cited in Geoffrey Serle, *The Rush to be Rich*, p. 159.

38. C.N. Connolly, 'Class, Birthplace, Loyalty', pp. 228–29.

39. Graeme Davison, 'Sydney and the Bush', pp. 192ff.

40. Victor Daley, 'The Call of the City', in *Wine and Roses*, Sydney, 1911.

41. Cited in Bernard Smith, *Australian Painting*, p. 88.

42. Cited in Graeme Davison, 'Sydney and the Bush', p. 208.

43. George A. Taylor, '*Those were the Days*', pp. 54–60.

44. A.G. Stephens (ed), *The Bulletin Story Book 1881–1901*, Sydney, 1901, pp. vi–viii.
45. In his painting, 'Anzacs Bathing',
46. Cited in Russel Ward, *The Australian Legend*, p. 233.
47. George A. Taylor, '*Those were the Days*', p. 20.
48. Arthur W. Jose, *The Romantic Nineties*, pp. 34–35.
49. *Ibid.*, p. 40.
50. R.H. Croll (ed), *Smike to Bulldog*, pp. 21–23.
51. Victorian College of the Arts, *Von Guerard to Wheeler: The First Teachers at the National Gallery School 1870–1939*, Melbourne, 1978 (photos and prize lists); Janine Burke, *Australian Women Artists 1840–1940*, Melbourne, 1980, pp. 24–37.
52. Graeme Davison, 'Sydney and the Bush', pp. 207–09.
53. Ian Turner (ed), *The Australian Dream*, pp. 219, 225.
54. A.B. Paterson, 'Clancy of the Overflow'.
55. Arthur W. Jose, *The Romantic Nineties*, pp. 19, 47.
56. Cited in Russel Ward, *The Australian Legend*, p. 227.
57. *Ibid.*, p. 252.
58. Cited in C.M.H. Clark, *Select Documents in Australian History 1851–1900*, p. 806.
59. Bernard Smith, *European Vision and the South Pacific 1768–1850*, p. 154.
60. Frank Wilkinson, *Australia at the Front*, p. 68. See also L.M. Field, *The Forgotten War: Australian Involvement in the South African Conflict of 1899–1902*, Melbourne, 1979, pp. 135, 186.
61. Cited in Russel Ward, *A Nation for a Continent*, p. 12.
62. For examples see John Barnes (ed), *The Writer in Australia*, pp. 3, 17, 38, 47–48, 57; Ken Levis, 'The Role of the *Bulletin* in Indigenous Short-Story Writing during the Eighties and Nineties', in Chris Wallace-Crabbe (ed), *The Australian Nationalists: Modern Critical Essays*, Melbourne, 1971, pp. 49–52.
63. Leslie Stephen cited in James Laver, *The Age of Optimism*, p. 176.
64. Ian Turner (ed), *The Australian Dream*, pp. 101–02. See also Bernard Smith (ed), *Documents on Art and Taste in Australia*, pp. 135–38.
65. Helen Baker Proudfoot, 'Botany Bay, Kew, and the Picturesque', pp. 30–45; Bernard Smith, *European Vision and the South Pacific 1768–1850*, pp. 133–34.
66. A.G. Stephens (ed), *The Bulletin Story Book 1881–1901*, pp. vi–viii.
67. Cited in Arthur W. Jose, *The Romantic Nineties*, p. 10.
68. Bernard Smith (ed), *Documents on Art and Taste in Australia*, pp. 274–75.
69. *Ibid.*, p. 263.
70. John Barnes (ed), *The Writer in Australia*, p. 52.
71. Peter Coleman, *Obscenity, Blasphemy, Sedition: 100 Years of Censorship in Australia*, Sydney, 1961, pp. 105–06; Australian Writers' and Artists' Union, *Rules*, Sydney, 1910; Geoff Sparrow (ed), *Crusade for Journalism: Official History of the Australian Journalists' Association*, Melbourne, 1960, pp. 23–24; *Bookfellow*, June 1912, p. 156.
72. Edwin J. Brady, *Australia Unlimited*, pp. 123–24.

Chapter 7   Young, White, Happy and Wholesome

1. Ethel Castilla, *The Australian Girl and other verses*, Melbourne, 1900.
2. Rosemary Pringle, 'Public Opinion in the Federal Referendum Campaigns

in New South Wales, 1898–99', *Journal of the Royal Australian Historical Society*, 64(4), March 1979, p. 245.

3. Gavin Souter, *Lion and Kangaroo: The Initiation of Australia, 1901–1919*, Sydney, 1976, p. 41.
4. *Ibid.*, p. 80.
5. C.M.H. Clark, *Select Documents in Australian History 1851–1900*, p. 790.
6. Mimmo Cozzolino, *Symbols of Australia*, Penguin, 1980, pp. 33–55.
7. Cf. R.W. Connell and T.H. Irving, *Class Structure in Australian History: Documents, Narrative and Argument*, Melbourne, 1980, p. 207.
8. Dion H. Skinner, *Renniks Australian Coin and Banknote Guide*, 10th ed, Adelaide, 1976, pp. 67, 76.
9. R.W. Connell and T.H. Irving, *Class Structure in Australian History*, p. 217.
10. Bernard Smith (ed), *Documents on Art and Taste in Australia*, p. 277.
11. 'Arthur Streeton', *Australian Encyclopaedia*, Sydney, 1926.
12. Arthur W. Jose, *The Romantic Nineties*, p. vi.
13. G.R. Searle, *The Quest for National Efficiency: A Study in British Politics and Political Thought, 1899–1914*, Oxford, 1971; Michael Roe, 'Efficiency: the Fascist Dynamic in American Progressivism', *Teaching History*, 8(2), 1974.
14. See the career and publications of Richard Arthur, activist for national purity, in *Australian Dictionary of Biography*, vol. VII.
15. John Barnes (ed), *The Writer in Australia*, pp. 44–45.
16. *Ibid.*, p. 57.
17. S.G. Firth, 'Social Values in the New South Wales Primary School', p. 142.
18. Joseph McCabe, 'Australia as a Forecast of the Future', *Lone Hand*, 2 October 1911, p. 485.
19. *Sydney Morning Herald*, 22 June 1907, p. 6.
20. W.J. Sowden, *Outline History of the Wattle Blossom Celebration in Australia*, Adelaide, 1913; A.J. Campbell, *Golden Wattle: Our National Floral Emblem*, Melbourne, 1921, p. 9; S.G. Firth, 'Social Values in the New South Wales Primary School', p. 146.
21. W.J. Sowden, *Outline History of the Wattle Blossom Celebration in Australia*, p. 12; Henry Lawson, 'Australia! Australia!'
22. Agnes L. Storrie, *Wattle Day League Leaflet* no. 2, 1910.
23. A.J. Campbell, *Golden Wattle: Our National Floral Emblem*, p. 15; Edward S. Sorenson, 'The Wattle: Australia's National Flower', *Lone Hand*, September 1912, pp. 386–87.
24. K.R. Cramp, *Wattle Day and its Significance*, Sydney, 1938.
25. R. Wynn *et al.*, *The Late Alfred Cecil Rowlandson: Pioneer Publisher of Australian Novels*, Sydney, 1922, pp. 3, 6, 20.
26. *Bulletin*, 2 February 1907.
27. *Lone Hand*, May 1907, pp. xxi–xxii.
28. *Ibid.*, July 1907, p. 307.
29. Colin Roderick (ed), *Henry Lawson Criticism 1894–1971*, Sydney, 1972, p. xxxii.
30. *Ibid.*, pp. 216–17.
31. *Ibid.*, p. 230. See also John Barnes, '"What Has He Done for Our National Spirit?"—A Note on Henry Lawson Criticism', *Australian Literary Studies*, 8(4), October 1978, pp. 485–91.
32. Arthur W. Jose, *The Romantic Nineties*, pp. 15, 17.
33. *Lone Hand*, June 1914, pp. 18–19; Marguerite Mahood, *The Loaded Line: Australian Political Caricature 1788–1901*, Melbourne, 1973, p. 182.

Chapter 8   Diggers and Heroes

1. Joseph Bowes, *The Young Anzacs*, London, 1917, p. 215.
2. C.E.W. Bean, *The Official History of Australia in the War of 1914–1918*, Sydney, 1921–1942, vol. VI, p. 1095.
3. Cited in Humphrey McQueen, *A New Britannia: An Argument concerning the Social Origins of Australian Radicalism and Nationalism*, Melbourne, 1970, p. 83.
4. *Sydney Morning Herald*, 22 June 1907, p. 6.
5. *Methodist School Hymnal*, Australasian Supplement, London, 1911, p. 8.
6. *Commonwealth School Paper*, 1 June 1910.
7. Henry Lawson, 'The Star of Australasia'.
8. Cited in Humphrey McQueen, *A New Britannia*, p. 87.
9. J. Foster Fraser, *Australia*, p. 124.
10. Frank Fox, *Australia*, London, 1910, p. 101.
11. *Sun*, 14 August 1911, cited in F.K. Crowley (ed), *Modern Australia in Documents 1901–1939*, p. 178.
12. Richard Arthur, *Keep Yourself Fit: The Dangers of Venereal Disease: An Address given at the Camps in Queensland and New South Wales*, Australasian White Cross League, Sydney, 1916, p. 11.
13. Rosemary Pringle, 'Octavius Beale and the Ideology of the Birth-Rate', *Refractory Girl*, 3, Winter 1973.
14. L.L. Robson (ed), *Australia and the Great War 1914–1918*, Melbourne, 1969, p. 40.
15. *Sydney Morning Herald*, 26 July 1897, Supplement.
16. L.L. Robson (ed), *Australia and the Great War 1914–1918*, pp. 46–47.
17. John Masefield, *Gallipoli*, London, 1916, pp. 19, 183.
18. L.L. Robson (ed), *Australia and the Great War 1914–1918*, pp. 44–45.
19. Edwin J. Brady, *Australia Unlimited*, p. 101.
20. Cf. John Masefield, *Gallipoli*, p. 18.
21. Cited in David Walker, *Dream and Disillusion: A Search for Australian Cultural Identity*, Canberra, 1976, p. 98.
22. R.W. Connell and T.H. Irving, *Class Structure in Australian History*, p. 267.
23. *Sydney Morning Herald*, 6 July 1907, p. 7.
24. C.E.W. Bean, *The Official History of Australia in the War of 1914–1918*, vol. I, pp. 45–47.
25. K.S. Inglis, *C.E.W. Bean, Australian Historian*, Brisbane, 1970, p. 6.
26. John Monash, *The Australian Victories in France in 1918*, London, 1920, pp. 290–91.
27. C.J. Dennis, *The Moods of Ginger Mick*, Sydney, 1916; K.S. Inglis, 'The Anzac Tradition', *Meanjin*, 24(1), 1965; David Walker, 'The Getting of Manhood', in Peter Spearritt and David Walker (eds), *Australian Popular Culture*, Sydney, 1979, p. 143.
28. George Blaikie, *Remember Smith's Weekly? A Biography of an Uninhibited National Australian Newspaper*, Adelaide, 1975, p. 159.
29. Joynton Smith, *My Life Story*, Sydney, 1927, pp. 263–64.
30. C.E.W. Bean, *The Official History of Australia in the War of 1914–1918*, vol. I, pp. 47–48.
31. C.E.W. Bean, 'Sidelights of the War on Australian Character', *Journal of the Royal Australian Historical Society*, 13(4), 1927, p. 216.
32. A.J. Smithers, *Sir John Monash*, London, 1973, p. 158.
33. John Monash, *The Australian Victories in France in 1918*, pp. 291–92.
34. A.J. Smithers, *Sir John Monash*, p. 203.

35. D.H. Lawrence, *Kangaroo*, London, 1955, pp. 68–88, 96–110.
36. A Psychologist and a Physician, *Whither Away? A Study of Race Psychology and the Factors leading to Australia's National Decline*, Sydney, 1934, pp. 71ff.
37. Cited in Tim Rowse, *Australian Liberalism and National Character*, Malmsbury, Victoria, 1978, p. 61.
38. Cited in K.S. Inglis, *C.E.W. Bean, Australian Historian*, p. 28.
39. Michael Roe, 'The Establishment of the Australian Department of Health: Its Background and Significance', *Historical Studies*, 17(67), October 1976, p. 184.
40. Cited in Fred Alexander, *Australia Since Federation: A Narrative and Critical Analysis*, Melbourne, 1967, p. 67.
41. W.K. Hancock, *Australia*, Brisbane, 1961, p. 248.
42. Cited in Philip Kitley, 'Anzac Day Ritual', *Journal of Australian Studies*, 4, June 1979, p. 58.
43. H.W. Dinning, *Australian Scene*, Sydney, 1939, p. vii.
44. Australian War Memorial, *Guide*, Canberra, 1950, p. x.
45. A.G. Butler, *The Digger: A Study in Democracy*, Sydney, 1945, pp. 22–23.
46. Cited in Keith Amos, *The New Guard Movement 1931–1935*, Melbourne, 1976, p. 27.
47. *Ibid.*, pp. 10–12.
48. G.L. Kristianson, *The Politics of Patriotism: The Pressure Group Activities of the Returned Servicemen's League*, Canberra, 1966, p. 13; Robert Murray, *The Confident Years*, Melbourne, 1976, p. 27.

Chapter 9   Growing Up

1. P.R. Stephensen, *The Foundations of Culture in Australia: An Essay towards National Self Respect*, Sydney, 1936, p. 90.
2. Cited in R.B. Nye and J.E. Morpurgo, *A History of the United States*, Penguin, 1964, p. 651.
3. Cited in David Potts, *The Twenties 1919–1929*, Melbourne, 1971, p. 18.
4. Peter Colemen, *Obscenity, Blasphemy, Sedition*, pp. 13, 82.
5. Cited in Michael Roe, 'The Establishment of the Australian Department of Health', p. 186.
6. Cited in George Blaikie, *Remember Smith's Weekly?*, pp. 227–28.
7. Richard White, '"Americanization" and Popular Culture in Australia', *Teaching History*, 12(2), August 1978.
8. Louis Esson, 'Nationality in Art', *Bulletin*, 1 February 1923, Red page.
9. Cultural Defence Committee, *Mental Rubbish from Overseas: A Public Protest*, Sydney, 1935, pp. 11, 14.
10. *Sydney Morning Herald*, 13 July 1927, p. 13.
11. *Bulletin*, 6 September 1923, p. 11.
12. Cited in Chris Wallace-Crabbe, *The Australian Nationalists*, p. 83.
13. *Sydney Morning Herald*, 29 January 1927, p. 14.
14. P.R. Cole, 'The Development of an Australian Social Type', p. 56.
15. *Bulletin*, 13 December 1923, Red page.
16. James Hume-Cook, *The Australian Industries Protection League: A Historical Review*, Melbourne, 1938, p. 9.
17. *Souvenir of the Australian Made Preference League and the Great White Exhibition Train*, Sydney, 1926, pp. 16, 22.
18. *Ibid.*, p. 1.

19. James Hume Cook, *The Australian Natives' Association: Its Genesis and History*, Melbourne, 1931, p. 25.
20. *Argus*, 9 January 1926, p. 31.
21. Lionel Lindsay, 'Australian Art', in Sydney Ure Smith (ed), *The Exhibition of Australian Art in London, 1923*, Sydney, 1923.
22. *Vision: A Literary Quarterly*, no. 1, May 1923, p. 3.
23. P.R. Stephensen, *Kookaburras and Satyrs: Some Recollections of the Fanfrolico Press*, Sydney, 1954, pp. 21–22.
24. Frank Crowley (ed), *A New History of Australia*, p. 448.
25. A Psychologist and a Physician, *Whither Away? A Study of Race Psychology and the Factors leading to Australia's National Decline*, Sydney, 1934.
26. Frank Crowley (ed), *A New History of Australia*, p. 448.
27. Cited in C. Hartley Grattan, *Introducing Australia*, Sydney, 1944, pp. 155–56.
28. P.R. Stephensen, *The Foundations of Culture in Australia*, pp. 89, 98.
29. Cultural Defence Committee, *Mental Rubbish from Overseas*, p. 6.
30. Cited in Geoffrey Serle, *From Deserts the Prophets Come*, p. 132.
31. Terry Smith and John Storey, 'Two Other Sesquis: The Royal Easter Show and May Day, 1938', *Australia 1938*, Bulletin no. 1, 1980, p. 51.
32. *Man*, March 1945, pp. 5, 100; Richard White, 'The Importance of Being Man', in Peter Spearritt and David Walker (eds), *Australian Popular Culture*, Sydney, 1979, p. 156.
33. P.R. Stephensen, *The Foundations of Culture in Australia*, pp. 76–77.
34. *Ibid.*, pp. 66–71.
35. Sidney J. Baker (1946) in C.B. Christesen (ed), *On Native Grounds*, Sydney, 1968, p. 458.
36. Miles Franklin, 'Amateurs but Proletarians', *Australian Writers Annual*, Sydney, 1936, p. 45.
37. Australian News and Information Bureau, *Australia at Home to the Yanks*, New York, 1944, pp. 15ff.
38. Ian Mudie (ed), *Poets at War*, Melbourne, 1944, p. 14.
39. *Australia National Journal*, no. 1, 1939, p. 15; no. 4, 1940, p. 14.
40. P.G. Edwards (ed), *Australia Through American Eyes 1935–1945: Observations by American Diplomats*, Brisbane, 1979, pp. 17, 45–46, 54.
41. *Ibid.*, p. 17.
42. Geoffrey Serle, *From Deserts the Prophets Come*, pp. 151–54; L.G. Churchward, *Australia and America 1788–1972*, p. 139.
43. Tim Rowse, *Australian Liberalism and National Character*, pp. 134–38.
44. R.M. Crawford, *An Australian Perspective*, Melbourne, 1960, pp. 68–69; Peter Coleman (ed), *Australian Civilization: A Symposium*, Melbourne, 1962, p. 1; J.D. Pringle, *Australian Accent*, London, 1958, p. 170; Geoffrey Serle, *From Deserts the Prophets Come*, pp. 148–49. See also Tim Rowse, *Australian Liberalism and National Character*, p. 228.
45. P.R. Stephensen, *The Foundations of Culture in Australia*, p. 90.
46. Adrian Lawlor, *Arquebus*, Melbourne, 1937, p. 208.
47. *Australian Writers Annual 1936*, p. 14.
48. Frank Dalby Davison, 'Australian Writers Come to Maturity', *Australia National Journal*, no. 2, 1939, p. 68.
49. A. Grenfell Price, *Australia Comes of Age: A Study of Growth to Nationhood and of External Relations*, Melbourne, 1945, pp. 139–40.
50. Geoffrey Serle, *From Deserts the Prophets Come*, p. 154.
51. Ian Turner (ed), *The Australian Dream*, pp. 304–05. See also Tim Rowse, *Australian Liberalism and National Character*, p. 181; John Docker,

Australian Cultural Elites: Intellectual Traditions in Sydney and Melbourne. Sydney, 1974, pp. 102f.
52. Cited in John Barnes (ed), *The Writer in Australia*, p. xiv.
53. Ian Reid, 'In Memoriam, Ned Kelly', *Meanjin*, 39(4), December 1980, p. 599.
54. Janine Burke, *Australian Women Artists*, p. 74.
55. *Daily Telegraph*, 7 February 1938, p. 6.
56. *History of the Bondi Surf Bathers' Life Saving Club 1906–1956*, Sydney, 1956, p. 31.
57. *Walkabout*, November 1938, p. 4; December 1939, p. 53.
58. *Argus*, 27 January 1938, p. 1.
59. *History of the Bondi Surf Bathers' Life Saving Club*, p. 5.
60. Geoffrey Serle, *The Golden Age*, pp. 186–87; R.D. Walshe, 'The Significance of Eureka in Australian History', *Historical Studies, Eureka Supplement*, 1954, pp. 76–80.
61. E.g. E.A. Ross, 'Look at Australia', *Publicist*, no. 44, 1 February 1940, p. 8; P.G. Edwards (ed), *Australia Through American Eyes*, p. 45.
62. C. Hartley Grattan, *Introducing Australia*, pp. 167–69.

Chapter 10 Everyman and his Holden

1. Photographed in *The Good Neighbour*, April 1954, p. 1.
2. Richard White, '"The Australian Way of Life"', *Historical Studies*, 18(73), October 1979, pp. 528–29.
3. Elizabeth Webb, *Stet*, Brisbane, 1950, p. 179.
4. George Caiger (ed), *The Australian Way of Life*, Melbourne, 1953; W.V. Aughterson (ed), *Taking Stock: Aspects of Mid-Century Life in Australia*, Melbourne, 1953; Ian Bevan (ed), *The Sunburnt Country: Profile of Australia*, London, 1953.
5. W.V. Aughterson (ed), *Taking Stock*, p. i.
6. Oswald L. Ziegler (ed), *Official Commemorative Book: Jubilee of the Commonwealth of Australia*, Sydney, 1951, p. 40.
7. Institute of Public Affairs, *Report on the Activities of the I.P.A.*, Sydney, 1949.
8. Geoffrey Blainey, *The Tyranny of Distance: How Distance Shaped Australia's History*, Melbourne, 1966, p. 334.
9. *The New Australian (Official Organ of the Big Brother Movement)*, 1(1), February 1928, p. 7.
10. Cited in W.D. Borrie *et al.*, *A White Australia: Australia's Population Problem*, Sydney, 1947, p. 151.
11. *The Good Neighbour*, August 1950, p. 1.
12. 'Nino Culotta' (John O'Grady), *They're a Weird Mob*, Sydney, 1957, p. 204.
13. Elizabeth Webb, *Stet*, p. 49.
14. George Johnston, 'Their Way of Life', in Ian Bevan (ed), *The Sunburnt Country*, pp. 151, 158.
15. W.E.H. Stanner, 'The Australian Way of Life', in W.V. Aughterson (ed), *Taking Stock*, pp. 3–4.
16. Australian News and Information Bureau, *Australia: Portrait of a Nation*, Canberra, 1955.
17. George Caiger (ed), *The Australian Way of Life*, p. 6.
18. W.V. Aughterson (ed), *Taking Stock*, p. 8.

19. Brian Fitzpatrick, *The Australian Commonwealth: A Picture of the Community 1901–55*, Melbourne, 1956, p. 15.
20. Roy Morgan, *Australian Public Opinion Polls*, February 1958, 1299–312.
21. Donald Horne, *The Lucky Country: Australia in the Sixties*, Penguin, 1966, pp. 82–85.
22. Emery Barcs, 'The Australian Way of Life', in Oswald L. Ziegler (ed), *Official Commemorative Book: Jubilee of the Commonwealth of Australia*, p. 40.
23. Henry Lawson, 'The Spirit of Sydney'.
24. Thomas Wood, *Cobbers*, London, 1934, p. 168.
25. J.D. Pringle, *Australian Accent*, London, 1958, p. 18.
26. Peter Spearritt, *Sydney Since the Twenties*, Sydney, 1978, p. 105.
27. *Commonwealth Year Book*, 1963, pp. 217–20.
28. Alan Trengove, *'What's Good for Australia . . . !' The Story of B.H.P.*, Sydney, 1975, p. 191.
29. *Commonwealth Year Book*, 1963, pp. 604–09.
30. *I.P.A. Review*, 3(1), January-February 1949, p. 14.
31. *Ibid.*, 18(1), January-March 1964, pp. 9–10.
32. David Kemp, 'Political Parties and Australian Culture', *Quadrant*, 21(12), December 1977, p. 7.
33. *Argus Woman's Magazine*, 24 September 1947, pp. 4–5.
34. *Commonwealth Year Book*, 1963, pp. 195, 321.
35. George Johnston, *Clean Straw for Nothing. A Novel*, London, 1969, p. 99.
36. Cited in National Capital Development Commission, *Tomorrow's Canberra*, Canberra, 1970, p. 21.
37. Rupert Lockwood, *America Invades Australia*, Sydney, 1954?, p. 93. See also Richard White, '"Combating Cultural Aggression": Australian Opposition to Americanisation', *Meanjin*, 39(3), October 1980, p. 284.
38. 'Editorial', *Overland*, December 1960, p. 8.
39. Robin Boyd, *Australia's Home: Its Origins, Builders and Occupiers*, Melbourne, 1961, p. 278. (1st ed 1952).
40. Alan Ashbolt, 'Godzone: 3) Myth and Reality', *Meanjin*, 25(4), December, 1966, pp. 373–74.
41. Noel McLachlan, 'Godzone: 4) The Australian Intellectual', *Meanjin*, 26(1), March 1967, p. 7.
42. Humphrey McQueen, *A New Britannia*, pp. 15–20.
43. Australian Council for the Arts, *Annual Report*, 1973, p. 9.
44. Geoffrey Serle, *From Deserts the Prophets Come*, p. 229.
45. Australian Broadcasting Commission, *Guest of Honour*, 28 June 1980.

Index